just don't marry one

interracial dating, marriage, and parenting

Edited by George A. Yancey
and Sherelyn Whittum Yancey

Foreword by Curtiss Paul DeYoung

Judson Press
Valley Forge

D0365962

just don't marry one:
interracial dating, marriage, and parenting

The editors and Judson Press have made every effort to trace the ownership of all quotes. In the event of a question arising from the use of a quote, we regret any error made and will be pleased to make the necessary correction in future printings and editions of this book.

Bible quotations in this volume are from *The Holy Bible*, King James Version (KJV); *HOLY BIBLE: New International Version* (NIV), copyright © 1973, 1978, 1984, used by permission of Zondervan Bible Publishers; and *The Living Bible* (TLB), copyright © 1971, used by permission of Tyndale House Publishers, Inc., Wheaton, IL 60189, all rights reserved.

Library of Congress Cataloging-in-Publication Data

Just don't marry one : interracial dating, marriage, and parenting / edited by George and Sherelyn Yancey ; foreword by Curtiss DeYoung.
    p. cm.
    Includes bibliographical references.
ISBN 0-8170-1439-X (pbk. : alk. paper)
1. Interracial marriage–Religious aspects–Christianity. 2. Interracial dating–Religious aspects—Christianity. 3. Interracial adoption–Religious aspects–Christianity. I. Yancey, George A., 1962- II. Yancey, Sherelyn.

BT707.3 .J87 2003
261.8'35846–dc21
2002073073
Printed in the U.S.A.

08 07 06 05 04 03 02
10 9 8 7 6 5 4 3 2 1

❦ DEDICATION ❧

TO THOSE BRAVE SOULS ON WHOSE SHOULDERS WE INTERRACIALLY married couples now stand—ones who have walked this path before us, who have endured scorn and unjust oppression, and whose sacrifices transformed the racism of our families, churches, and nation and challenged them to finally accept the love we have for each other.

❦ CONTENTS ❦

CONTENTS

SECTION 3
Parenting Issues

APPENDIXES

❧ FOREWORD ❧

IN MINNESOTA, WHEN A WEDDING NOTICE FOR AN INTERRACIAL couple or an article about a multiracial family appears in the *St. Paul Pioneer Press,* it is likely that the couple or family will receive a letter from a man in St. Paul who believes he is called to defend God-ordained racial separatism. At first glance he seems like a relic from a bygone era—a time when one could be killed for crossing the line of race. Yet his sentiments are still shared by people in our society, especially as it relates to members of their own families. For some, interracial coupling represents one of the last taboos in human relations—an aberration of God's design for the human family.

At the same time, others celebrate the increase in the number of interracial marriages and families, pointing to this trend as *the* solution to racism in the United States. They believe that racism will cease to exist when the human family becomes thoroughly mixed racially. Between these two extremes we find George and Sherelyn Yancey and the authors included in this book. They certainly do not back down from challenging those who oppose interracial marriage, nor do they fully embrace a utopian vision. *Just Don't Marry One: Interracial Dating, Marriage, and Parenting* offers a well-reasoned perspective. The authors included in this collection edited by the Yanceys provide us with good scholarship and real-life human stories.

George and Sherelyn Yancey have written a very timely book. As the United States becomes increasingly racially diverse, family relationships will more and more reflect the same diversity. Also interracial and multiracial family relationships are more prevalent as subjects in the public discourse. No longer are these issues only whispered about in private circles or used as fodder for white supremacist ravings. Even our nation's presidents have wittingly or unwittingly joined the discussion. A postmortem debate on Thomas Jefferson's sexual liaisons across the boundaries of race has generated much interest. In an attempt to be elected president of the United States, George Bush, the father, spoke of his "brown" grandchildren and George W. Bush, the son, had his mixed-race Spanish-speaking "brown" nephew, George P. Bush, working on his campaign. This book provides a thoughtful and comprehensive discussion of the relevant issues driven by moral and pastoral concerns rather than by market share or political ambitions.

Sherelyn and George Yancey have brought together a thoughtful group of commentators in this edited volume. I am impressed by the diversity of the contributors. They are pastors, parents, scholars, social workers, scientists, counselors, and theologians. They are Asian Americans, Latinos, African Americans, Native Americans, whites, and persons with multiracial lineages. They all bring a wide range of experiences and perspectives. I am particularly encouraged by the fact that a majority of the contributors not only speak from much study of the issues, but also have lived what they write about. I was moved by the words of individuals who themselves are of multiracial descent. Their voices spoke of the juxtaposition of struggle and joy. Yet their voices resonated with the affirmation that they were not mistakes but were created in the image of God with a divine purpose. This book exudes honesty, vulnerability, transparency, and authenticity.

In whatever role you find yourself as it relates to interracial couples and families, *Just Don't Marry One* has a word for you. If you are in an interracial marriage or contemplating dating someone of a different race, if you are the parent of a child whose race differs from yours, if you provide support for others in such situations as a pastor, counselor, professor, grandparent, or friend—this book is for you. The topics included cover the gambit: self-esteem, stereotypes, history, culture, the Bible, identity, racism, religion, and the like. While there are no easy answers, this book offers much wisdom.

I also deeply appreciate this book for very personal reasons. For eighteen years I have been married to a magnificent woman named Karen who is an African American. Two amazing teenage children—Rachel and Jonathan—have resulted from our union. We have centered our lives in our faith in Jesus Christ, and thanks to God's grace and the support of families and friends, we have enjoyed an incredible journey together. It has not always been easy. We could have used a book like this along the way.

So I am grateful to the Yanceys and to Judson Press for having the courage and foresight to publish this volume. As far as I know it is the first resource of its kind from a Christian perspective. For a religious faith that claims the interracially married Moses as one of its greatest prophets and the multiracial Jesus of Nazareth as its Savior, this book is long overdue. Hopefully this book will help move us to a day when our primary identity as individuals and families is rooted in the fact that we are children of God and created in God's image.

—Curtiss Paul DeYoung

§ ACKNOWLEDGMENTS §

IN A BOOK ABOUT FAMILIES, WE WANT TO ACKNOWLEDGE OUR families: Rose Taylor, George's mom, who encouraged him to strive for his best; Aunt Ann, who graced our wedding with her poem; Vincent, Justin, and Robert Howard, who grew up with George and always had his back; and Marjorie Pedigo Otto Whittum, Sherelyn's mom and Abe Lincoln's fourth cousin, who instilled in her a love for God and her family's pioneer spirit. We genuinely thank our contributors, who patiently worked with us to make this book a reality. We are deeply indebted to the attendees of our workshop "Ten Top Myths about Interracial Marriage" at the 2000 National Multiracial Ministry Conference in Indianapolis, whose requests for this multidisciplinary handbook inspired our efforts. We are grateful for the courage of this ongoing conference to address the reality of interracial love in the Christian community. We thank Judson Press for understanding the vision and the need for this book and believing in that vision enough to publish it. We thank Mary Alice Stevens for her willingness to read our manuscript and for her helpful comments. Finally, and most important, we thank our Lord and Savior, Jesus Christ, who offers hope and welcome to those of us whom God has joined together but who are unjustly accused of betraying our races when we interracially marry or when we embrace our multiracial heritage.

❦ OUR WEDDING DAY POEM ❦
by Sherelyn Whittum Yancey

On the outside
    We look so different
I am black
    I am white
    I am male
      I am female
Yet on the inside
    We seem so similar
Created from the same clay
    The LORD GOD formed us
I say, "At long last ...."
    I say, "Finally I have found ...."
Bone of my bone
    Soul of my soul
My wife
    My husband
My sweetheart
    My friend
I leave my family
    You cleave to me
We are now a couple
    And still individuals
Oneness in calling
    United in purpose
Sojourners in following
    Our Lord Jesus Christ
Let us return to the Garden
    Let us dance in the Son
Let us celebrate the love
    That has joined us as ONE.

❦ INTRODUCTION ❦

Sherelyn's Story

"What color is she?" George's mom asked. Her oldest son, a college professor, had finally called to announce that he had discovered the woman he wanted to marry. As I (Sherelyn) watched my future husband describe me to his African American mother, I realized that she had not asked about the color of my hair or eyes; she wanted to know the color of my skin. I felt uneasy, suddenly nervous to speak with my future mother-in-law over the telephone. I wondered, *Does she hope I am black? Will she be disappointed I am white?* A white daughter-in-law was nothing new to her, since George's three younger brothers had children with white women. Racism did not drive this probing question of color. Rather, it was her knowledge that skin color, unlike hair or eye color, does matter for her children and grandchildren in America.

After George introduced me as his future wife, I asked his mother if I could call her by her first name, since I felt unsure how to address her. (In my white family, we call all in-laws by their first names.)

"No, that won't do; don't call me by my first name," she replied.

I felt stuck. As we struggled over a few awkward moments, trying to figure out a respectful title that would be mutually acceptable, I began to realize this was going to be more complicated than just loving George. I felt perplexed by what other social barriers related to racial differences we might encounter as we created our new interracial family. With God's love, today Mama T. and I share a rich, warm relationship.

George's Story

I (George) already knew that an interracial relationship is complicated. When I was in graduate school, I fell for a young, white Christian woman. Her mother refused to even meet me, because I was black. My girlfriend did not want to risk losing her mother's approval, so she ended our relationship. I felt stunned and rejected, because this was the first time in my life when being black was a barrier I could not overcome. Suffering this discrimination created a crisis of my faith in God. Even my girlfriend's Christian confidants questioned the legitimacy of our romantic relationship.

This experience changed the direction of my personal and professional life. I began to research resistance to interracial marriage from scriptural and sociological perspectives.

When I met Sherelyn, we developed a solid friendship based in Christ. I saw the depth and openness she had about race relations, having already wrestled with issues of white privilege and exploitation of Native Americans. Our common love in Jesus enabled us to embrace and yet transcend our racial differences.

I was not as optimistic about her brother from Idaho. I insisted that Sherelyn call to inform him that I was black before we met in person. Later we realized that I was testing her resolve to remain committed to me in view of the very real possibility that Sherelyn might be ostracized by her white family for marrying me. Such was not the case—I was warmly welcomed. While I had been raised to believe in myself and in what I could accomplish, my earlier romantic relationship had taught me that because of a family member's racism, interracial relationships bring with them the emotional danger of rejection.

Where Our Story Encounters Yours

Interracial marriages are growing in America. In 1970, just three years after the U.S. Supreme Court ruled that state laws against interracial marriages were unconstitutional, there were only about 310,000 interracial marriages in the United States.[1] In 1980, this had more than doubled to 651,000. By 1987, the number of interracial marriages had increased to 799,000. According to the 2000 Census, the number of interracial marriages is about 1.2 million, representing a quadrupling of the number of such marriages over the past thirty years.

In 1998 the census also indicated that 5.16 percent of all marriages are multiracial. This percentage has risen dramatically from 0.39 percent in 1960 to 2.1 percent in 1980 and to 2.17 percent in 1990.

This growing population of interracial couples and multiracial individuals creates unique cross-cultural family dynamics that are virtually ignored by churches in America.

Multiracial Christian couples challenge their families and churches to rethink previously held misconceptions about American race relations. Christian marriage and family writers have historically discouraged interracial marriage overtly or by ignoring the topic altogether.[2] Resources that Christians are producing to reach out to interracial families are nil. Believers today are compelled to revisit the issue of interracial marriage presented from an authentic biblical perspective free from racial superiority bias. In their new book, *Divided by Faith*, Emerson and Smith point out that white evangelicals generally isolate themselves from cross-racial fellowship.[3] We suggest that this lack of social interaction between races creates a void filled with benign cultural differences, mistrust, negative racial stereotypes, and unwritten rules against interracial marriage.

This book is directed toward Christians with a twofold purpose. First, it is intended to affirm, nurture, and encourage believers in interracial marriages and families. Second, it is a multidisciplinary handbook intended to provide biblical insight to equip pastors, seminary faculty and students, youth and campus ministers, counselors, and social workers with reference chapters that can stand alone to act as compasses to navigate the uncharted waters of ministering to Christian interracial couples and families.

While looking for specific Christian resources to strengthen interracial marriages and families, we naturally contacted Focus on the Family, headed by Dr. James Dobson. In response, all we received was a resource sheet listing various international and national adoption services. Even then, nothing was offered regarding interracial marriage or transracial adoption. We believe that this disconnection leaves many men, women, and children without essential biblical tools necessary to address the unique pressures Christian multiracial families face in our "racialized" society. One can only speculate that Focus on the Family might lose financial support if Dr. Dobson publicly supported Christian interracial marriage.

This silence in the Christian sector may be understandable, since a significant number of white Christians still oppose interracial marriage.[4] These objections are culturally based, because nothing in Scripture supports these prejudices. While this ostrichlike head-in-sand stance is a safer choice to avoid controversy among a vast listening audience, it also highlights the need for biblically based resources supporting Christian multiracial families. We hope and pray that this resource book, being the first of its kind to minister to Christian interracial marriages and families, will challenge those who choose to ignore multiracial families.

We decided to respond to the requests by creating this book based upon our experiences as a Christian interracial couple, our professional endeavors, and our confidence in the expertise of our contributing authors. We have coauthored two academic articles on premarital interracial formation. George, a sociologist, has published several journal articles on interracial marriage and a book called *Beyond Black and White: Reflections on Racial*

Reconciliation, which contains three chapters about interracial unions.[5] Sherelyn, a parish nurse, who has worked cross-culturally, has also created an Interracial Family Calendar that features pictures of real interracial families and multiracial historical events.

The vision for this book was conceived when we presented a workshop on interracial marriage at the Fourth National Multiracial Ministry Conference, held in Indianapolis in 2000, when attendees asked us to bring together thoughtful Christian leaders who could speak to the various needs of interracial families. This multidisciplinary handbook is written from a biblical perspective by authors of various racial identities. It can be used to help both seekers and leaders understand the unique dynamics surrounding multiracial families. This is a book that, quite frankly, is long overdue.

This handbook is grouped together into three major sections composed of stand-alone reference chapters. The first section is "Foundations for Christian Leaders," followed by "Support for Interracial Couples and Multiracial Families" and then "Parenting Issues."

Section one, "Foundations for Christian Leaders," is intended to aid Christian leaders in the helping professions serve multiracial families. This multidisciplinary section contains five essays. First, from a *theological* perspective, Rev. Dr. Craig Keener, in a chapter entitled "The Bible and Interracial Marriage," exposes the inadequate theology that has guided generations of white Christians opposed to interracial marriage. Second, from a perspective of *pastoral care,* Dr. A. Charles Ware's contribution, "Pastoral Counseling of Multiracial Families," draws upon his years of premarital and postmarital counseling of interracial couples. Next, from a *sociological* perspective, Dr. George A. Yancey exposes subtle racism still held by American Christians in his chapter, "Debunking the Top Stereotypes about Interracial Couples." Then Ken Ham explores a *biological* perspective in his reprinted abridged chapter "One Race" from the book *One Blood,* showing how physical differences among the races can be scientifically explained from Genesis and how the theory of evolution has been used to justify racism. Finally, Sherelyn Whittum Yancey provides a *historical* perspective on interracial marriage and children in her chapter, "Interracial Sexual Relations in Early American History," recounting how early American slave society outlawed yet enjoyed interracial sexual relations, producing multiracial children who were unjustly denied their place in traditional families and churches.

Of special interest to those in interracial relationships, or who are considering such relationships, are five essays in section two: "Support for

Interracial Couples and Multiracial Families." First, Sundee Frazier, a former staff member and worship leader for InterVarsity, presents her insider's perspective as a biracial child in her chapter, "What about the Children? I Am One," in which she provides assurance for interracial couples that the children from these unions will be as happy and healthy as other children, while still providing advice for such couples as to how they may best guide their kids. Second, Rev. David Tatlock tackles tough premarital questions about interracial relationships in his chapter, " 'What about My Family?' and Other Premarital Questions." Third, Pastor Art and Debbie Lucero, a Hispanic/Asian couple, share humorous but valuable insights about the cross-cultural differences in their chapter, "And Two Shall Become One: Merging Two Racial Cultures in Christian Love." Fourth, Randy Woodley's autobiography, "Mixed Blood: I Am a Bridge," explores how people of mixed-blood heritage can become powerful healers of the racial pain that remains in our country. Fifth, Rev. Bob and Jean Chin speak from their own experience in their chapter, "Interracial Marriage: An Asian American Christian Perspective." Last, Olga Soler challenges whites interested in interracial relationships with her contribution, "Being Brave Enough to Love in Color."

Finally, section three, "Parenting Issues," concludes this handbook with three important chapters. First, Dr. Michael and Joni Emerson, who intentionally moved their white children into multiracial neighborhoods, suggest what may be helpful for parents who fear the inevitable consequences of interracial contact at church, school, and neighborhoods in their reflection, "What If Our Children Date Interracially?" Next, a white parent, Rev. Dr. Fred Prinzing, candidly writes to update the only Christian book specifically addressing interracial marriage, *Mixed Messages,* in his chapter, "Do I Have Your Blessing?" Dr. Prinzing provides valuable wisdom to help Christian parents understand the issues that develop from interracial love. Finally, Deborah Johnson, an Asian American, provides startling insight during her interview, "When Our Children Do Not Look Like Us: Transracial Adoption in the Church."

A word about racial classifications used by the authors of this book. What are considered acceptable terms for racial groups seem to change every few years. For that reason, we have chosen to be flexible in our use of racial terms. We will use the terms "African American" and "black" interchangeably. The same is true for "European American" and "white," "Hispanic American" and "Hispanic," "Asian American" and "Asian," and "Native

American" and "American Indian." We also will freely interchange the terms "people of color" and "racial minorities" despite the well-intentioned objections others may hold. These various labels will continue to change, especially as multiracial people define themselves outside the narrow constraints of today's racial identification system.

For practical application, at the end of each chapter a set of challenging questions can be found for use in both personal reflection and small-group discussions in classrooms, homes, and churches. We pray that this book will be useful for you. We hope that this handbook provokes needed conversations as well as provides intellectual, emotional, and spiritual support for interracial couples and families.

Finally, it is our intention that this unique resource capture the attention of Christian leaders who are dedicated to strengthening Christian marriages and families but seem unaware of the distinctive dynamics brought about by the increasing number of interracial families and singles. The spirit of this book is to provide a forum among interracial families, helping to heal wounds inflicted by well-meaning, though often misguided, Christians. We pray that this work will challenge long-held notions spiritualizing racial superiority. In addition, we ask those active in the movement for racial reconciliation and social justice to welcome us as we live out racial reconciliation on the most intimate level—in our marriage and family lives. If any of these intentions are fulfilled as a result of this book, we will celebrate with you at our multiracial family reunion with God, as described in Revelation 7:9–10:

> After this I looked and there before me was a great multitude that no one could count, from every nation [*ethnos,* or "ethnicity," in Greek], tribe, people and language, standing before the throne and in front of the Lamb. They were wearing white robes and were holding palm branches in their hands. And they cried out in a loud voice:
> *"Salvation belongs to our God,*
> *who sits on the throne,*
> *and to the Lamb." (NIV)*

Notes

1. *These numbers do not count marriages of Hispanics to whites since they are based upon census data that tend to label Hispanics as a white ethnic group.*

2. *Furthermore, the recent public spat between Kenneth Hagin Jr., and Frederick Price over whether parents should forbid their children to interracially date is another example of how some Christians still resist romantic interracial relationships.*

3. *Michael Emerson and Christian Smith,* Divided by Faith: Evangelical Religion and the Problem of Race in America *(New York: Oxford University Press, 2000).*

4. *George Yancey, Michael Emerson, and Karen Chai. "Who Can We Marry? A Look at the Hierarchical Construction of Marriage Preferences in the United States" (paper presented at Southern Sociological Society Meetings, New Orleans, 2000).*

5. *The book can be purchased at our website: www.racialreconciliation.com.*

foundations for christian leaders

❧ ONE ❧

The Bible and
Interracial Marriage

Craig S. Keener

FAR FROM OPPOSING INTERRACIAL MARRIAGE, THE BIBLE GIVES us examples of prominent servants of God who were themselves interracially married. It also provides a theological groundwork for challenging objections to interracial marriage. In fact, one cannot truly accept the gospel of Christ and reject the possibility of interracial marriage. Before we can address the biblical perspective on interracial marriage, however, we must define what we mean by interracial marriage.

What *Is* Interracial Marriage?

In the beginning, interracial marriage was a nonissue. Adam and Eve, and later Noah and his family, included the genetic roots of all races in the world today. Those who are against "race mixing" because they fear mixed-race offspring should consider that multiracial children are actually closer to the way God created humanity than are the rest of us! We are all descended from people who, like multiracial individuals today, possessed the genetic strands of many races.

But the nonracial origin of humanity raises for us another issue: What is a race? The genetic differences linked to each race are fewer than the genetic differences between individual members of any particular race. One need not even suppose, as some have, that Noah's three children gave birth to each of the three racial categories we have today (Caucasian, Mongoloid, Negro); marriage among their descendants would have yielded various combinations of genetic traits. Since traits such as complexion are among the quickest to change, differences in complexion and other racial traits may have reflected inbreeding due to migrations as humanity scattered over the face of the earth. Scattering and the division of languages occurred specifically as a judgment at Babel (Genesis 11:7–9), leading to a scattering of cultures and consequently to some genetic differences as well. Because nations united against God, God scattered them. But in Christ, God reverses this division at Pentecost (Acts

2:6–11).[1] The potential for distinctions is part of the beautiful diversity in God's creation, but separatism was never God's ideal for humanity.

The idea of three (or four) clearly definable racial categories is a myth fostered by nineteenth-century racist anthropology, now abandoned by the vast majority of anthropologists.[2] Race, as we have defined it in the United States, relates to the specific history of African slavery and black segregation here. When slaveholders raped African slaves and produced racially mixed offspring, the same system that allowed these atrocities also labeled the children (and future descendants) "black" so they could remain slaves. Yet, peoples across the globe exhibit a wide variety of complexions and physical features; some fit into clearly defined physical categories, but many do not. The genetic picture is even murkier. Some even suggest that Europeans' genetic stock is 65 percent Asian and 35 percent African.[3] So much for Nazi desires to maintain white racial purity. Whatever the disputes about the site of Eden, no one places it in Europe.

That is not to deny that race is a reality; it is in fact a defining reality for tens of millions of people in the United States and many others elsewhere. But it is a cultural reality more than one based on physical traits. That means that the sort of dynamics involved in an interracial marriage in the U.S. may resemble the sort of dynamics involved in a Tamil-Sinhalese marriage in Sri Lanka, a Serbian-Albanian marriage in the former Yugoslavia, a marriage between Lingala and Munukutuba speakers in Congo-Brazzaville, a Hutu and Tutsi marriage in Rwanda, or marriage between an Ibo and a Hausa-speaking northerner in Nigeria. In fact, given the recent history of strife between many of these groups, the social conflicts involved in these examples are often much more dramatic than those experienced by interracial couples in most parts of the United States.

These dynamics also resemble those among some peoples in the ancient Mediterranean world. Yet the one kind of union some passages in the Bible specifically discourage is the union between Israelites and Gentiles. Cultural (not always physical) traits separated Jews from Gentiles, but these kinds of characteristics also separated one group of Gentiles from another. The specific reason for prohibiting Jewish-Gentile marriage in Scripture was not ethnic or cultural but religious.

Positive Biblical Examples of Interethnic Marriages
If the Old Testament warned against Israelites marrying Gentiles, it is interesting that the New Testament opens with an emphasis on the mixed heritage

of the Savior. In Matthew's genealogy, Jesus descends not only from David and Abraham (Matthew 1:1) but also from some Gentile women![4] Jewish people regarded genealogies as significant in part because they recognized God's providence in bringing about marriages; later rabbis even declared that this required as much miraculous oversight as the parting of the sea.[5]

Matthew's examples. That Matthew wants us to recognize this emphasis on Jesus' descent from Gentiles is clear. Whereas Jewish people used genealogies to emphasize, where possible, the purity of their Israelite lineage, Matthew does precisely the opposite for Jesus.[6] Ancient genealogies usually omitted women, but Matthew includes four of them, thereby drawing attention to them. If a genealogy included a few women, one might expect to find the four matriarchs of Israel: Sarah, Rebekah, Rachel, and Leah (though Rachel was not an ancestor of Judah). Instead, Matthew includes four women with Gentile associations (Matthew 1:3,5–6). The fact that he includes them is more critical than which Gentiles he names (only two of them represent very positive examples). But we will pause to look at all four.

First, Matthew mentions Tamar. As with the final woman he mentions in the genealogy, Tamar's story does not recall great moral purity. More important, however, she is a Gentile. Unlike his grandfather Isaac and his father, Jacob, Judah does not journey back to Mesopotamia to find a wife; instead, he marries a Canaanite (Genesis 38:2). Presumably Tamar, the wife he acquires for his son Er, is also a Canaanite; her family home is not far away (38:11).

When Er died childless, Judah followed the custom of sending in another son to impregnate Tamar on behalf of Er. This was a way to continue Er's name and line and would also guarantee that Tamar would share in the wealth of the family into which she had married. If the other son, Onan, got Tamar pregnant and she had a boy, her son would be the heir of Er, the first-born heir of Judah. Unfortunately, Onan also realized the other implications of this outcome: Tamar's son would get half the inheritance, whereas Onan would get only a quarter. If Tamar could not conceive, however, then Onan himself would count as the firstborn of two sons—and get two-thirds of the inheritance. More concerned about wealth than about his brother's honor or his sister-in-law's need, he tried to avoid impregnating her. So God struck him dead. God was acting in part to vindicate the honor of a Canaanite woman who had married into Israel.

Judah, however, fears that Tamar is the cause of his two sons' sudden deaths; hence, he does not want to give her to his third son, Shelah. In this culture, he would bear great dishonor for refusing to give her Shelah, so he simply says that she can marry him later. She waits and does not remarry—until she realizes that he has been cheating her (Genesis 38:14). But in some Middle Eastern cultures, if a brother of the husband were unavailable, one could use the father to sire offspring.[7] To Judah's discredit, Tamar apparently knows his character well enough to surmise that he will stop for a prostitute. After his wife's death, Tamar disguises herself as a prostitute and becomes pregnant through him. Not realizing that he was the father, he wants to burn her to death for her sin—till she confronts him with his role in it. At that point, he realizes that he is guiltier than she (38:26). She had used the only means available to her to acquire what was legally hers.

Although her behavior is not a positive role model for us, it becomes a turning point in Judah's life. In the previous chapter, Judah had taken the lead in selling Joseph into slavery (Genesis 37:25–27). But in the chapters that follow, he gradually comes to prefer being a slave himself to letting another brother be enslaved (44:16–34). It was his sinful encounter with a Canaanite woman that first led to an open recognition of guilt in his life (38:26). Her moral standards proved higher than his own. (The contrast between Judah's behavior with Tamar and Joseph's behavior with Potiphar's wife will prove instructive below.)

Next, Matthew mentions Rahab, adding a Gentile emphasis to Israel's royal line not already stressed by the Old Testament. Joshua's orders were to exterminate all the inhabitants of the land, but Rahab could be spared because she sided with Israel rather than with her own people. In essence, she feared and obeyed Israel's God; her faith mattered more to God than her ethnicity.

Matthew's ironic use of Rahab as a Gentile ancestor of the chosen line echoes her surprising role in the Book of Joshua. The story of Jericho (Joshua 3–7) includes two main new characters: Rahab and Achan. Rahab is a Canaanite who survives the destruction of her city; she saves herself and her family by following Israel's God. By contrast, Achan is a Judahite who dies along with his family for disobeying Israel's God, though his people are blessed. Rahab (presumably with some of her family's knowledge) hides the spies on her roof; Achan (certainly with his family's knowledge) hides his loot under his tent. Rahab's house survives when the city is destroyed; Achan's tent is burned. In other words, the Book of Joshua is not just about one people annihilating another.[8] Israelites and Gentiles could switch places—based on their obedience or disobedience to God! Rahab becomes a model of faith

(Hebrews 11:31; James 2:25) and, according to Matthew, a righteous Gentile ancestor of Jesus. She married into Israel.

Third, Matthew mentions Ruth, the ancestor of David. The law prohibited a Moabite (like a few other of the most hostile peoples) from becoming an Israelite (Deuteronomy 23:3), but God did not allow this general rule to bar an exceptional person like Ruth, who embraced the God of Israel (Ruth 1:16). The romantic story of Ruth and Boaz teaches many lessons, including God having good purposes for us even when our sufferings make us feel that God has abandoned us (Ruth 1:21; 4:14–15). But the story of Ruth, like the story of Jonah and some other sections of the Old Testament (e.g., 1 Samuel 5–6), shows God's compassion and desire for Gentiles to understand who God is. Most ancient Israelites who heard the story of Ruth for the first time might think that it was just a nice romance—until they reached the surprise ending! Ruth, it turned out, was part of God's plan for carrying on a line that quickly yielded King David (Ruth 4:18–22). This intercultural marriage proved to be directly providential and related to the messianic line.

Fourth, Matthew mentions Uriah's widow. In this case, in contrast to the other women he mentions in this genealogy, Matthew names her only by her former husband's name. This may be because Bathsheba may have been the daughter of a prominent Jewish family (2 Samuel 11:3; 23:34) but had married into Uriah's Hittite family, although Uriah or his ancestors seem to have adopted Israel as their home (2 Samuel 11:11; 23:39).[9] Since her own Gentile connection is less clear than that of the three women Matthew mentions before her, Matthew associates her directly with Uriah, whom the Old Testament calls "the Hittite" no fewer than ten times. Even the mother of King Solomon had Gentile associations!

Matthew does not provide these four examples—Tamar, Rahab, Ruth, and Bathsheba—in isolation. Rather, they are part of his larger theme of the Gentile mission (e.g., Matthew 15:22; 24:14; 28:19; see further below). For Matthew, godly interracial marriages are signs of ethnic reconciliation and the church's mission to reconcile representatives of all nations under Christ's Lordship.

Joseph and Asenath. In contrast to his big brother Judah, Joseph resisted sexual sin. In fact, he ended up in the prison of Potiphar, one of Pharaoh's officials, because he refused to sleep with Potiphar's wife (Genesis 39:1,7–20; 40:3). Ironically, Pharaoh himself later arranged Joseph's marriage with the daughter of a prominent priest whose name is only slightly different from Potiphar's. This wife, Asenath, bore Joseph two sons in Egypt (Genesis 41:50; 46:20).

How important is this item of information in the larger scheme of things? Was Joseph's fathering two children by Asenath simply an event without moral significance, or was it part of God's benevolent plan for him? The answer seems clear when we consider that Jacob gives Joseph the birthright that Reuben had forfeited: Joseph would receive the double portion, so that his first two sons would become two tribes in Israel (Genesis 48:5–6; 1 Chronicles 5:1–2). That means that Asenath was the mother of two of Israel's tribes; the Israelites had some Egyptian genes!

Further, Joseph's marriage to this Egyptian noblewoman was part of God's blessing to him. After building suspense with a detailed account of Joseph's long sufferings, Genesis reveals Joseph's exaltation (Genesis 41:40–45). The ironic contrasts in this account show us that God was reversing Joseph's previous sufferings. Like Israel in Egypt in a later generation, Joseph went from slavery to exaltation. Joseph's brothers had stripped him of the fine robe his father had given him (Genesis 37:3,23,31–33), and Potiphar's wife had stripped him of another robe (39:12). Now, by contrast, Pharaoh has him clothed in royal garments (41:42). The bowing of Egypt (41:43) is a first installment on the promise that ultimately even his own family would bow before him (37:10; 42:6; 43:28).

These contrasts also reveal that God was providentially rewarding Joseph for his faithfulness. Judah had surrendered his ring to a woman with whom he had committed sexual immorality (Genesis 38:25); by contrast, Joseph, who had resisted immorality (39:8–12), receives Pharaoh's ring (41:42)! Likewise, Joseph, who refused Potiphar's wife, now marries the daughter of another man whose name is a variant form of "Potiphar." Given that almost none of the Egyptians in the story (including Pharaoh, his officials, and Joseph's personal aide, Genesis 40:1–2; 44:1) are named, the naming of these two "Potiphars" is significant; there is a deliberate literary connection between them. Further, Asenath's status as daughter of the prominent priest is significant enough that Genesis repeats it with every mention of her name (Genesis 41:45,50; 46:20). God rewarded Joseph's faithfulness by giving him a wife who was Egyptian!

We cannot know for certain whether Asenath was primarily Semitic (one of the Hyksos rulers of the period) or native Egyptian, but ancient Israelites who read this story would not have known of such distinctions in Egypt's earlier history. They knew the Egyptians as an Afroasiatic people, a mixture of Asian peoples to the northeast and the Nubians to the south. Egyptians were generally dark, and some were very dark (the complexions on average darkened further to the south).[10] In any case, this was an interethnic marriage, and God intended it as a blessing. Other ethnic Egyptians presumably married Israelites, though those in Jacob's household would have followed Israel's God (see Genesis 17:27). A number of Abraham's servants were from Egypt (Genesis 12:16; 16:1); others hailed from elsewhere, such as Damascus (15:2). Their descendants would have remained part of Jacob's household when he traveled to Egypt (25:5,33). When Egypt later enslaved Israel, it is hardly likely that they would have freed Israel's slaves; rather, the slaves would have blended into Israel's tribes.

Moses' marriage(s). Joseph was not the only leader in Israel's early history to marry a Gentile while in exile from his home. Joseph married an Egyptian after being exiled from Canaan; Moses married a Midianite after fleeing from Egypt. In fact, the connection between these accounts is surely deliberate. Joseph was a slave who became a prince of Egypt; Moses was a prince of Egypt who chose to identify with the slaves. Both were rejected by their own people as deliverers (see Acts 7:9,27,35–39,52). God raised up one to bring Israel to Egypt and the other to bring Israel out of Egypt. Both marry the daughters of local priests (Genesis 41:45; Exodus 2:16,21). Midianites enslaved Joseph (Genesis 37:36), but he married an Egyptian; Moses fled for his life from Egypt but married a Midianite (Exodus 2:15,21). Each woman bore her husband at least two sons during his time of exile, and in each case one son's name reflected the fact that the father was in a foreign land (Genesis 41:51–52; Exodus 2:22; 18:3).

The circumstances in which Moses met Zipporah the Midianite also fit a pattern that indicates God's design. He met her by a well (Exodus 2:16), the sort of place where Abraham's servant found a wife for Isaac and where Jacob met Rachel (Genesis 24:11,15; 29:9–10). Moses helps her and her sisters water their flock, just as Jacob did for Rachel (Exodus 2:17,19; Genesis 29:10). Moses meeting Zipporah was God's plan!

Moreover, God did not provide this marriage merely for Moses' comfort with no regard to his future calling; the narrative implies that this incident is part of God's redemptive plan for Moses' work. The image of "drawing water" (despite different terms) recalls the circumstances of his early rescue from the water for which he was named, in the same context (Exodus 2:10,16,19).[11] This rescue in turn reminds readers of God's redemptive work in Moses' time: Moses was in the water because Pharaoh wanted the Israelite boys drowned in the Nile (Exodus 1:22), but God would remind Egypt of its offenses when he sent Moses back to them. The first plague would turn the

Nile to blood (Exodus 7:20–21); the last plague would kill Egypt's most esteemed baby boys (12:29–30); and finally, God would drown Egypt's armies in the sea (14:27–28). Further, Moses' deliverance was possible only through the women God used, such as the midwives, Moses' mother, and Moses' sister (Exodus 1:15–21; 2:2–4,7–8). The other woman who helped rescue him is most relevant here—a foreign woman, one of Pharaoh's own daughters whose compassion for a baby would ultimately undermine her father's policy (Exodus 2:5–10). Given the other women God used as a blessing to Moses, it is reasonable to regard Zipporah in the same way. Moses' connection with Zipporah's family certainly did prove to be a blessing to Israel (Exodus 18).

Still, the marriage must have required some cultural adjustments, especially for Zipporah. She appeared none too happy about circumcising their child, though she was willing to do it to save Moses' life (Exodus 4:24–26).[12] Although Jethro had accepted Israel's God as one among many, he realized only later that Israel's God was the greatest of gods (Exodus 18:11). Nor did this cross-cultural marriage imply that all other unions with Midianites would be sacred: Midianite women who would lead Israel to worship other gods were dangerous (Numbers 25:15,18; 31:17–18). But in the case of Moses, this marriage was divinely arranged.

It is no coincidence that Stephen, preaching that God is not localized in Jerusalem, mentions that Moses had sons in the land of Midian (Acts 7:29). Here, as in Matthew, an interethnic union becomes an example of God's concern for all peoples.

How would Israel have felt about their own leader being married to a foreigner when, as a rule, such behavior was forbidden them? One passage does mention leaders resenting Moses' marriage to a foreign woman. Whether this woman was Zipporah or another woman is not clear, though Numbers 12:1 sounds as if this is another wife. In any case, she was a Nubian, perhaps from Egypt, if she was not Zipporah.[13] In this instance, leaders no less influential than Miriam and Aaron criticized Moses' marriage to a foreign woman—but no one less than God defended Moses. Whatever range of complexions was found in Israel, the Nubians were certainly black by everyone's definition (cf. Jeremiah 13:23).[14] In this case Moses' foreign wife was notably black, so God judged Miriam by turning her white—with leprosy! He turned her "as white as snow" (Numbers 12:10). (Leprosy was associated with whitened skin—Leviticus 13:3,13,20,25; 2 Kings 5:27). Even in ancient Israel, some interethnic marriages had God's full blessing.

Other examples. In the case of Esther, her marriage to the king of Persia may not have been voluntary; she was taken and added to his harem before being chosen as queen (Esther 2:8–9). This is certainly not an ideal marriage, regardless of the races involved; thus, we treat her here only briefly. At the least, however, we can see God preparing and working through this marriage to rescue the chosen people. God's favor is clear in the story. King Xerxes divorced or demoted Vashti for refusing to come when he summoned her (Esther 1:12,19); he forgave Esther when she came unbidden (Esther 5:2). Vashti lost Xerxes' favor at a banquet (Esther 1:3,12), but Esther was installed at one (Esther 2:18) and further secured the king's favor at others (Esther 5:6). God protects and exalts Mordecai at Haman's expense, in the end even giving him Haman's job (Esther 6:4,6,10,13; 7:9; 8:2)! God had clearly raised up Esther for "such a time as this" (Esther 4:14).

Probably many interethnic marriages occurred that are not mentioned in Scripture because the couples were not prominent like Joseph or Moses. (We will deal with less savory examples, like Solomon, below.) While Israelites were not supposed to marry foreign wives who would turn their hearts from God, foreigners who settled in Israel were to be welcomed into the covenant of God. This principle is affirmed repeatedly in the Law of Moses (Exodus 12:19,48–49; 20:10; 22:21; 23:9,12; Leviticus 16:29; 17:8–15; 18:26; 19:10; 22:18; 24:22; Numbers 9:14; 15:14–30; 19:10; 35:15; Deuteronomy 1:16; 5:14; 10:18–19; 14:29; 16:11,14; 24:14–21; 26:11–13; 27:19; 29:11–12; 31:12) and in the Prophets (Isaiah 14:1; Jeremiah 7:6; 22:3; Ezekiel 22:7,29; 47:22–23). Presumably, therefore, all of them could marry into Israel, with the exceptions of Ammonites and Moabites (Deuteronomy 23:3); Egyptians and Edomites were explicitly permitted (Deuteronomy 23:7–8). For that matter, the Book of Ruth shows that God made exceptions even for Moabites.[15] Some immigrants probably had spouses when they came; others, like Uriah the Hittite, apparently did marry into Israel. Such cases must have been fairly frequent. David's Cherethite and Pelethite (Philistine) bodyguards (2 Samuel 8:18; 15:1; 20:7,23; 1 Kings 1:38,44), Ebed-melech the Nubian (Jeremiah 38:7–12; 39:16–18), and the Nubian courier in 2 Samuel 18:21–32 are all examples of foreigners who settled in the land, just as Moses and Joseph had settled among foreign peoples.[16] Some children of mixed marriages in foreign lands also seem to have retained some attachment to Israel even when the father was foreign (probably implied in 1 Kings 7:13–14; 2 Chronicles 2:13–14).

Because most Gentiles in the Old Testament period did not follow Israel's God, it is not surprising that we read of only a few positive cases of inter-marriage. Yet even among Israel's greatest leaders, we find some. In the New Testament period there were few Gentiles living in the parts of Palestine that the Gospels cover, but we do learn of a Jewish-Gentile marriage in the Book of Acts. Timothy's mother was Jewish and his father was Gentile. Though Timothy had not been circumcised, he apparently was raised in the Jewish faith. His mother and grandmother were both godly Jewish women even before the gospel came to them (Acts 16:1–3; 2 Timothy 1:5; 3:15). Given the few marriages mentioned outside Palestine in the New Testament, this one constitutes a significant example. Timothy was racially mixed.[17]

Objections to Interracial Marriage

According to the Bible, God created boundaries between peoples, and in the case of Israel, God enforced these boundaries. Some have exploited the Bible's claim for such boundaries to seek to justify racial separation, whether in marriage or in society at large. Those who appeal to this argument often cite Acts 17:26—as if acknowledging God's sovereignty over the times and places when and where nations exist implies that their boundaries are eternally fixed or genetically defined!

To say that God is sovereign over which peoples settled where, however, is a descriptive and not a prescriptive statement. It certainly does not imply that God will not continue sovereignly mixing peoples! These boundaries reveal God's greatness by showing the diverse cultures as well as diversity in nature that God created (Genesis 10; cf. Genesis 1). The same God who created the boundaries of peoples has also sovereignly readjusted those boundaries through history; God freely moves nations around (Amos 9:7). After all, we rarely meet Philistines, Hittites, Edomites, Moabites, or Ammonites anymore. Nor can one turn the fact of some peoples predominating in some regions into an argument of natural law: the same history that explains this predominance in a given period attests to plenty of mixing and migration before it. Indeed, an argument from nature would support rather than oppose interracial unions: the more diverse the genetic stock, the healthier the offspring are likely to be![18]

If one is to make a specific argument from the Bible against interracial marriage, one might prefer to turn to the Old Testament practice of endogamy: Israelites were told to marry Israelites. Before there were technically Israelites to marry, Abraham secured a member of his clan for Isaac, and Rebekah did the same for Jacob; apparently these women were closer to the faith than the geographically nearer women were (Genesis 24:3–4; 27:46; 28:1–2). Yet God's promise to Abraham ultimately challenges the need for such limitations. Abraham would become the ancestor of many nations (Genesis 17:4–5), a promise that the New Testament applies to the church (Romans 4:17).[19] Through Abraham, all peoples would be blessed (Genesis 12:3; 18:18; 22:18; 26:4; 28:14), for from his faithful seed would come salvation even to the Gentiles. For Christians, "endogamy" simply means marrying fellow Christians (1 Corinthians 7:39; 9:5; cf. 2 Corinthians 6:14–18).

Likewise, God told the Israelites that they were special and were forbidden to intermarry with the Canaanites, specifically because the foreigners might turn Israel's hearts from God (Deuteronomy 7:3–4). The Old Testament contains many examples of bad mixed marriages along with the good ones, but what made them bad was that they were *religiously* mixed marriages, not that they were ethnically mixed marriages. Because religion and culture were closely intertwined, intercultural marriages could pose dangers to Israel, but these were never racial matters. Further, the exceptions we viewed above show that even the cultural barriers could be overcome. Most of these positive exceptions involved Jewish men marrying foreign wives, because in patriarchal societies men had more influence in shaping the marriage and the faith of the children—though as we note here, only men with strong faith would lead in faith. But cases like Esther and Timothy's mother, Eunice, show that women with strong faith could also have a positive influence on their families.

Some mixed marriages did bring serious dangers to those involved. For example, Samson married a Philistine woman who then pried a secret out of him (Judges 14:17). The union was part of God's plan, but only so that Samson's personal pain would make him an enemy of the Philistines (14:4). The Book of Judges virtually skips over twenty years of his public ministry (15:20) in its hurry to move on to his subsequent liaison with a Philistine prostitute (16:1). His new relationship with a Philistine woman picks up the earlier story line; apparently the dysfunctional relationship of his youth still haunted him. Ignoring the danger from which he had barely escaped, he soon began sleeping with another Philistine, who pried a more important secret out of him—despite the fact that she betrayed him a few times before he finally gave in (16:8–17)!

But again, the story of Ruth demonstrates that the problem was not these Philistines' ethnicity. (Since they were historically more "European" than the

Israelites, Moabites, or Egyptians, most white readers would be happy to know that the Philistines' ethnicity was not the problem.) The problem was that Samson kept being attracted to women who were loyal to a people hostile to Israel. What began with adolescent rashness (Judges 14:2–3) apparently led to a desire to fulfill a better relationship with a Philistine, the ethnicity itself being a primary factor in his desire. This is a good warning for Christians not to date or marry people who do not serve our God, but it says nothing about committed Christians from different peoples marrying. It does sound the caution, however, that one should marry the right person and not simply seek to fulfill an attraction to a race.

Solomon married many foreign wives as part of his international diplomacy, in which kings or leaders gave their daughters in marriage to other kings. But whereas he was apparently a "good witness" to some foreign royal women, like the queen of Sheba (1 Kings 10:4–9), the multitude of his foreign wives eventually turned his heart from God and led him to compromise with their religious practices (1 Kings 11:1–8).[20] The Law of Moses had already warned against this danger for kings, again for the specific reason that their hearts would be turned from God (Deuteronomy 17:17), just as could happen to other Israelites (Deuteronomy 7:3; 1 Kings 11:2). Again, the problem was not the wives' ethnicity but their religion. A foreign princess was explicitly welcome if she truly adopted Israel as her new home, along with its faith (Psalm 45:10–11).[21]

After the exile, many Israelites repented of marrying foreign wives and demonstrated this repentance by divorcing them (Ezra 10; see Numbers 13:23–29; contrast 1 Corinthians 7:12–14). Again, however, the problem was that Israel, meant to be a people set apart to the Lord, had adopted pagan practices of the most wicked surrounding nations (Ezra 9:1–2,11–12); they were raising their children according to the ways of the other nations, not according to Israel's heritage (Nehemiah 13:24). Had the foreigners adopted Israel's God and heritage, they would have been treated differently (Leviticus 19:33–34; 23:22; 24:22; 25:35; Zechariah 7:10; Malachi 3:5), like Rahab, Ruth, or Uriah; it was those who continued to practice paganism who were to be exterminated (Leviticus 20:2; 24:16; Numbers 15:30; Ezekiel 14:7–8).[22] All Gentile Christians are converts to faith in Israel's God (Romans 11:17); we are one spiritual race (1 Corinthians 10:32). Those grafted into Israel's faith as Abraham's spiritual descendants (Galatians 3:29; cf. Romans 2:29) are free to marry their fellow followers of Christ.

Even if one insisted on reading these texts ethnically rather than religiously, however, the argument would not go very far. God told only Israelites not to intermarry with other peoples. That would still allow any ethnic Gentiles to intermarry with each other! But the ethnic application of these texts today is impossible for Christians. Even with regard to food customs, the New Testament reverses the Old Testament practice of separation (Mark 7:19; Acts 10:12–15; 11:3; Romans 14:3,20; Galatians 2:12), and the ultimate point of this is that we may no longer consider other groups of people as unclean (Acts 10:28; 11:18; cf. Romans 14:20–21). God called Israel to be separate lest the nation compromise with Gentile ways (which often happened); God calls the church to evangelize the nations, and today the church is made up of many nations.

The Racist Ideology behind Objections to Interracial Marriage

Those who object to interracial marriage have applied their objections selectively. For example, one hears few complaints about the romantic story surrounding the marriage of John Rolfe to Pocahontas in 1614. Still, the ideas promoting racial purity have been around in this country for a long time. For example, in 1878 some Californians publicly worried that some whites would intermarry with Chinese immigrants. They felt that this would "debase" the white race even more than intermarriage with blacks. By 1880 a California law prohibited whites from marrying anyone with even a Chinese or black grandparent. In 1921, after Los Angeles allowed Filipinos to marry whites, California's attorney general filed suit to prevent such support for mixed marriages. The state legislature banned these marriages in a unanimous decision; it was not until 1948 (the year that Israel became a nation) that California's laws against interracial marriage were declared unconstitutional.[23]

Through most of human history, people did not object in general to interracial marriage, although many objected to marrying ethnic enemies of their people. Ethnocentrism, of course, has always been common, and such ethnocentrism ultimately laid the foundations for opposing interracial marriage. Greeks, for example, looked down on other peoples, and some even came up with pseudoscientific reasons for their racism.[24] Although in general Greeks respected the legendary "Ethiopians," by which they meant sub–Saharan Africans,[25] some believed that peoples to the south were less intelligent because the heat overcooked their brains, just as peoples to the north were less intelligent because their brains were frozen. Muslim Arabs adopted these sorts of stereotypes, which helped bolster their involvement in the African slave trade.[26]

In the ninth century, some Arabs began applying the myth of Ham, a perversion of the story of Ham in Genesis 9. In Genesis, only Canaan is cursed, and the curse was fulfilled by some of the story's audience as they conquered the land of Canaan. But by claiming that Ham was cursed, these Arabs justified the further enslavement of Africans, even when (against Islamic law) these were Africans converted to Islam.[27] They also perpetuated stereotypes that Africans were stinky, oversexed, and lazy.[28] This bias did not, however, prevent interracial unions. Most slave cultures in human history included exploitation of female slaves, and Arabs seemed to prefer female African slaves to male ones, for use in their harems.[29] Although they employed a racist ideology to justify their enslavement of Africans and practiced racial discrimination, they did not practice sexual segregation on these grounds. (Marriage was often problematic mainly because of the class issue, and intercourse was expected.)[30] Despite enslavement and discrimination, the Spanish and Portuguese also did not prohibit interracial unions with locals and imported Africans, as the large mixed populations in many parts of Latin America testify.

U. S. history, however, took a different turn. Originally the settlers could use indentured servants of any color, but British law regulated their treatment of subjects of the crown. They discovered that exploiting African workers, who could not appeal to the crown for redress, was more profitable than exploiting whites.[31] In time, economic incentive required ideological justification, and whites caricatured Africans in much the same way as their slave-trading Arab predecessors had. This time, however, colonies devised laws to ensure that children of interracial unions remained slaves, and ultimately they devised laws ruling against such unions.[32] The laws were, of course, frequently flouted in practice, but polite white society chose not to take much notice.

Even states that came to reject slavery rejected racial mixing, fearing that it could lead to interracial unions.[33] Many abolitionists accommodated this prejudice because they feared they would undermine popular support by appearing too radical.[34] Some, however, like evangelical businessman Lewis Tappan, vocally supported "amalgamation," the mixing of races. To those who protested fearfully that social mixing could lead to interracial marriages (and sometimes did, as in the case of Frederick Douglass), he replied that in a thousand years everyone in America would be copper-colored.[35] Fear of interracial unions remained one of the major arguments supporting racial segregation in the Jim Crow era.

Some claimed scientific reasons for their opposition to interracial unions. In the mid-nineteenth century, a leading evolutionary scientist at Harvard contended that whites and blacks were separate species. He avoided blacks and considered interracial unions to be as dangerous as incest, although an evangelical biology professor there argued against his case.[36] In the twentieth century, Nazi eugenicists sought to produce a master Aryan race by eliminating Jews, Eastern Europeans, Africans, and other potential threats to a pure gene pool. Today, despite the claims of some whose discipline is not genetics, geneticists have refuted such pseudoscientific claims.[37]

Opposition to interracial marriage derives from the same racist ideology and spirit that undergirded slavery, U.S. segregation, and South African apartheid. It is simply the final piece of segregation to require dismantling, and to tolerate it is to tolerate the spirit of racism that created it. Racism and its moral siblings constitute human sin or selfishness on a corporate level—our group's interests versus those of others. As we shall quickly observe, it is impossible to remain faithful to the gospel of Christ while permitting racial separatism, in marriages or otherwise.

Theological Basis for Supporting Interracial Marriage

Although the Bible provides some examples of interracial marriages, it provides much more than that: it provides a theology of ethnic and cultural reconciliation that defies all racial separatism as inimical to the gospel of Christ.[38] While God encouraged a form of cultural separatism for ancient Israel to prevent religiously corrupting influences (e.g., Leviticus 20:26), the Lord moved the early Christians to reverse this separatism (e.g., Acts 10:28). Mission, rather than preservation, was the new primary paradigm for intercultural contact.

Paul. One can hardly imagine Paul, apostle to the Gentiles, supporting segregation among different groups of Gentile Christians. He strenuously argued against it even between Jewish and Gentile Christians, regarding the latter as spiritual converts to Israel's faith and heritage. In fact, when Peter allowed for a segregated lunch counter to avoid offending more conservative elements in the church, Paul publicly accused him of denying the gospel of Christ (Galatians 2:11–14). Jesus and Judaism both advised private reproof,[39] but because the gospel itself was at stake, Paul rebuked Peter publicly.

Some time before Paul wrote his letter to the Romans, Jewish Christians previously expelled from Rome had returned there (Romans 16:3,7; cf. Acts 18:1–2). Because most Jews lived in their own sections in Rome, the house churches may have been divided along Jewish-Gentile lines. Paul reconciles believers by reminding them that both Gentiles (Romans 1) and Jews (Romans 2–3) are lost, that ethnic descent from Abraham is not sufficient (Romans 4), since all are descended from Adam (Romans 5:12–21), and that the law by itself cannot justify (Romans 7). Jewish people claimed superiority because they were chosen in Abraham, but Paul reminds them that neither Ishmael nor Esau received the full promise, so it is not physical descent from Abraham but God's will that determines who will be saved (Romans 9). He also warns Gentile Christians not to despise ethnic Israel, because God still has a purpose for Israel, and ethnic Jews can embrace more easily their spiritual heritage than can Gentiles (Romans 11).

In other words, all of us have to come to God on the same terms— through Jesus Christ. None of us dare look down on any other. That is why Paul keeps stressing that the gospel is for all, both Jew and Gentile alike (Romans 1:16; 2:9–10; 3:9,29; 9:24; 10:12). Paul now applies this principle practically: we must serve one another (12:3–16); the heart of the law is loving one another (13:8–10). We should not look down on each other's food customs or holy days (Romans 14)—the main complaints Roman Gentiles offered concerning Roman Jews. We should follow the examples of Jewish-Gentile reconciliation we find in the ministries of Jesus (15:3–12) and Paul (15:14–27). Finally, we should beware of those who cause division (16:17)! Paul reasons from the gospel how we are to treat one another. If all of us are saved on the same terms, then our diversity is not a cause for separatism.

Paul himself refused to compromise his gospel to the Gentiles. He ended up in prison because of it (Acts 21:28–29; 22:21–22). When he writes to his fellow Christians near Ephesus, they know full well why he writes to them from detention (see Acts 21:27,29). They know that he was accused of having taken a Gentile past the dividing wall in the temple that separated Jews from Gentiles (Acts 21:28). To them, Paul declares that Christ has shattered that wall of partition and established a new, spiritual temple that includes both Jew and Gentile (Ephesians 2:14,19–22).[40]

Gospels and Acts. When Matthew lists the four women with Gentile associations in his opening genealogy, they represent merely examples of part of his larger agenda. These interracial marriages introduce his emphasis on the

Gentile mission: his Jewish-Christian readers must evangelize Gentiles. Thus, we learn in Matthew

- Jesus was sought from the East (2:1–2)
- Abrahamic descent is not primary (3:9)
- Jesus settled in "Galilee of the Gentiles" (4:15)
- Jesus finds special faith in a Roman army officer (8:10–11)
- Jesus delivers demoniacs in Gentile territory (8:28–32)
- foreign cities matter as much to God as Israel's (10:15; 11:21–24; 12:41–42)
- Jesus responds to the great faith of a Canaanite woman (15:28)
- Peter confesses Jesus in an area whose paganism was well known (16:16)
- the gospel must be preached among all the nations before the end comes (24:14)
- all nations will be judged according to it (25:32–34)
- the first to recognize Jesus as God's Son after his death are his Roman execution squad (27:54)
- the heart of the church's mission is discipling the nations (28:19)

Matthew opened this theme with interracial marriage, a tangible symbol of God's bridging the chasm created by human sin.

Mark includes some of the same examples, but we will focus on only one. In the Old Testament, Gentiles were welcome in the temple (1 Kings 8:41–43); more rigid application of purity laws, however, led to Gentiles being kept further out in Herod's temple. Just as Paul paid a price for challenging the temple's ethnic segregation, so did Jesus. The Pharisees had plotted to kill him earlier, but they never got past the plotting stage; after all, they held little political power (Mark 3:6). But when Jesus overturned the tables in the temple, he challenged the hegemony of the Sadducean establishment, the political elite of Jerusalem. Within a week they had him handed over to the Romans and executed as a criminal (Mark 14:1; 15:1).

Why did Jesus overturn the tables? His quotes from Scripture may help indicate at least one reason (Mark 11:17). He quotes Isaiah 56:7, which declares God's purpose for the temple: it was to be a house of prayer for all nations. Then he quotes Jeremiah 7:11, which calls the temple a "robbers' den"—the place where robbers feel safe to store their loot after committing their crimes. The context in Jeremiah 7 warns that the temple will be destroyed. Jesus is warning about the impending destruction of God's house because of corruption, including the treatment of the

Gentiles (Mark 13:2). Within a generation, his words were fulfilled (cf. Mark 13:30).

The Gospel of Luke also shows that God's purposes for Gentiles were rooted in the Old Testament. Jesus introduces his mission, for instance, by speaking of some prophets' ministries to a Syrian general and to a widow in Phoenicia (Luke 4:26–27). He also deals favorably with Samaritans (Luke 9:52; 10:33–37; 17:16). He embraces the marginalized and closes the Gospel with the Gentile mission (Luke 24:47).

In the Book of Acts, Luke's second volume, however, the mission to the Gentiles reaches center stage (Acts 1:8). First, God leads the apostles to install Hellenist Jews in positions of leadership (Acts 6:5). These Hellenists are bicultural, foreign Jews, and ultimately they form the bridge for the Gentile mission (Acts 11:19–20). Among them, Stephen lays the theological groundwork for the mission by showing that God is not localized in Jerusalem or the Holy Land (Acts 7). One of his examples, in fact, involves an interracial union (Acts 7:29). Philip—another of the Hellenists—pioneers the mission to Samaria and reaches the first Gentile Christian (Acts 8). Paul's conversion and call to the Gentiles inaugurates a new stage in the Gentile mission (Acts 9), as does the church's reception of a Gentile convert and the possibility of eating with him despite his lack of circumcision (Acts 10–11). This mission continues on into the heart of the Roman Empire (Acts 28:16–31). And yet, while this mission was God's agenda, the Jerusalem church was dragged into it against its own prejudices (Acts 10:28; 11:2–3; 15:5; 21:21). God's Spirit today continues to challenge us to move beyond human prejudices and accept the Spirit's call.

When Jesus prays for all his followers to be one (John 17:21), part of the answer to that prayer is ethnic and cultural unity among his followers. Despite prejudices against Samaritans even among his own disciples, Jesus ministers to the Samaritan woman and her community (John 4:4–42). He promises her a coming time when the true place of worship will be neither in Jerusalem (where Judeans worshiped) nor on Mount Gerizim (where Samaritans worshiped) but in the Spirit (John 4:21–23).[41] Here Jesus probably is implying the spiritual temple that Paul, Peter, and others later emphasized.

Revelation likewise offers a vision of the future in which representatives from all peoples gather to worship God (Revelation 5:9–10; 7:9).[42] This is the goal and climax of God's plan—a united people from all the peoples God has created, a plan God had in mind already when calling Abraham so that all the families of the earth would be blessed in him (Genesis 12:2–3). From start to finish, the gospel message involves reconciliation. Through Christ we are reconciled to God, and the resulting church must demonstrate lives of reconciliation with one another in Christ.

This means that racial prejudice and apartheid, the foundations for opposition to interracial marriage, are inimical to the gospel. If we really believe the gospel's claim that what matters most is Christ, then the chief divider in humanity will be between those who trust him and those who do not. All other divisions are relative, and true unity in Christ can surmount them. Without such divisions, one cannot segregate Christians of different cultures or races. (It is understandable and not, in my opinion, wrong that individual Christians may continue to feel more comfortable culturally among those who share their culture, especially if they belong to minority cultures. But they dare not objectify their comfort as God's will or prescribe it for others.) Marriage is the ultimate joining of two persons into one (Genesis 2:24; Mark 10:8), so an interracial marriage that involves a godly unity in diversity is the ultimate challenge to racial segregation, striking it at the deepest level.

Those who oppose interracial marriage in our culture for pragmatic reasons ("they will have a hard time"; "it will be hard on the children") are not necessarily racist in the direct sense, but they compromise with the racist system rather than challenging it. After all, others have endured opposition for their commitment to relocate to other cultures for ministry, yet we as Christians support them. Can God not have a purpose in calling two people together in a cross-cultural way even without relocating them? The objective in contemplating a potential interracial union, as in any union, must be how it fits God's will for those involved. Obviously some interracial unions, like some single-race unions, are not God's will. But Scripture shows that we cannot determine God's will in any given case simply by color codes.

Conclusion

Christians cannot affirm the gospel faithfully and yet refuse to share unity as brothers and sisters in Christ. Further, we cannot share this unity in Christ and yet prohibit fellowship and marriage based on ethnicity. Scripture prohibits absolutely some kinds of sexual unions (homosexual, extramarital, and premarital intercourse). It also strongly discourages marrying outside the faith. But both testaments portray godly interracial marriages, some of which become divine models of ethnic reconciliation. A biblical theology of ethnic reconciliation, which is central to the gospel, invites rather than discourages more interethnic social relations, including marriage, in the body of Christ.

The only theological prejudices against it, in principle, are ultimately those undergirding slavery and segregation, which we regard as heretical, diabolic institutions. Prejudice against interracial marriage should be confronted no less firmly than other manifestations of racism.

On a personal note, I have defended these convictions for many years, including in footnotes of various books.[43] They seemed clear to me from the gospel even shortly after my conversion, when witnessing Christians were in the minority and the faith of my witnessing partners mattered more than their complexion. Eventually I felt compelled to defend them with somewhat greater personal significance in a letter to my grandmother, who was very kind and dear to me but held a different view.[44] The issue arose when my younger brother Chris was preparing to marry his fiancée, Minglan, who is from Shanghai, China. While defending them, I was defending myself in advance, because I am white and yet was active in the black church (which has a lot of godly single women); given my setting, I was already expecting at that time that my future wife would probably be black. I have proved wrong in expecting that she would be African American, though she has turned out to be black.

In 1989 Médine Moussounga came to Duke University for a year of research while writing her dissertation at the University of Paris. She was one of my closest friends from the graduate InterVarsity Fellowship at Duke, and she was also one of the most vibrant witnesses on campus. Our friendship grew in the years that followed, until we lost contact during a civil war in the Congo, her home country. She remained in hiding in the forest for eighteen months. Unknown to me, both before that time and even in the forest, some people of prayer who knew nothing about me told her that she would marry a white man with a big ministry, just as I had felt things about my future wife that fit only her. After she reached safety, we realized that our love had stood the test of time and we should take the next step.

When I agreed to write this chapter, Médine was still in the forest, and I did not yet know that she would become my future wife. When I finished writing this chapter, we were engaged. Médine and I finally married on March 13, 2002, so we now have personal reasons for joyfully reading this book other than academic interest in the subject.

Discussion Questions

1. Since the American notion of biological race was not applicable during the time the Bible was written, how can we use the Bible to

inform us about racial issues in general and interracial marriage issues in particular?

2. Why do you think Matthew would go out of his way to include Gentile women in his description of Jesus' genealogy? What is the implication of the inclusion of these women for multiracial families?

3. Which of the objections to interracial marriages do you think has the most merit? Why? How would you answer this objection?

4. The author contends that there is a racist ideology behind many of the objections to interracial marriage. What is his strongest argument for this contention? How convincing do you think this argument is?

5. Should Christians allow pragmatic, instead of racist, opposition to stop interracial marriages? Why or why not?

Notes

1. *See e.g., F. F. Bruce,* Commentary on the Book of Acts, *New International Commentary on the New Testament (Grand Rapids, Mich.: Eerdmans, 1977), 64; B. B. Dominy, "Spirit, Church, and Mission: Theological Implications of Pentecost,"* Southwestern Journal of Theology 35, no. 2 (1993): 34–39; D. Smith, "What Hope after Babel? Diversity and Community in Genesis 11:1–9, Exodus 1:1–14, Zephaniah 3:1–13, and Acts 2:1–13," *Horizons in Biblical Theology 18, no. 2 (1996): 169–91; David Hill,* New Testament Prophecy *(Atlanta: John Knox, 1979), 95; and F. Scott Spencer,* Acts *(Sheffield, England: Sheffield Academic, 1997), 32–33. Some caution is appropriate regarding Luke's intention (C. K. Barrett,* A Critical and Exegetical Commentary on the Acts of the Apostles, *2 vols. [Edinburgh: Clark, 1994, 1998], 112, 116, 119; J. D. G. Dunn,* The Acts of the Apostles *[Valley Forge, Pa.: Trinity, 1996], 24), but the church's appropriation of the account this way remains legitimate (G. D. Cloete and D. J. Smit, " 'Its Name Was Called Babel … ,' "* Journal of Theology for Southern Africa *no. 86 [1994]: 81–87).

2. *See more details in W. E. B. DuBois,* The World and Africa: An Inquiry into the Part Which Africa Has Played in History, *rev. ed. (New York: International, 1965), 115–16; cf. Sharon Begley, "Three Is Not Enough: Surprising New Lessons from the Controversial Science of Race,"* Newsweek, *February 13, 1995, 67–68; Bruce G. Trigger, "Nubian, Negro, Black, Nilotic?" in* The Arts of Ancient Nubia and the Sudan—The Essays, *vol. 1 of* Africa in Antiquity *(Brooklyn, N.Y.: Brooklyn Museum, 1978), 26–35; Colin Renfrew and Paul Bahn,* Archaeology: Theories, Methods, and Practice *(London: Thames & Hudson, 1991), 371; Edward G. Olsen, "What Shall We Teach about Race and Racism?" in* Teaching in the Inner City: A

Book of Readings, *eds. J. C. Stone and F. W. Schneider (New York: Thomas Y. Crowell, 1970), 356–60.*

3. *Sribala Subramanian, "The Story in Our Genes: A Landmark Global Study Flattens The Bell Curve," Time, January 16, 1995, 55; R. W. Mack, ed., Race, Class, and Power, 2d ed. (New York: D. Van Nostrand, 1968), 57; Begley, "Three Is Not Enough," 68.*

4. *To be sure, if this is Joseph's genealogy (Matthew 1:16), it does not speak to Jesus' genetic heritage, but it does speak to his legal heritage, to the royal line God had chosen in the Old Testament. If one is interested only in genetic lineage, what "race" was Abraham? If that question is not easily answered, we should note that clearly the Israelites who came out of Egypt were thoroughly mixed with Egyptian and other Near Eastern blood, since the servants of Jacob's house would have assimilated into the family after all were enslaved (see Glenn Usry and Craig Keener, Black Man's Religion [Downers Grove, Ill.: InterVarsity Press, 1996], 73; Genesis 12:16; 16:1; 25:5,31–34; 27:29; cf. Genesis 13:6–8; 14:14).*

5. *E.g., b. Sanh. 22a; Gen. Rab. 68:4; Pes. Rab. Kah. 2:4; cf. Lev. Rab. 8:1; Num. Rab. 3:6.*

6. *Jos. Apion 1.30; cf. b. Pes. 62b; p. Ter. 7:1; M. D. Johnson,* The Purpose of the Biblical Genealogies: With Special Reference to the Setting of the Genealogies of Jesus, *2d ed., Society for New Testament Studies Monograph 8 (Cambridge: Cambridge University Press, 1988), 88–95.*

7. *See Hittite laws, tablet 2, law 193 (trans. Goetze, in* Ancient Near Eastern Texts Relating to the Old Testament, *ed. J. B. Pritchard [Princeton, N.J.: Princeton University Press, 1955], 196); also Cyrus Gordon,* The Common Background of Greek and Hebrew Civilizations *(New York: W. W. Norton, 1965), 95.*

8. *I owe these observations about Rahab to J. Scott Duvall and J. Daniel Hays,* Grasping God's Word *(Grand Rapids, Mich.: Zondervan, 2001), 297–8.*

9. *If Eliam, her father (2 Samuel 11:3), is the same warrior of that name (2 Samuel 23:34), her marriage to his colleague in David's elite troop, Uriah (2 Samuel 23:39), is understandable. So also is the later hostility of one Ahithophel the Gilonite (2 Samuel 15:12,31), Eliam's father (2 Samuel 23:34).*

10. *See* Black Man's Religion, *64–68, and the documentation for these pages on 165–8. The later Jewish romance "Joseph and Asenath" fills in details creatively but was especially designed to promote Jewish faith.*

11. *The rescue image is clear; the writer of Genesis and Exodus uses the term for "ark" only with reference to what Moses was floating in and what Noah's family floated in (see Nahum Sarna,* Exploring Exodus *[New York: Schocken, 1986], 28–29, 32).*

12. *Circumcision may appear here as a sign of adoption by God, whose children the Israelites were; God would slay the children of his children's oppressors (Exodus*

4:22–23). On this complex passage, see Umberto Cassuto, A Commentary on the Book of Exodus *(Jerusalem: Hebrew University Press, 1967), 58–61; Peter Enns,* Exodus, NIV Application Commentary *(Grand Rapids, Mich.: Zondervan, 2000), 133–4.*

13. *Some early Jewish interpreters offered the same guess, suggesting that she was a Nubian princess Moses had married (Jos. Ant. 2.252).*

14. *The Egyptian and Hebrew term "Kush" seem to reflect the indigenous African name for an African people south of Egypt (see W. L. Hansberry,* Africa and Africans as Seen by Classical Writers *[Washington, D.C.: Howard University Press, 1981], 8–9). The term also has this meaning in later sources such as the following: Petronius Sat. 102; Seneca Dial. 5.27.3; Sextus Empiricus Against the Ethicists 3.43; Philo Allegorical Laws 2.67; Gen. Rab. 73:10; 86:3.*

15. *Later rabbis understood Deuteronomy 23:3 as excluding only male Moabites (m. Yeb. 8:3; Sifre Deut. 249.1.1–2; Pes. Rab. 49:2).*

16. *Cf. also the Egyptian tale of Sinuhe, who married locally while in exile (Sinuhe 79), though he later returned happily to Egypt.*

17. *On interracial children today, see Sundee Frazier,* Check All That Apply *(Downers Grove, Ill.: InterVarsity Press, 2002).*

18. *E.g., Olsen, "What Shall We Teach?" 359.*

19. *The Ishmaelites and Midianites descended from Abraham, but the point of Genesis is that Abraham's chosen seed would multiply (cf. Genesis 48:19); together with the blessing of all nations, however, this implies Gentiles coming to faith.*

20. *We leave aside the question as to whether Solomon had relations with the queen of Sheba, though Ethiopian tradition (possibly from the early Christian era) claims it. On the tradition, see William Leo Hansberry,* Pillars in Ethiopian History *(Washington, D.C.: Howard University Press, 1981), 33–59; on this queen as queen of Ethiopia in early Jewish tradition, see also James M. Scott, "Luke's Geographical Horizon," in* The Book of Acts in Its Greco-Roman Setting, *6 vols. (Grand Rapids, Mich.: Eerdmans, 1994), 2:483–544, esp. 536; on the story's historicity, see David Tuesday Adamo, "The Place of Africa and Africans in the Old Testament and Its Environment" (Ph.D. diss., Baylor University, 1986), 131–7. The writer of 1 Kings does not place her among Solomon's foreign wives (1 Kings 11) but among his foreign policy achievements, such as impressing the king of Tyre (1 Kings 10:11–12).*

21. *Since he turned from God in his old age (1 Kings 11:4), possibly his earlier marriage to Pharaoh's daughter had not had this effect on him by itself (1 Kings 3:1; 11:1). Deuteronomy 17:17 specifically warns about "multiplying" wives (both in the Hebrew original and in the Greek version), suggesting many of them; the context*

probably indicates that foreign wives are in view (Deuteronomy 17:15–16). But since 1 Kings 11:2 cites Deuteronomy 7:3, it recognizes that even one spouse could turn a person away from God.

22. *Even Leviticus 25:47 points in this direction, because it addresses only the permanent land rights of the original Israelite settlers. This did not grant them first-class status (Deuteronomy 14:21; 28:43; even more severe in 2 Chronicles 2:17–18, but this includes Gibeonites and others who did not worship Israel's God—2 Chronicles 8:7–8; cf. 2 Samuel 1:13; 2 Chronicles 6:32–33), but it does not eliminate the welcome mentioned above. Further, presumably future generations could become Israelites—at the very least, any descendants with an Israelite father, so all but the purely male line.*

23. *See Frazier,* Check All That Apply, *182–3. Immigrants from Japan, India, and elsewhere protested they were white because of a 1790 law limiting naturalization to whites; the law was repealed only in 1952 (Ellis Cose, "One Drop of Bloody History,"* Newsweek, *February 13, 1995, 70), shortly before the civil rights movement!*

24. *See e.g., Aristotle,* Politics *1.1.4, 1252b; 1.2.18, 1255a; 3.9.3, 1285a.*

25. *See most thoroughly Frank M. Snowden Jr.,* Blacks in Antiquity: Ethiopians in the Greco-Roman Experience *(Cambridge, Mass.: Harvard University Press, 1970); idem,* Before Color Prejudice: The Ancient View of Blacks *(Cambridge, Mass.: Harvard University Press, 1983).*

26. *Bernard Lewis,* Race and Slavery in the Middle East *(New York: Oxford University, 1990), 46–48. For the Greco-Roman source, see e.g., Pliny Natural History 2.80.189 (in Snowden,* Before Color Prejudice, *86–87); Y. Talib with F. Samir, "The African Diaspora in Asia," in* Africa from the Seventh to the Eleventh Century *(Berkeley: University of California Press, 1988), 704–33, esp. 721–22.*

27. *Murray Gordon,* Slavery in the Arab World *(New York: New Amsterdam, 1989), 32; Lewis,* Race and Slavery, *55.*

28. *Lewis,* Race and Slavery, *92–94, 97; Gordon,* Slavery in the Arab World, *102–3. Sexual stereotypes about slaves are a common form of projection in slave cultures.*

29. *Gordon,* Slavery in the Arab World, *57, 79–104, 150; cf. Lewis,* Race and Slavery, *91. For sexual abuse of slaves in many cultures, see e.g. my* Paul, Women, and Wives: Marriage and Women's Ministry in the Letters of Paul *(Peabody, Mass.: Hendrickson, 1992), 197, 217. Some in precolonial Africa employed slaves in this manner (see J. K. Henn, "Women in the Rural Economy," in* African Women South of the Sahara, *eds. Margaret Jean Hay and Sharon Stichter [New York: Longman, 1984], 1–18, esp. 5–6).*

30. *Lewis,* Race and Slavery, *85–86, 91; Gordon,* Slavery in the Arab World, *43; Yusuf Fadl Hasan,* The Arabs and the Sudan: From the Seventh to the Early Sixteenth Century *(Edinburgh: University of Edinburgh Press, 1967), 43.*

31. *C. Eric Lincoln,* Race, Religion, and the Continuing American Dilemma *(New York: Hill & Wang, 1984), 35. On the ease of recapture as a factor, see Lerone Bennett Jr.,* Before the Mayflower: A History of the Negro in America, *1619–1964, rev. ed. (Baltimore: Penguin, 1966), 37.*

32. *Bennett,* Before the Mayflower, *37; also noted by C. Eric Lincoln in a public lecture at Duke Divinity School, November 9, 1990. Cf. also Bennett,* Before the Mayflower, *43–44, 242–73. That monogamy was honorable may have played a part, but the enslavement of children of such unions for economic purposes also played its role.*

33. *For fear of interracial unions supporting slavery and segregation, see e.g. David R. Roediger,* The Wages of Whiteness: Race and the Making of the American Working Class *(New York: Verso, 1991), 156; "God's College and Radical Change,"* Christian History *7, no. 4 (1988): 27.*

34. *See e.g., Nancy A. Hardesty,* Women Called to Witness: Evangelical Feminism in the Nineteenth Century *(Nashville: Abingdon, 1984), 118; Dorothy Sterling,* We Are Your Sisters: Black Women in the Nineteenth Century *(New York: W. W. Norton, 1984), 115.*

35. *On Tappan's stance, see e.g., Hardesty,* Women Called to Witness, *118; "The Gallery: Arthur (1786–1865) and Lewis (1788–1873) Tappan,"* Christian History *7, no. 4 (1988): 17–18; Donald Dayton,* Discovering an Evangelical Heritage *(New York: Harper & Row, 1976), passim.*

36. *Erskine Clarke,* Wrestlin' Jacob: A Portrait of Religion in the Old South *(Atlanta: John Knox, 1979), 108; David N. Livingstone,* Darwin's Forgotten Defenders: The Encounter between Evangelical Theology and Evolutionary Thought *(Grand Rapids, Mich.: Eerdmans; Edinburgh: Scottish Academic Press, 1987), 59–60; for the evangelical biologist Asa Gray, see Livingstone,* Darwin's Forgotten Defenders, *60–64.*

37. *See especially Begley, "Three Is Not Enough"; Subramanian, "Story in Our Genes," citing Princeton University Press's thousand-page* History and Geography of Human Genes *against the conclusions of nongeneticist* Bell Curve *authors.*

38. *I have addressed the issues in this section at greater length and with fuller documentation in "The Gospel and Racial Reconciliation," in* The Gospel in Black and White, *ed. D. L. Ockholm (Downers Grove, Ill.: InterVarsity Press, 1997), 117–30.*

39. *See my* A Commentary on the Gospel of Matthew *(Grand Rapids, Mich.: Eerdmans, 1999), 453–4. In fairness to Peter, he probably saw himself as doing cultural accommodation (1 Corinthians 9:19–23). But when this excludes people on the basis of*

their ethnicity, it is unacceptable, as Peter himself acknowledged in less strenuous times (Acts 11:3,17; 1 Peter 2:5,9–10).

40. *For documentation, see Keener, "Gospel and Reconciliation," 118–21.*

41. *For further detail and documentation, see my forthcoming commentary on John (Peabody, Mass.: Hendrickson, in press).*

42. *For background and documentation, see my "Revelation,"* NIV Application Commentary *(Grand Rapids, Mich.: Zondervan, 2000), 189, 249–50.*

43. *Including my first one, … And Marries Another (Peabody, Mass.: Hendrickson, 1991), 167, n. 30.*

44. *August 10, 1990.*

§ TWO §

Pastoral Counseling of
Multiracial Families

A. Charles Ware

A PASTOR HAS AN AWESOME RESPONSIBILITY TO SPEAK THE MIND of God to the people of God as revealed in the Word of God. We do not simply study the crowd, find out what they want, and give it to them. While the Bible must be applied to the times, it is not to be subservient to the times. Thus unity across economic, cultural, and ethnic lines should be proclaimed not because it is the latest fad but rather because it is the clear teaching of the eternal Word of God. The church is not a human's creation but God's. The manual describing the church's parts and operation is the Bible (1 Timothy 3:14–15; 2 Timothy 3:16–17). It is vital that Christian counselors and pastors draw from the Bible as they minister to the members of their churches. The purpose of this chapter is to correct some of the biblical abuse that pastors have previously used against interracial couples as well as to provide advice for Christian leaders who have the responsibility to counsel interracial couples and to help create an atmosphere where interracial families may be comfortable within their churches.

Commitment to the Bible was the reason that numerous fundamentalist and evangelical leaders gave for opposing interracial marriages in the past.[1] For example, one common argument was that interracial marriage was contrary to the Word of God. It was further reasoned that since interracial marriage is sin at its worse and unwise at its best, segregated churches, schools, and colleges would keep racial groups from the temptation to date and possibly marry across racial lines. Therefore, pastoral counsel concerning interracial marriage was primarily limited to denouncing or discouraging such unions and encouraging people to attend a church with their own people.

This line of thinking is illustrated by a pastor's concluding argument against integration: "Christ said plainly there would be no marrying and giving in marriage in heaven, therefore, there will be no need for segregation in heaven. But there is marrying and giving in marriage down here, therefore,

28

segregation is imperative to preserve the purity of the races and to prevent the mongrelization which has taken place in every country where integration has prevailed."[2] Another nationally known Christian radio speaker stated his view clearly by counseling, "I feel Negroes and Whites should never intermarry, but where possible live in their own social and religious groups and churches."[3]

I have previously written concerning the use of Scripture that when supporting racism "misinterpretation leads to misapplication, which leads to misdirection."[4] Pastors must rightly divide the Word of God on this issue and provide supporting resources for their congregations. Yet resources to assist the clergy in redirecting the church along the track of biblical truth in regards to interracial families are scarce today. Thus, it is critical that leaders invest some time and funds to gather as much solid information as possible.

Since Dr. Keener has correctly asserted that interracial families are biblical, the clergy must be prepared to address the inevitable and sometimes unique issues that such unions face in a society and in a church with a long history of racial struggles. The growing number of interracial marriages, blended families, and transracial adoptions demands clear and practical counsel from today's clergy. According to the U.S. Census Bureau's 2000 Current Population Survey, the number of mixed-race marriages, once legally prohibited, has risen from 140,000 in 1960 to 1.5 million in 2000 and is steadily growing.

The challenge of facilitating biblical change in this environment calls for hard work. In fact, some may argue that a homogenous church is less demanding. Cross-cultural issues will only add more fuel for dissent in a church that is already known for its divisions. When one begins to consider the political views, music tastes, worship styles, historic and contemporary heroes, who would ever seriously consider a cross-cultural church? God is who would make such a consideration! A church for people of different histories and cultures and, yes, even past hostility is precisely what the New Testament teaches. A church for Jews and Gentiles was a church of great diversity (Ephesians 2:11–3:7).

The New Testament pastor was charged to work hard at maintaining unity and peace with such diversity rather than segregating the church along Jewish and Gentile lines (Ephesians 4:3). Hard work it may well be, but let us not forget that if anyone desires the office of a bishop, that person desires a good work (1 Timothy 3:1)! Great musicians and athletes will attest that those who excel must work hard. Good churches are no exception.

Healthy relationships are built upon the foundation of truth and nurtured in the garden of love. Wise pastoral counseling begins with a wise pastor. A wise pastor is one who has gathered accurate data. Like a skilled surgeon, the intelligent pastor must use the Bible to separate truth and error. Illusions, whether they are personal or societal, must be clearly identified and surgically removed from the hearts and minds of Christians.

The truth is that we, especially in America, have created a racial identity myth that divides families. The concept that one drop of black blood makes a person black came from twisted minds who desired to maintain the purity of the white gene pool.[5] It allowed white fathers to be freed from their biblical responsibilities to their biological children—children who were denied the knowledge of their full heritage and were denied their rights. Such a twisted concept is still causing individuals to deny their full heritage and churches to be confused about their diverse identity. The result is that many interracial families are disconnected within the church, and the church does not have a clue as to how to reach them.

Proper biblical counseling must be based on the fact that the entire human family originated from Adam and the three sons of Noah.[6] Furthermore, as Christians, we know that the Christian family is a covenant relationship in which two people leave their father and mother and cleave together as one and seek to raise godly seed (Genesis 2:24; Malachi 2:14–16; Ephesians 5:22–6:4). Knowing the truth about race is critical, yet one must still be able to address the cultural challenges of a society constructed on the lie of racial superiority and injustice. The reality is that we are still living in a society that is racially divided. From the census to education, from economics to racial profiling by police, racial identity is still culturally experienced even if it is not a scientific fact.

Cross-cultural relationships involving other ethnic groups have challenges; however, black/white relationships have a long and unique history in the U.S. A white woman shared with me how she and her black husband were pulled over by a police officer one night while driving to their suburban home. The officer asked her to get out of the car, then pulled her aside and asked whether she was okay. She answered the officer by stating that she was okay and was headed home with her husband. She mentioned that such incidents happened to them on more than one occasion.

Good pastoral counseling will assist individuals in understanding the culture in which they live. They must be taught the truth so that the pressures of a twisted society might not cause their relationship to crumble under the weight of social criticism. Couples, including interracial marriages, must accept the fact that the strength of their relationship is more dependent upon their personal character and trust in God than upon society's approval. Love, as described in 1 Corinthians 13, must characterize not only their love for one another but their love toward others as well. It is necessary for them to respond to stares of curiosity or condemnation in a Christlike manner. They must accept being the odd couple at social gatherings as their choice.

Laura Fazio lists the following irritants interracial couples may face:

1. Acquaintances, who, upon finding out that you are in an interracial relationship, ask you very personal questions about your relationship. My favorite one is: "What did your parents say when they found out you were dating a black man?"

2. Television shows that only pay lip service to interracial couples. If a character becomes interracially involved, the relationship will last no longer than one or two episodes. The partners usually break up because of the family or community pressures. The message given is that successful interracial relationships are unlikely.

3. Men who automatically assume that any white woman who dates a black man is a slut.

4. Women who ask the female partner in a black/white interracial relationship "if it's true what they say about black men," referring to black men's sexuality.

5. Bookstores that put all the interracial books in the "African American" section, as if interracial relationships are a "black problem" and only black people are interested in reading about them.

6. Wedding invitations and accessories that depict white or black couples, but never interracial couples.

7. People who assume that when an interracial couple has relationship problems, it's because of racial differences, not because of personality or personal conflicts.

8. White people (unaware that a person is involved in an interracial relationship) who "feel safe" making racist comments in front of other white people, as if they will agree just because they are white.

9. Being treated as if your interracial relationship is just a fling, something you'll "grow out of" rather than a serious, committed relationship.

10. People of all ethnicities who accept interracial relationships, in general, but who are against interracial couples having children—"but what about the children?"[7]

While interracial couples must be prepared to respond to such annoyances, the church should help them by creating an accepting atmosphere. And good pastoral counsel includes helping to create such a healthy environment. The church environment is, at least in part, the pastor's responsibility.

Interracial relationships will develop issues that should be confronted. What are some issues that may be unique to interracial relationships? It can be helpful to create or use a model similar to one composed by Deborah Young-Ware and Darol Ware. Deborah explained her rationale for their model as follows: "As an interracially married mental health clinician, I am dismayed at the lack of general information on interracial couples. Nowhere in the literature have I come across an interracial couple development model. Most published work on interracial couples is negative, written by biased outsiders.... My husband and I have been married over four years and have a very solid relationship which has survived many hardships. We have a connection far beyond the physical body and appearance."[8]

This model provides clarification for the differing perspectives of black male/white female partnerships. However the processes are similar regardless of the gender of the black or white partner. Their model can be seen in table 1.

Sometimes the normal premarital questions, even those discussing cultural differences, fail to probe the individual struggles a couple may be facing due to the interracial nature of the relationship. The Ware model may assist a counselor in helping a couple to face issues normally not discussed

TABLE 1: Stages in Young-Ware and Ware's Interracial Development Model		
Black Male:	*Partner's Perspective:*	*White Female:*
Recognition	*Stage 1*	Initial introduction
Pursuance of relationship	*Stage 2*	Hypothetical intellectualizing
Denial	*Stage 3*	Pursuance of relationship
Isolation	*Stage 4*	Shared response
Self-evaluation	*Stage 5*	Self-doubt and guilt
Anger	*Stage 6*	Immersion and advocacy
Rejection	*Stage 7*	Realization of "white privilege"
Fear	*Stage 8*	Seeking equilibrium
Happy medium	*Stage 9*	Depression
	Stage 10	Cognizance of "reality"
	Stage 11	Happy medium

in premarital counseling. Asking a couple to read the model and share their thoughts on the different stages will give insight into a couple's concept of the challenges that they might face simply because of the interracial nature of their relationship.

Greater than the concern of cultural criticism is the possibility of rejection by extended family. Some parents may be caught in the cultural web of racial superiority or solidarity to the point of rejecting their child's desire to marry outside his or her race. Other parents may be concerned about the rejection of extended family members or their social circles. Personal prejudice is never more severely tested than when one's child desires to marry "one of them."

Couples, and especially counselors, must not assume that all parental objections to interracial relationships are motivated by prejudice. The parents may know something about their child that they believe demonstrates the child is not ready for marriage to anyone. Perhaps the child is generally rebellious and is seeking an interracial relationship simply to strike out at society or his or her parents. Perhaps the potential challenges of an interracial relationship cause the parents great concern over their child's ability to handle such a relationship.

A wise counselor will want to explore an individual's motives for marriage to be sure that they are biblical. Furthermore, the counselor should use caution in encouraging a couple to consummate any marriage without parental consent. The couple should listen to the parents' concerns and seek to address them, not merely verbally but by an exemplary life. Sometimes a little patience on a couple's part can change a parent's mind.

The pastor should also, where possible, speak to the parents to assess their objections. If the parents have unscriptural objections to the marriage, the pastor should confront them with truth. If the parents have reasonable objections, the pastor should discuss these with the couple, guiding them in all things to seek to do the will of God as revealed in the Bible.

Certainly the pastor must confront interracial couples with the gravity of consummating a marriage when there are strong parental objections. Emotional ties built over twenty to thirty years are not easily broken. Is the couple prepared not to visit parents or attend family reunions? Have they counted the cost of having children whose grandparents refuse to establish any kind of relationship with them? How will they explain such an estranged relationship to the children?

Unresolved issues with parents can adversely affect a marriage. It is better to love parents, educate them, and win their approval when possible. Some couples have waited, prayed, and married without complete parental approval, but these efforts have helped them to build a strong relationship with the extended family over time.

Meanwhile, pastors should not confront parents and their children with such emotional decisions only when an interracial marriage is an issue within their family. The pulpit should have prepared the congregation through faithfully communicating the mind of God through sound biblical teaching. In addition, the congregation should have been exposed to positive interracial role models both from the Bible and current life. Some biblical examples of interracial marriage include Moses and Zipporah (Exodus 2:15–22; Numbers 12:1–2) and Ruth and Boaz (Ruth 4:10; Matthew 1:5). Godly interracially married families should be exposed to congregations just to make the visual statement that God blesses such unions. The desire is to create an environment in the church where color is not the issue. Rather, truth, personality, and culture are the focuses in disciplining families to glorify God.

But what about the children? Pastors will need to address various societal issues facing children from interracial families and/or transracial adoptions. Children from cross-cultural marriages still live in a society that pressures them to choose or accept racial identification with only one parent's heritage while denying the other. In the film *Black Indian: An American Story*, the unscientific, shallow, deceptive, erroneous nature of the American racial classification is clearly depicted as individuals from cross-cultural parentage, including Native Americans, discuss how society has sought to impose upon them a single racial identity.[9]

Children of interracial parentage can be affected by society's distorted concept of racial identity. For example, an Asian woman who was married to a black man sought my counsel concerning her son, who had taken a course on African American history at a secular university and had come home to inform her that she did not understand him because she was not black. I told her that she needed to look him squarely in the eyes and inform him that she understood what it was like to carry him in her womb for nine months, give birth to him, clean his dirty diapers, and raise him for eighteen-plus years. Clearly the young man needed to be confronted with the truth that he has his mother's genes as well as his father's.

Pastors need to build a foundation of truth that will help saints stand when hit with the storms of life. Self-identity is a critical issue in human development. The truth that we belong to one humanity in Adam and one body in Christ needs to be knitted into the very fabric of every church member.

Both the Bible and life illustrate that children from biracial parentage have made significant contributions to society. Let it not be forgotten that the recipient of two New Testament letters, Timothy, was the offspring of an interracial marriage (Acts 16:1–5). Counselors can benefit from having a list of children of interracial marriages who have struggled with these issues and yet can be positive role models. Keep in mind that many such children have been identified with a single race due to the American system of classification. It should be clear that the racist culture of this country was rooted in a twisted rather than biblical understanding of race. Therefore, cultural misconceptions and abuse must be separated from the love of God. The church should be (although it often is not) a shelter from the storms of hostility in the world.

Transracial adoptions have created some intriguing arguments over the years. Shortly after moving to the Midwest, I received a call from an administrator of a Christian adoption agency. At a conference on adoption, some presenters had strongly advanced their argument that it is not in the best interests of a black child to be placed in a white home. The administrator asked my counsel. We discussed issues such as family heritage, racial identity, schooling, neighborhoods, dating, and marriage. The basic question was whether racial and cultural identity is of greater importance than Christian nurturing. My counsel was that Christian nurturing is a greater issue in child rearing than color.

My wife and I were invited to a blended family support group where we met a number of white couples who had adopted black or biracial children. These couples were diligent to incorporate cultural sensitivity within their Christian nurturing. The couples were studying African American history, using literature in their home that depicted ethnic diversity, finding a church that provided support and sensitivity, and seeking to move into a neighborhood that was more racially diverse. This racially blended family support group provided opportunities to build relationships with other parents and children. White Christian homes can provide both Christian nurturing and cultural exposure for transracially adopted children.

A child's racial identity often becomes more of an issue when he or she reaches the dating age. For example, a young man from a dysfunctional home was taken to church weekly through a bus ministry. The young man developed a close relationship with a couple in the church that lasted through high school and several years at a Christian college. But when the young man expressed interest in dating a girl ethnically different from him, the couple's rejection of him left the young man feeling betrayed. Pastors need to prepare their congregation to biblically answer the question of how intimate Christians can become across ethnic lines. Views on intermarriage should not be a late discovery in long-term relationships.

Seeking a safe harbor from society's color-coded caste system, many interracial couples seek in vain for supportive materials, resources, or organizations, such as churches. A wise pastor will call a congregation to a commitment to truth and love rather than comfort and preference, and will seek to develop resources. A pastor should be sure that the church library has books, magazines, audiotapes, and videos that biblically address the various issues facing interracial families and dating. The pastor should also identify helpful Web sites, conferences, and support groups. And finally, the pastor should establish a list of successful role models, families, and churches as references for families who desire to explore or expand their relationships beyond your congregation.

Interracial families are not the only ones needing accurate information. The entire church must be educated. Teaching from the pulpit and Bible studies needs to weave these issues into lesson materials. Do sermon illustrations and applications promote unity with diversity or segregation, even within families, along racial lines? After all, the New Testament church was an interracial body of believers (Colossians 3:10–11). Church literature, bulletins, and decorations should display a rich diversity in the body of Christ. Classes and counseling should be developed that help people honestly and biblically deal with American and church history, especially as it relates to racial issues. Small groups for spiritual and social support may be formed to assist interracial families to process their unique challenges and see how they connect within the larger body of Christ.

Interracial families can encourage the church in several ways. For instance, they can encourage appreciation for differences. They can become models of hope in a society of despair. Validation of the single origin of humanity may be illustrated by interracial marriage. Successful models become a strong antidote to the stereotypical claim that interracial marriages fail. Racially blended families may become a powerful advertisement of a church for all people in an increasingly diverse society and may well serve as a microcosm of heaven on earth.

Biblical pastoral counseling is a holistic challenge. The best counseling begins before the counselee ever seeks an appointment with the pastor. Faithfully speaking the truth in love will help Christians grow up in Christ and thereby build one another up in love. A healthy, diverse church environment can be a powerful antibiotic against the destructive bacteria of racial prejudice. Resources that expose the church to racial diversity should create an appreciation, rather than apprehension, of differences. Explaining the reality of our history and culture helps us to understand why things are the way they are and what is needed to set us back on the track of truth that leads toward heaven. A church that offers pastoral counseling and teaching that seek to create an environment reflecting heaven's diversity is a church where interracial families will feel a sense of belonging.

Discussion Questions

1. Why is it so important for Christians in interracial marriages to know that there is biblical support for their families?
2. How can Christians make an effort to accommodate and encourage interracial families? How can the church you go to be more accommodating to interracial families?
3. Which irritant on Fazio's list do you think is the most frustrating for interracial couples? Why do you feel this way? What do you think would be the best way to handle this irritant?
4. What are some of the issues that emerge from the Ware model that are unique problems for interracial couples?
5. Do you have interracial families in your church? If so, can you think of ways that those families have encouraged the members of your church?

Notes

1. *See chapter 1 by Craig S. Keener, "The Bible and Interracial Marriage," pages 2–27.*
2. M. L. Moser Jr., The Case against Integration *(Little Rock: Challenge, 1974)*, 23.
3. M. R. DeHaan, M.D., Answers to Bible Questions *(Grand Rapids, Mich.: Radio Bible Class, 1961)*, 2:266.
4. A. Charles Ware, Prejudice and the People of God: How Revelation and Redemption Lead to Reconciliation *(Grand Rapids, Mich.: Kregel, 2001)*, 89.
5. Plessy vs. Ferguson, *1856, legalized this concept.*
6. *Ken Ham, Carl Wieland, and Don Batten,* One Blood: The Biblical Answer to Racism *(Green Forest, Ark.: Master, 1999)*, 11–29.
7. *Laura Fazio, "Ten Annoyances Faced as Part of an Interracial Relationship,"* Interrace 7, *no 3 (1996): 11. Reprinted by permission.*

8. *Deborah Young-Ware and Darol Ware, "An Interracial Development Model: A Thoughtful Presentation of the Components of Developing an Interracial Couple Relationship and Identity,"* Interrace 8, *no 3 (1998): 12.*

9. Black Indian: An American Story. *Dallas: Rich Heape-Sims, 2000.*

ৡ THREE ৡ

Debunking the Top Stereotypes about Interracial Couples

George A. Yancey

I WAS WALKING WITH A PROFESSOR FROM AFRICA ON THE CAMPUS of a small Midwestern college. We were discussing matters involving local campus politics. As an African professor, he was frustrated with the actions of some of the African American professors on campus.[1] It was then that he dropped a bombshell on me. He told me that some of the black professors thought I was a poor role model for the black students on campus because I was interracially married. I was disappointed that this was the opinion of my fellow African American colleagues. Their attitude did not dampen my relationship with my wife, Sherelyn, nor did it damage my self-esteem. I did, however, feel sad to learn that black professors on campus were judging my ability to serve students not by my actions but by the color of my wife's skin.[2]

The attitude of those highly educated professors is directly connected to one of the prevailing social stereotypes directed at interracial couples—that a person in the interracial marriage is a "sellout," or traitor, to his or her race. It is particularly troubling that well-educated professors (precisely the individuals I would least expect to accept stereotypes) were the ones who clung to this myth. This incident served to remind me of the resistance that interracial couples still face in our society inside and outside the church. Because of that resistance, a large number of stereotypes tend to dominate our understanding of interracial relationships.

The tendency to stereotype others is a good example of human depravity. Humans will hold on to stereotypes despite evidence to the contrary, even when holding on to such stereotypes works to their disadvantage. Sociologists define ethnocentrism as a means by which a group establishes who they are, as opposed to who they are not. Racial self-esteem is a positive result of ethnocentrism, while stereotyping is a negative effect of this phenomenon. Humans tend to use stereotyping in order to elevate their group above other groups. By doing this, they dehumanize other groups, which helps them feel superior to those groups.

Debunking a stereotype does not mean that it is false all of the time. The notion that Hispanic Americans are lazy is a stereotype. There is no evidence showing that Hispanic Americans are lazier than people of other racial groups. However, there are lazy Hispanic Americans, just like there are lazy people of all races. Likewise, some of the stereotypes surrounding interracial relationships tend to imply that these relationships are more dysfunctional than monoracial relationships. Quite obviously, there are some dysfunctional interracial relationships. But these bad relationships do not prove negative stereotypes about interracial couples any more than a lazy Hispanic American proves the stereotype about Hispanic Americans. Debunking stereotypes about interracial relationships means challenging the notion that interracial relationships are more dysfunctional than same-race romantic relationships. Therefore, I am intending to illustrate that, on average, those in interracial relationships are no worse off than those in intraracial relationships. Keeping this goal in mind, let us examine the major stereotypes about interracial relationships.

Stereotype 1: Interracial Relationships Are about Being Rebellious

Many people believe that individuals enter into interracial unions because they want to express rebellion against their parents or society. Interracial unions can serve to shock one's parents or to stick the proverbial finger in one's parents' eyes. Of course, this strategy is possible only because of the unfair hostility such couples face. If Americans accepted and loved interracial couples the way God would want us to, then there would be no shock value in dating interracially.

Developmentally, it is important for children to learn how to separate from their parents. The rebellion that we often see in teenagers and young adults can represent this process, which is vital for helping a child to internalize his or her own values and beliefs. Of course, there are many ways by which a young person can rebel and thus establish those values and beliefs. Because of the social resistance that exists against interracial relationships, a child can choose to enter into an interracial relationship to rebel. Therefore, we should not be surprised to find that some individuals will enter into interracial relationships to rebel against authority figures.

However, my experience with people involved in interracial relationships, along with the research that I have conducted, indicates that rebellion is not an important factor for explaining why interracial marriages are formed.[3] Furthermore, relationships that are based upon rebellion, whether interracial or intraracial, generally do not last. Those of us in interracial relationships do so for love and companionship—just like everyone else. It is true that we have challenged the social norms that state that we must stay within our own race when we date and marry. However, this type of rebellion is not dysfunctional; rather, it is just the realization that the love we share is not limited to people of our own skin color.

Stereotype 2: Most Interracial Couples Are Comprised of a White Woman and a Minority Man

This statement is true if we look only at interracial relationships between whites and blacks. Currently, about 65 percent of all black-white interracial relationships have a black man and a white woman. This stereotype has developed because we tend to think of interracial relationships as only black-white relationships. More white men than women create interracial relationships with Hispanic Americans and Asian Americans. If we look at interracial relationships that contain nonblack racial minorities, then more white men are in interracial relationships than are white women.

To debunk this myth, we must broaden our thinking of interracial relationships beyond those between blacks and whites. We tend to notice black-white interracial couples much more than other types of interracial couples. For example, if there is a black-white couple sitting at one table in a restaurant and a white-Asian couple sitting at another table, which couple will get the most stares? We all know that it is the black-white couple that will get the stares. I believe the black-white relationship is the hardest for people to accept in part because of the unresolved legacy of slavery and subsequent racial hostility.[4]

It is true, however, that more white women are paired with black men than vice versa. Angry black women have voiced their protest in Christian circles: "Why are all the white women stealing our few good black men?" In part they are reacting to the fact that our society has made it harder for black men to succeed economically and easier for them to be incarcerated. These factors decrease the number of "quality" black men available to them. Black women who resent seeing a white woman with an economically solid black man take note that there is one less good marital prospect for them. It seems that white women, rather than black men, tend to be more sensitive to the anger of these black women. This tendency may exist, in part, because of greater feminine sensitivity, because of less preparedness of whites in general to deal with racism, or perhaps because the blame is

41

directed specifically at white women rather than at black men. It is this last possibility that I want to address.

The allegation that white women have somehow "tricked" black men into an interracial relationship is as ludicrous as earlier notions in our history that black women "bewitched" white men into bed with them. Black men and white women have freely chosen to enter into interracial relationships with each other. Black men who have gone to college are more likely to interact with nonblack women. So it is not surprising that financially successful black men are more likely to intermarry than are black men who do not attend college. This can account for the tendency of "quality" black men to be with white women.

One may wonder why black women, who attend college in greater numbers than black men, do not interracially marry as often as black men. There are two possible reasons why this is the case. First, black women have historically suffered sexual abuse at the hands of white men, thereby making it harder for black women to build romantic interest in white men. Second, white women and black men may share a greater affinity toward one another due to a shared experience of discrimination by white men. Black women experience both sexism and racism, whereas white men set up the power structure. This gives those two groups little chance for developing an affinity for each other. As we get further away from the period of time when white men were free to sexually abuse black women, we may witness an increase in the number of black women who enter into interracial relationships.[5] This will remove some of the pressure causing this resentment.

Ultimately, the black woman who is unwilling to enter into an interracial relationship for personal reasons, rather than because of scriptural convictions, must recognize that her decision limits her pool of potential marital partners. While a black Christian woman has the right to make such a personal decision, she does not have the biblical authority to condemn others who choose to interracially marry. If we belong to the Lord, we cannot steal anyone from anybody (1 Corinthians 6:19-20). To marry outside one's own race is neither sexual nor racial betrayal, while judging those marriages is sin (James 4:11-12).

Stereotype 3: Interracial Couples Will Not Be Welcomed Anywhere

There is a common stereotype about interracial couples—and for that matter, multiracial people—that they are unwelcome to either race. This stereotype is used to keep the races separated, since it is assumed interracial couples will not receive the same level of social support as monoracial couples.[6]

Historically, much of this concern was warranted. Interracial couples generated a good deal of anger, since our existence challenges the social notion of racial purity. Seventeen states had laws against interracial marriage that were enforced as late as 1967, when the Supreme Court declared such laws unconstitutional. In truth, there will always be people who do not accept interracial couples. That is their loss. Yet Sherelyn and I have always found many friends wherever we have gone who accept us as just another Christian couple. It is true that we have to endure the stares that most interracial couples face. But beyond stares and a bigoted comment or two, we have been able to enjoy our married life with the support of the friends God has sent our way. In fact, there have been situations in which we have enjoyed relatively high social status because of my position as a college professor and Sherelyn's profession as a registered nurse. In those situations, our racial status hardly seems to matter.

I do not say this to minimize the various levels of hostility waged against interracial couples in our churches and society. As recently as 2000, there was a ban on interracial marriage in the state constitution of Alabama. This ban was removed by a referendum, yet 42 percent of the people in that state voted to keep the ban. That means that two out of every five people in Alabama still wanted a ban on interracial marriage on the books.

But while this type of hostility still exists, it is also important to note that overt support for interracial families has never been as high as it is today. Interracial families have a level of political and social representation in society that we have never experienced before. While there are churches that still are not welcoming to such couples, the number of those churches is shrinking as some Christians begin to take the issue of racism more seriously today. Many large cities now have support groups for interracial families that can be located through the Internet (see appendix A), although few can be found in churches. While partners in interracial marriages do experience more resistance than those in same-race marriages, we now have access to resources that can help us make our marriages more socially satisfying.

Stereotype 4: Only Desperate People Choose Interracial Relationships

Some people wonder why a white person would want to deal with the hostility that comes from an interracial relationship. Others wonder if racial minorities who enter into interracial relationships do so because they feel inferior about their own racial identity. These ideas revolve around the notion that people who enter into interracial relationships are desperate individuals who cannot date within their own race.

This stereotype is especially troublesome for whites seen as dating or marrying beneath themselves. It has even been argued that poor white women are willing to marry middle-class black men because that gives them an opportunity to use their status as a white person to gain a marital partner with a higher economic status.[7] The implication of this theory is that those women cannot attract a white middle-class husband.

If whites entering into interracial relationships are "desperate," then members of racial minorities in interracial relationships should have more physical beauty, economic, and educational resources than their white partners. However, at least some of the social science research in this area has indicated that whites entering into interracial relationships tend to share the same level of economic and educational resources as their minority partners.[8] This seems to indicate that whites entering into interracial relationships are just as desirable as the racial minorities in those relationships.

Once again, I am not saying that there are not people who enter into interracial relationships out of desperation. Singles groups at churches run the gamut from psychologically disturbed to emotionally healthy men and women. Individuals who enter into interracial relationships also run such a gamut. But the exception does not prove the rule. The vast majority of interracial relationships are not based upon desperation but are the coming together of two people seeking love with someone whom they view as an equally yoked partner.

Stereotype 5: Interracial Relationships Are Driven by Sexual Curiosity—"Jungle Fever"

This stereotype suggests that people in interracial relationships are driven by sexual curiosity. Supposedly, the different racial features of one's sexual partner make him or her seem more exotic and mysterious. It is a stereotype that has been held in both white and nonwhite communities. In fact the term "jungle fever" is the title of a Spike Lee movie in which a black man has an affair with a white woman. In the film *Jungle Fever* the motivation for the interracial relationship is portrayed as being based on sexual curiosity instead of common interests or companionship. This stereotype has also been directed at Asian American women who are seen as "exotic."[9]

This is unfortunately one of the most damaging and pervasive stereotypes about interracial couples, because the underlying notion is that those of us in interracial unions are preoccupied by sexual deviancy and are not spiritually mature. Because of their biblical commitment to premarital sexual abstinence, some Christians who believe this myth discourage others from interracial dating to avoid the appearance of sexual promiscuity.

The truth or falsity of this stereotype was one of the first questions I tackled when I originally started conducting research on interracial couples. My colleague Dr. Richard Lewis sent out a survey to hundreds of interracial couples.[10] People surveyed were asked why they started to date their eventual marriage partner. When we analyzed the data, we found that interracial couples generally were formed for the same reasons as same-race couples: companionship, compatibility, or personal attraction. Only a tiny minority of the sample stated that they were sexually attracted to people of certain races. Our findings are not surprising. People who enter into marriage are not likely to do so for immature reasons, such as they want to know what it is like to have sex with someone of another race.[11]

But what about the dating couples who do not marry? Is it the case that nonmarried interracial couples are more likely to be sexually promiscuous than other dating couples? Research I conducted addresses that question by assessing sexual attitudes of Americans in general. The results found that single adults who have an experience with interracial dating are no more likely to have sexually promiscuous attitudes than are other single adults.[12] Once again the evidence shows that those who choose to engage in interracial relationships do so for the same reasons as everyone else.

Having a preference for certain physical attributes (skin color, hair texture) belonging to members of certain races has no association with whether that person is going to be sexually promiscuous. We all have physical preferences when we search for potential mates. These issues are merely matters of personal taste and do not have any moral implications. The quicker that we as the body of Christ come to that realization and provide support for interracial couples, the sooner we will be able to minister to them.

Stereotype 6: Members of Interracial Couples Do Not Have a Problem with Racism

This is one stereotype I wish were true. But the notion that interracially marrying will end one's own racial prejudices is false.

For example, late one night, after Sherelyn and I arrived in Jackson, Mississippi, for a racial reconciliation conference, we pulled up to a grocery store parking lot. The store was in a poverty-stricken area on the black side of the town. Before getting out of the car, Sherelyn peered inside the front store windows. I waited in the car while she went into the store. Turning to me, her black husband, she exclaimed, "George, they are all black in there!"

Rather than condemning her for blurting out her gut-level reaction, I understood that she lives in America, where we live in a racialized society that has taught her to fear young, poor black men. That a white woman can feel safe in a store full of whites, but not of blacks, is an indictment on America. This society has taught her that race matters and that a white woman is not supposed to feel safe around blacks.

The strength of our interracial marriage centered in Christ provides us a sacred space where we can confess our faults to each other and help to heal the subtle sin of racism hidden within our hearts. In my first book I illustrated that many of us, myself included, are affected with the poison of racism since we live in a society where racism is the norm.[13]

People who interracially marry are not necessarily more accepting of people of other races than are those who marry within their own race. Being interracially married means that we have chosen to love someone of a different race. However, while marrying across racial lines does not eliminate racism within an individual, it does provide opportunities for growth.

To her credit, Sherelyn has shown remarkable depth in her understanding of the plight of African Americans and other racial minority groups. She is the one who is often dragging me to black history events or movies. Unlike many whites, Sherelyn does not subscribe to the notion that we can ignore race, since she recognizes the damage of historical racism.

An interracial marriage does offer an opportunity for racial healing, but it is a mistake to assume that it eliminates the racism a person previously had or that such a marriage indicates that a person is not racist at all.

Stereotype 7: Interracial Children Will Suffer

Almost everybody who enters into an interracial relationship will be questioned, "What about the children?" The concern about the children is probably the reason most often given today to discourage interracial couples. This concern is tied to a stereotype that biracial children are going to have miserable lives because they will be racially confused. Because this concern is used against interracial couples so often, it becomes important to challenge this stereotype.

In my previous book, *Beyond Black and White*, I note that sociological research has indicated three major findings concerning multiracial children. First, there is slight racial identity conflict within biracial children. Second, these children tend to enjoy multiple cultures more than other children. Third, these children do not seem to have any more negative psychological effects than other children.

The first finding is the only one that indicates that multiracial children may have unique problems. However, it should not be surprising that multiracial children have slight racial identity problems, since they have to think about definitions of race in a way that other children do not. As a child, I never had to wonder whether I was black or not. If I had a socially defined white parent, then I would have wondered about my own racial identity. I do not have any confusion about my race, because during my whole life I was told that I was black. This is not the case for a growing number of multiracial children.

The fact that biracial children have to deal with racial issues says more about the importance American churches and society place upon race than it does about the psychological health of multiracial children. Nobody worries about our social identity if we are a redhead, blue-eyed, or short. We are concerned about skin color because our American society states that we should be concerned about skin color. The concern multiracial children have about race represents the level of importance we currently and historically have placed upon racial issues. I argue that the racial identity confusion of these children reflects our society's embedded racial hierarchy rather than the psychological problems of those children.

Finally, some argue that white partners should be discouraged from having interracial children because then those children will be kids of color. The motivation for this discouragement is the belief that white parents are not equipped to teach their biracial children how to cope with prejudice. However, these same individuals contend that whites can and should have white children who will not have to inherit the problems of American racism.

There are two problems with this argument. First, the whole notion that biracial children assume the identity of the parent who is a person of color, instead of being white or biracial children, adheres to the racist one-drop rule that has defined black racial identity since slavery was justified by white supremacy. Reinforcing the one-drop rule, whether done by blacks to secure political numbers or by whites to claim racial superiority, is not conducive to solving any of the racial problems in our society. Second, minority parents, by definition, have to raise children of color. There is a bit of arrogance in thinking that the raising of minority children is beneath white parents in multiracial relationships, when it is all right for minority parents to raise these same children.

Stereotype 8: Race Doesn't Matter in Interracial Relationships

There is a romantic notion in American society that love is all you need to sustain a relationship. Many disappointed couples have discovered that feelings of love, as wonderful as they are, cannot sustain a marriage. An extension of the "love will conquer all" myth is that love can automatically overcome the racial tensions that may develop within interracial relationships.

Some Christians assert that we should be "color-blind" in our interracial relationships, thus ignoring the racial difference between us. But to ignore the racial identity of one's partner is to ignore a vital part of that person. Our racial identity is part of our social, personal, and spiritual reality. People who enter into interracial relationships need to recognize that they have contrasting racial identities that will bring about unforeseen issues they will have to work through.

To take a color-blind approach into such encounters is to invite possible disaster. Rather, I believe that we should learn how to embrace our cultural differences.

From my own marriage, I can tell you that being interracially married does bring its own challenges as well as rewards. Sherelyn and I are much more likely to deal with common marital problems (e.g., communication skills and financial decisions) than any special problem that comes out of being interracially married. In fact, I believe that 95 percent of all our marital issues have nothing to do with racial issues. But that 5 percent still exists, and interracial couples cannot ignore the racial issues that develop. A healthier perspective is to tackle those racial issues head-on rather than try to pretend that race is not important.

Let me give you a personal example. Sherelyn grew up in an all-white atmosphere that instilled within her a sense of patriotism, especially since an ancestor of hers suffered at Valley Forge with George Washington. This sense of patriotism is fairly common among European Americans, especially those who are Christians. I, however, share an attitude that many racial minorities have, in that we are skeptical about American patriotism. I recognize that Independence Day represents a wonderful holiday for European Americans, but that holiday does not mean as much to me. I do not see it as a cause for celebration, since blacks were not freed on that day but rather at that time were labeled three-fifths of a person. Before I was married, I rarely celebrated this holiday.

Sherelyn and I have had to come to terms with these cultural differences. I am now willing to celebrate Independence Day with her, but she has developed more of an understanding as to why this holiday does not have much meaning for me. In addition, Sherelyn has sought out African American celebrations of Juneteenth, the day we revere as when the Emancipation Proclamation came to Texas slaves. We have not avoided this issue but rather we have talked about it and gained a new perspective from each other. In this way our social world has been enriched as I learn from Sherelyn's perspective and she learns from mine.

As long as racial issues continue to traumatize our American society, we can never ignore issues of race in interracial relationships. It has been documented that whites entering into interracial marriages tend to learn more about the racial privilege they have inherited.[14] This often develops when these whites care about the racism their marital partners experience. I know that when Sherelyn learns about an incident of racism against African Americans, she personalizes it. Our marriage has made her a more powerful advocate for people of color. Likewise, my relationships with Sherelyn and with other whites have helped me to understand their fears and perspectives.

In a society that seems to constantly work to separate people from different races, interracial relationships allow us to transcend those barriers with those we love the most. On the most intimate, familial level, we embrace the promise of "your people will be my people and your God will be my God" (Ruth 1:16).

Stereotype 9: A Person in an Interracial Marriage Is a Sellout to His or Her Own Race

Of all the stereotypes in this list, being a sellout is the one that racial minorities are more likely to accept than whites. However, some whites do perceive other whites in interracial unions as "traitors" to their race.

Such whites are holding on to notions of racial purity based in overt white supremacy. In today's society, accepting such supremacist notions is

49

discouraged. Most whites do not openly subscribe to the idea that whites are sellouts, although many may subtly accept the inference that whites are better than racial minorities. Thus they may wonder what is wrong with the white person who consents to date or marry a member of a racial minority.

On the other hand, many racial minorities resent interracial families because they appear to disrupt the attempt to build a racially unified community that can confront white society politically. People of color may suspect that those of us in interracial families are trying to escape the problems associated with being a racial minority by merging ourselves with a white person. They fear that the children we have will try to pass as white and minimize the concerns of racial minorities.

The sellout stereotype is shortsighted since it assumes that we racial minorities in interracial relationships are going to be influenced by our white partners but that the reverse is not going to occur.

When I married Sherelyn, I brought someone into my life who became a greater advocate for racial minorities. She has always had a concern about the problems racial minorities face. But now, when she hears about a hate crime or racial profiling, it becomes personal to her because she has a black husband who might be targeted. Through our conversations, she has developed more of an understanding of why blacks do not trust the American system of justice and why we think that society often works against us.

It has been argued that whites living a lifestyle by which they often come into contact with African Americans are better able to understand the perspectives of American blacks.[15] Being interracially married allows whites to have the ultimate chance to understand American society from the perspective of an oppressed group and thus be allies for their causes.

Those of us in these marriages might actually be helping our respective racial communities by teaching our white family members about American racism and prejudice in a personal way. For racial minorities to reject those of us in interracial marriages is similar to the social rejection people of color often received from whites who refused to trust nonwhites. Racial minorities should be exceptionally sensitive to promulgating this type of prejudice.

Conclusion

Multiracial couples and children are sometimes seen as abnormal and unusual in America. This attitude is changing, but it is still present, especially among conservative Christians. Multiracial Christian couples are just like same-race couples in terms of our commitment to strengthen our marriages

and families. We are unusual, however, because the love of God has motivated us to cross the color line despite poor theology and sinful social stereotypes, which makes it more difficult for us to gain the social support that we
all want for our marriages and families.

For me as a sociologist, it is my job to examine and debunk the preceding
stereotypes. Perhaps you can think of others I have not listed. Examine your
own heart and ask God if you have believed any of these stereotypes, so that
you can cleanse them from your mind. As Christians, we want to challenge
these stereotypes in ourselves, our churches, and our circles of friends. As
Christians confront these stereotypes, we can create an atmosphere to welcome multiracial families with affirming social support. Doing so will help us
to heal some broken hearts of multiracial couples who have been previously
rejected by Christian churches.

Discussion Questions

1. How does stereotyping harm the individuals who are stereotyped? How
   does it harm those who engage in stereotyping?
2. How do we evaluate whether generalizations about certain groups are
   true or not? Why do we often believe that stereotypes are true, despite
   evidence to the contrary?
3. Which stereotypes about interracial couples are not mentioned in this
   chapter? What are they, and how can they be debunked?
4. After reading this chapter, do you still think that any of the stereotypes
   discussed are true? If so, which ones? How do you deal with the arguments of the author?
5. What can we, as Christians, do to confront our own stereotypes of multiracial families? How can we help multiracial families confront these
   stereotypes?

Notes

1. *Africans bring a different perspective to the American society than do American
   blacks. They are often critical of native-born African Americans. It is my experience
   that there is much greater cultural difference between Africans and African
   Americans than is generally recognized.*
2. *In fact, in some ways I was more active with black students on campus than I had
   ever been as a graduate student or in my previous teaching jobs. I was mentoring
   several black students and attending black cultural events, such as Kwanza and
   gospel choir performances.*

3. *See Richard Lewis, George Yancey, and Siri Blizer, "Racial and Nonracial Factors Which Influence Spouse Choice in Black/White Marriages,"* Journal of Black Studies *28, no. 1 (1997): 60–78.*

4. *Several other researchers and I have documented this fact. My research includes evidence from a mail-in survey (Richard Lewis and George Yancey, "Biracial Marriages in the United States: An Analysis of Variation in Family Member Support,"* Sociological Spectrum *15, no. 4 [1995]: 443–62) and from a national random telephone survey (George Yancey, Michael Emerson, and Karen Chai, "Who Can We Marry? A Look at the Hierarchical Construction of Marriage Preferences in the United States" [paper presented at the Southern Sociological Society Meetings, New Orleans, April 2000]). Other evidence of this fact can be found in Cedric Herring and Charles Amissah, "Advance and Retreat: Racially Based Attitudes and Public Policy," in* Racial Attitudes in the 1990s: Continuity and Change, *eds. Steve A. Tuch and Jack K. Martin (Westport, Conn.: Praeger, 1996), 121–43; and Abby Ferber,* White Man Falling: Race, Gender, and White Supremacy *(Lanham, Md.: Rowman & Littlefield, 1998), 34–40.*

5. *There is already some census evidence showing that while the number of black men in black-white marriages is greater than the number of black women, the number of black women is increasing at a faster rate than that of black men. If this continues, eventually there will be as many black women married to white men as there are black men married to white women.*

6. *Oswald J. Smith states in a Christian tract, "Those who marry other races will find themselves ostracized by both. You say it ought not to be. But it is, and no man can change it. . . . Nothing but sorrow, heartache, and regret will result"* (How to Choose a Wife *[Minneapolis: Osterhus Publishers]). His statement shows a common argument that Christians should avoid interracial marriage, not because it is wrong, but because society states that it is wrong. This is an example of how some Christians have used this stereotype to discourage interracial marriages.*

7. *Robert K. Merton, "Intermarriage and Social Structure: Fact and Theory,"* Psychiatry *4, no. 3 (1941): 361–74; Kingsley Davis, "Intermarriage in Caste Societies,"* American Anthropologist *43, no. 3 (1941): 376–95.*

8. *Thomas P. Monahan, "The Occupational Class of Couples Entering into Interracial Marriage,"* Journal of Comparative Family Studies *7, no. 2 (1976): 175–92; James Gadberry and Richard A. Dodder, "Educational Homogamy in Interracial Marriages: An Update,"* Journal of Behavior and Personality *8, no. 6 (1993): 155–63.*

9. *For more information about this, see Paul R. Spickard,* Mixed Blood: Intermarriage and Ethnic Identity in Twentieth-Century America *(Madison: University of Wisconsin Press, 1989), 39–40.*

10. *Lewis and Yancey, "Biracial Marriages."*

11. *Although there are a few interracial marriages shaped by "jungle fever," we have to consider how many same-race marriages are formed out of sexual obsession. It is likely that the percentage of "jungle fever" interracial marriages is no larger than the percentage of same-race marriages where there is sexual obsession.*

12. *George Yancey, "An Empirical Test of Differential Sexual Attitudes and Promiscuity among Individuals Involved in Interracial Relationships: Debunking 'Jungle Fever,' " Social Science Journal (forthcoming).*

13. *George Yancey,* Beyond Black and White: Reflections on Racial Reconciliation *(Grand Rapids, Mich.: Baker, 1996), 15.*

14. *Heather Dalmage,* Tripping on the Color Line *(New Brunswick, N.J.: Rutgers University Press, 2000), 63–68.*

15. *Michael Emerson and Christian Smith,* Divided by Faith: Evangelical Religion and the Problem of Race in America *(Oxford: Oxford University Press, 2000), 106–9.*

⚛ FOUR ⚛

One Race
Ken Ham

THERE IS REALLY ONLY ONE RACE—THE HUMAN RACE. SCRIPTURE distinguishes people by tribal or national groupings, not by skin color or physical appearance. Clearly, though, there are groups of people who have certain features (e.g., skin color) in common, which distinguish them from other groups. We prefer to call these "people groups" rather than "races."

All peoples can freely interbreed and produce fertile offspring. This shows that the biological differences among the "races" are not very great at all. In fact, the DNA differences are trivial.

Anthropologists generally classify people into a fairly small number of main racial groups, such as the Caucasoid (European, or "white"),[1] the Mongoloid (which includes the Chinese and the American Indians), the Negroid (black Africans), and the Australoid (the Australian Aborigines). Within each classification, there may be many different subgroups.

Virtually all evolutionists would now agree that the various people groups did not have separate origins; that is, in the evolutionary belief system, the different people groups did not each evolve from a different group of animals. So they would agree with biblical creationists that all people groups have come from the same original population. Of course, they believe that such groups as the Aborigines and the Chinese have had many tens of thousands of years of separation. Most people believe that there are such vast differences between groups that there had to be many years for these differences to somehow develop.

Editors' note: Too many biological myths are used to discourage interracial couples. We felt it was vital to find Christian biological work that refutes these myths. While support of interracial couples is not the main focus of this excerpt from the book One Blood, *the principles in this chapter are invaluable for helping Christians deal with those myths. For those who want a more in-depth treatment of the subject of evolution and racism, the postscript to this chapter provides information on how to obtain the book* One Blood. *Reprinted by permission.*

One reason for this is that many people believe that the observable differences come from some people having unique features in their hereditary makeup that others lack. This is an understandable but incorrect idea. Let's look at skin color, for instance. It is easy to think that since different groups of people have yellow skin, red skin, black skin, white skin, and brown skin, there must be many different skin pigments or colorings. And since different chemicals for coloring would mean a different genetic recipe or code in the hereditary blueprint in each people group, it appears to be a real problem. How could all those differences develop within a short time?

Here's how. We all have the same coloring pigment in our skin: melanin. This is a dark brownish pigment that is found in special cells in our skin. If we have none (as in the case of people called albinos, who suffer from an inherited mutation-caused defect, so that they lack the ability to produce melanin), then we will have a very white or pink skin coloring. If we produce a little melanin, it means that we will be European white. If our skin produces a great deal of melanin, we will be a very deep black. And in between, of course, are all shades of brown. There are no other significant skin pigments.[2]

In summary, from currently available information, the really important factor in determining skin color is melanin—the amount produced and the proportions and distribution of its two components.

This situation is true not only for skin color. Generally, whatever feature we may look at, no people group has anything that is, in its essence, uniquely different from that possessed by another. For example, the Asian, or almond-shaped, eye gets its appearance simply by having an extra fold of fat. Both Asian and Caucasian eyes have fat; the latter simply have less of it.

What does melanin do? It protects the skin against damage by ultraviolet light from the sun. If you have too little in a very sunny environment, you will more easily suffer from sunburn and skin cancer. If you have a great deal of melanin, and if you live in a country where there is little sunshine, it is much harder for your body to get adequate amounts of vitamin D (which needs sunshine for its production in your body). You may then suffer from vitamin D deficiency, which could cause a bone disorder such as rickets.

We also need to be aware that one is not born with a genetically fixed amount of melanin but rather with a genetically fixed potential to produce a certain amount, increasing in response to sunlight. For example, if you are in a Caucasian community, you may have noticed that when your friends headed for the beach at the beginning of summer, they may, if they spent their time indoors during winter, have all been more or less the same pale color. As the summer went on, however, some became much darker than others.

But how do we explain the formation of many different shades of skin color arising in such a short biblical time scale (a few thousand years)? Let's look at a few observations that can help us to explain this. From here on, whenever we use such words as "different colors," we are, strictly speaking, referring to different shades of the one color, melanin.

If a person from a very black people group marries someone from a very white group, their offspring (called "mulattos") are middle brown. It has long been known that when mulattos marry each other, their offspring may be virtually any color, ranging from very black to very white. Understanding this gives us the clues we need for our overall question, so we must first look, in a simple way, at some of the basic facts of heredity.

Heredity

Each of us carries information in our body that describes us similar to the way a blueprint describes a finished building. It determines not only that we will be human beings, rather than cabbages or crocodiles, but also whether we will have blue eyes, a short nose, long legs, etc. When a sperm fertilizes an egg, all the information that specifies how the person will be built (ignoring such superimposed factors as exercise and diet) is already present. This information is in coded form in our DNA.[3] To illustrate coding, a piece of rope with beads on it can carry a message in Morse code.

Can you see how the piece of rope, by using a simple sequence of short beads, long beads, and spaces (to represent the dots and dashes of Morse code) can carry the same information as the English word "help" typed on a sheet of paper? The entire Bible could be written thus in Morse code on a long enough piece of rope.

In a similar way, the human blueprint is written in a code (or language convention), which is carried on very long chemical strings called DNA. This is by far the most efficient information storage system known, surpassing any foreseeable computer technology.[4] This information is copied (and reshuffled) from generation to generation as people reproduce.

The word gene refers to a small part of that information that carries the instructions for manufacturing (for example) only one enzyme.[5] A small portion of the "message string," with only one specification on it, would be a simple way of understanding this gene concept.

For example, there is a gene that carries the instructions on how to make hemoglobin, the chemical (protein) that carries oxygen in your red blood cells. (Actually, there is more than one gene for hemoglobin, but that does not alter the principles of this necessarily simplified illustration.) If that gene has been damaged by mutation (such as when there are copying mistakes during reproduction), the instructions will be faulty, so it will make a crippled form of hemoglobin, if any. (There are a number of diseases, such as sickle-cell anemia and thalassemia, that result from such mistakes.)

So, going back to that cell and that egg that has just been fertilized, where does all of its information—its genes—come from? One half has come from the father (carried by the sperm) and the other half from the mother (carried in the egg). Genes come in matching pairs, so in the case of hemoglobin, for example, we have two genes that both contain the code (instruction) for hemoglobin manufacture, one from the mother and one from the father.

This is a very useful arrangement, because if you inherit a gene from one parent that is damaged and can instruct your cells to produce only a defective hemoglobin, you are likely to get a normal one from the other parent that will continue to give the right instructions. Thus, only half the hemoglobin in your body will be defective. (In fact, each of us carries hundreds of mistakes, inherited from one or the other of our parents, which are usually covered up by being matched with a normal gene from the other parent.)

Skin Color

We know that skin color is governed by more than one gene. For simplicity, let's assume there are only two,[6] A and B, with the correspondingly "more silent" genes a and b. The small letters in this case will code for a small amount of melanin in the skin. So, a very dark group of people who, on intermarriage, kept producing only very dark offspring would be AABB; the same situation for a very fair-skinned people would be aabb. The Punnett Square (see page 58) shows what combinations would result in a mulatto (the offspring of an AABB and aabb union).

What would happen, using the Punnett square, if two such middle-brown mulatto people were to marry (the shading of the squares roughly indicates the resultant skin color)?

Surprisingly, we find that an entire range of colors, from very white to very black, can result in only one generation, beginning with this particular type of middle-brown parents.

Those children born with AABB, who are pure black (in the sense of consistently having no other types of offspring), have no genes for lightness at all. If they were to marry and migrate to a place where their offspring could not intermarry with people of lighter color, all their children would be black—a pure "black line" would result.

Those with aabb are white. If they marry other whites and migrate to a place where their offspring cannot marry darker people, a pure (in the same sense) "white line" will result. They will have lost genes that give them the ability to be black, that is, to produce a large amount of melanin.

So you can see how it is easily possible, beginning with two middle-brown parents, to get not only all the colors but also people groups with stable coloring. But what about people groups that are permanently middle brown, such as we have today? Again, this is easily explained. Those of aaBB or

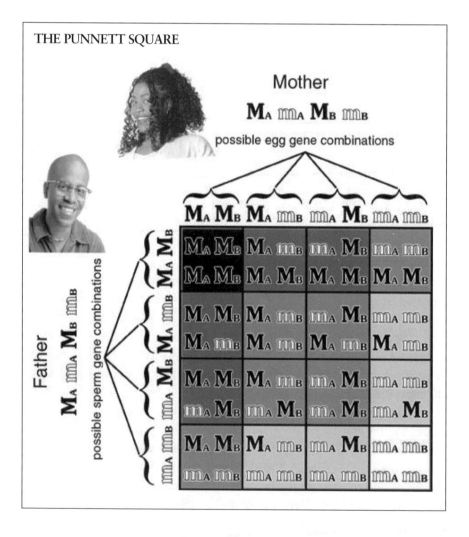

THE PUNNETT SQUARE

AAbb, if they no longer interact with others, will be able to produce only middle-brown colored offspring. (You may want to work this out with the Punnett square.)

If these lines were to interbreed again with other such lines, the process would be reversed. In a short time, their descendants would show a whole range of colors, often in the same family.

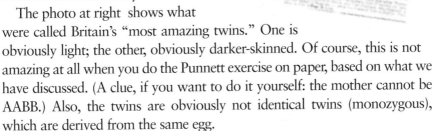

Two-tone twins

The photo at right shows what were called Britain's "most amazing twins." One is obviously light; the other, obviously darker-skinned. Of course, this is not amazing at all when you do the Punnett exercise on paper, based on what we have discussed. (A clue, if you want to do it yourself: the mother cannot be AABB.) Also, the twins are obviously not identical twins (monozygous), which are derived from the same egg.

If all the humans on earth were to intermarry freely and then break into random groups that kept to themselves, a whole new set of combinations could emerge. It may be possible to have almond eyes with black skin, blue eyes with black, tightly curled hair, etc. We need to remember, of course, that the way in which genes express themselves is turning out to be much more complex than this simplified picture. Sometimes certain genes are linked together. However, the basic point is unaffected.

Even today, close observation shows that within a particular people group you will often see a feature normally associated with another group. For instance, you will occasionally see a European with a broad flat nose or a Chinese person with very pale skin or Caucasian eyes. As pointed out previously, most biologists now agree that among modern humans, "race" has little or no biological meaning. This also argues strongly against the idea that the people groups have been evolving separately for long periods.

What Really Happened?

We can now reconstruct the true history of the "people groups" using:
- the information given by the Creator in the Book of Genesis
- the background information given above
- some consideration of the effect of the environment

The first man, Adam, from whom all other humans are descended, was created with the best possible combination of genes—for skin color, for example. A long time after Creation, a worldwide Flood destroyed all humans except a man called Noah, his wife, his three sons, and their wives. This Flood greatly changed the environment. Afterward, God commanded the survivors to multiply and cover the earth (Genesis 9:1). A few hundred years later, people chose to disobey God and to remain united in building a great city, with the Tower of Babel as the focal point of rebellious worship.

From Genesis 11, we understand that up to this time there was only one language. God judged the people's disobedience by imposing different languages on humanity, so that they could not work together against God and so that they were forced to scatter over the earth as God intended.

So all the people groups—"black" Africans, Indo-Europeans, Mongols, and others—have come into existence since that time. Some people sadly have promoted the false idea that dark skin is related to the so-called but nonexistent "curse of Ham."[7]

Noah and his family were probably middle brown, with genes for both dark and light skin, because a medium skin color would seem to be the most generally suitable (dark enough to protect against skin cancer, yet light enough to allow vitamin D production). As all the factors for skin color were present in Adam and Eve, they would most likely have been middle brown as well. In fact, most of the world's population today is still middle brown.

After the Flood, for the few centuries until Babel, there was only one language and one cultural group. Thus, there were no barriers to marriage within this group. This would tend to keep the skin color of the population away from the extremes. Very dark and very light skin would appear, of course, but people tending in either direction would be free to marry someone less dark or less light than themselves, ensuring that the average color stayed roughly the same.

The same would be true of other characteristics, not just skin color. Under these sorts of circumstances, distinct, "constant" differences in appearance will never emerge. This is true for animals as well as human populations, as every biologist knows. To obtain such separate lines, you would need to break a large breeding group into smaller groups and keep them separate; that is, not interbreeding anymore.

The Effects of Babel

This is exactly what happened at Babel. Once separate languages were imposed, there would have been instantaneous barriers. Not only would people tend not to marry someone they couldn't understand, but also entire groups that spoke the same language would have difficulty relating to and trusting those that did not. They would tend to move away or be forced away from each other, into different environments. This latter, of course, is what God intended. But this intention could not have included keeping "different races" apart—there were no such recognizable groups yet!

It is unlikely that each small group would carry the same broad range of skin colors as the original, larger group. So one group might have more "dark" genes, on average, while another might have more "light" genes. The same thing would happen to other characteristics: nose shape, eye shape, etc. And since they would interbreed only within their own language group, this tendency would no longer be averaged out as before.

As these groups migrated away from Babel, they encountered new and different climate zones. This would also have affected the balance of inherited factors in the population, although the effects of the environment are not nearly as important as the genetic mix with which each group began. As an example, let us look at people who moved to cold areas with little sunlight. In those areas, the dark-skinned members of any group would not be able to produce enough vitamin D and thus would be less healthy and have fewer children.

So, in time, the light-skinned members would predominate. If several different groups went to such an area, and if one group happened to be carrying few genes for lightness, this particular group could in time die out. This natural selection acts on the characteristics already present and does not evolve new ones.

It is interesting to note that in the Neanderthals of Europe (an extinct variety of man now recognized as fully human),[8] many showed evidence of vitamin D deficiency in their bones. In fact, it was this, plus a large dose of evolutionary prejudice, that helped cause them to be classified as "ape-men" for a long time. It is thus quite plausible to suggest that they were a dark-skinned people group who were unfit for the environment into which they moved because of the skin-color genes they began with. Notice that this natural selection, as it is called, does not produce skin colors but only acts on the created colors that are already there.

Conversely, fair-skinned people in very sunny regions could easily be affected by skin cancer, in which case dark-skinned people would more readily survive.

So we see that the pressure of the environment can (a) affect the balance of genes within a group, and (b) even eliminate entire groups. This is why we see, to a large extent, a fit of characteristics to their environment (e.g., Nordic people with pale skin, equatorial people with dark skin, etc.).

But this is not always so. An Inuit (Eskimo) has brown skin yet lives where there is not much sun. Presumably such people have a genetic makeup such as Aabb, which would not be able to produce lighter skin. On the other hand, native South Americans living on the equator do not have black skin. These examples show that natural selection does not create new information—if the genetic makeup of a group of people does not allow variation in color toward the desirable, natural selection cannot create such variation.

African Pygmies live in a hot area but rarely experience strong sunshine in their dense jungle environment, yet they have dark skin.

Pygmies may be a good example of another factor that has affected the racial history of the human race: discrimination. If a variation from the normal occurs (e.g., a very light person among a dark people), then historically it has been usual for that person to be regarded as abnormal and unacceptable. Thus, such a person would find it hard to get a marriage partner. People could also recognize the poor fitness of certain characteristics in their environment, and so these become incorporated into the selection criteria for marriage partners. This would further tend to eliminate light genes from a dark people near the equator, and dark genes from light people at high latitudes. In this way, groups have tended to "purify" themselves.

Also, in some instances, inbreeding in a small group can highlight any commonly occurring unusual features that would previously have been swamped by continual intermarriage. There is a tribe in Africa whose members all have grossly deformed feet as a result of this inbreeding.

To return to Pygmies, if people possessing genes for short stature were discriminated against, and if a small group of them sought refuge in the deepest forest, their marrying only each other would ensure a Pygmy "race" from then on. The fact that Pygmy tribes have never been observed to have their own languages, but instead speak dialects of neighboring non-Pygmy languages, is good evidence in support of this.

The Effects of Choice

People groups that were already equipped with certain characteristics may have made deliberate (or semideliberate) choices concerning the environments to which they migrated. For instance, people with gene combinations for a thicker, more insulating layer of fat under their skin would tend to leave areas that were uncomfortably hot.

Other Evidence

The evidence for the Bible's account of human origins is more than just biological and genetic. Since all peoples descended from Noah's family after the Flood a relatively short time ago, we would be surprised if, in the stories and legends of many of the groups, there were not some memory, albeit distorted by time and retelling, of such a catastrophic event. In fact, an overwhelming number of cultures do have such an account of a world-destroying Flood. Often these have startling parallels to the true, original account (eight people saved in a boat, a rainbow, the sending of the birds, and more).[9]

The following brief excerpt is from just one of the many Australian Aboriginal dreamtime legends that are no doubt changed records of the Flood account as given in Genesis:

> Long, long ago, … came the flood … with only the tops of the mountains standing up above it like islands. The water kept on rising, and finally even the mountain peaks disappeared. The world was one vast, flat sheet of water, and there was no place for the Nurrumbunguttias to live…. Slowly the flood waters receded. The mountaintops appeared again, and the spear heads of trees showed above the water. The sea went back into its own place, and the land steamed under the hot sun…. Animals, birds, insects, and reptiles appeared once more and made their homes on the quickly-drying plains.[10]

Some legends even mention three brothers (possibly the three sons of Noah):

> Unlike the majority of ancestors, who were products of the land they occupied, Yahberri, Mahmoon, and Birrum came from a distant land. The three brothers, together with their grandmother, arrived in a canoe made from the bark of the hoop pine tree, goondool.[11]

In summary, the dispersion at Babel, breaking a large interbreeding group into small, inbreeding groups, ensured that the resultant groups would have different mixes of genes for various physical features. By itself, this would ensure that in a short time there would be certain fixed differences in some of these groups, commonly called "races." In addition, the selection pressure of the environment would modify the existing combinations of genes, causing a tendency for characteristics to suit their environment.

There has been no simple-to-complex evolution of any genes, for the genes were present already. The dominant features of the various people groups result from different combinations of previously existing created genes, plus some minor changes in the direction of degeneration, resulting from mutation (accidental changes that can be inherited). The originally created (genetic) information has been either reshuffled or has degenerated, not been added to.

As one researcher put it, "It's kind of like if all of us are recipes. We have the same ingredients, maybe in different amounts, no matter what kind of cake we turn out to be."[12] In other words, just as someone can take a cake mix and make a number of different cakes, all with the same basic recipe but slight variations, so we can think of Adam and Eve as having the original DNA "recipe," if you like, and all their descendants have the same basic "recipe" with slight variations.

Consequences of False Beliefs about the Origin of "Races"

Rejection of the gospel. The accuracy of the historical details of Genesis is crucial to the trustworthiness of the Bible and to the whole gospel message.[13] So the popular belief that people groups evolved their different features, and could not all have come from Noah's family (contrary to the Bible), has eroded belief in the gospel of Jesus Christ.

Racism. One of the biggest justifications for racial discrimination in modern times is the belief that, because people groups have allegedly evolved separately, they are at different stages of evolution and some people groups are less evolved. Thus, the other person may not be as fully human as you. This sort of thinking inspired Hitler in his quest to eliminate Jews and Gypsies and to establish the "master race." Sadly, some Christians have been infected with racist thinking through the effects on our culture of evolutionary indoctrination, the idea that people of a different color are inferior because they are supposedly closer to the animals.[14]

Consider the ways in which people in America were indoctrinated in ideas that fueled prejudice and racism toward certain groups of people.

In 1907, a *Scientific American* article stated: "The personal appearance, characteristics, and traits of the Congo Pygmies ... [conclude they are] small, apelike, elfish creatures.... They live in dense tangled forest in absolute savagery, and while they exhibit many ape-like features in their bodies ...."[15]

Books such as *The History of Creation* by Ernst Haeckel were studied in the universities in the late nineteenth and early twentieth centuries. Students read such things as:

> Nothing, however, is perhaps more remarkable in this respect, than that some of the wildest tribes in southern Asia and eastern Africa have no trace whatever of the first foundations of all human civilization, of family life, and marriage. They live together in herds, like apes, generally climbing on trees and eating fruits; they do not know of fire, and use stones and clubs as weapons, just like the higher apes.... At the lowest stage of human mental development are the Australians, some tribes of the Polynesians, and the Bushmen, Hottentots, and some of the Negro tribes.[16]

And in 1924, the then *New York Tribune* newspaper carried an article about the Tasmanian Aboriginals, declaring: "Missing Links with Mankind in Early Dawn of History."[17]

Imagine what the people of England thought when they read an article in the *New Lloyd's Evening Post* about two Australian Aboriginals who were brought back to England: "They appear to be a race totally incapable of civilization ... these people are from a lower order of the human race."[18]

No wonder racist attitudes abound throughout America and other nations.

Influence on missionary outreach. Historically, the spread of evolutionary belief was associated with a slackening of fervor by Christians to reach the lost in faraway countries. The idea of savage, half-evolved, inferior peoples somehow does not give rise to the same missionary urgency as the notion that our "cousins," closely linked to us in time and heredity, have yet to hear the gospel. Even many of the finest of today's missionary organizations have been influenced, often unconsciously, by this deeply ingrained belief in the evolutionary view of how other peoples and their religions came about.

All Tribes and Nations Are Descendants of Noah's Family

The Bible makes it clear that any newly "discovered" tribe is not a group of people who have never had any superior technology or knowledge of God in their culture. Rather, their culture began with (a) a knowledge of God, and (b) technology at least sufficient to build a boat of ocean liner size. In looking for the reasons for some of this technological loss and cultural degeneration, Romans 1 suggests that it is linked to the deliberate rejection by their ancestors of the worship of the living God. A full appreciation of this would mean that, for such a group, we would not see the need to educate several generations and give them technical aid as a first priority, but rather we should see their real and urgent need for the gospel as first and foremost.

In fact, most "primitive" tribes still have a memory, in their folklore and religion, of the fact that their ancestors turned away from the living God, the Creator. Don Richardson, missionary of Peace Child fame, has shown that a missionary approach, unblinded by evolutionary bias, and thus looking for this link and utilizing it, has borne a bountiful and blessed harvest on many occasions.[19]

For instance, consider the following excerpt from a book on Australian Aborigine dreamtime legends. Notice the similarity to the account of the forbidden fruit and the Fall in Genesis. It can bring tears to one's eyes to realize these people once had the truth of the Genesis account:

The first man ever to live in Australia was Ber-rook-boorn. He had been made by Baiame. After establishing Ber-rook-boorn and his wife in a place that was good to live in, he put his sacred mark on a yarran tree nearby, which was the home of a swarm of bees. "This is my tree," he told them, "and these are my bees. You can take food anywhere you like in the land I have given you, but this tree, the bees, and the honey they make, you must never touch. If you do, much evil will befall you and all the people who will come after you." ... But one day, when the woman was gathering firewood, her search carried her to Baiame's tree.... A brooding presence seemed to hover above her, and she raised her eyes once more. Now that she was closer to the tree she saw the bees hovering round the trunk, and drops of honey glittering on the bark. She stared at them, fascinated by the sight. She had tasted the sweet excretion only once before, but here was food for many meals. She could not resist the lure of the shining drops. Letting her sticks fall to the ground, she began to climb the tree. Suddenly there was a rush of air and a dark shape with huge black wings enveloped her. It was Narahdarn the bat, whom Baiame had put there to guard his yarran tree. Ber-rook-boorn's wife scrambled down and rushed to her gunyah, where she hid in the darkest corner. The evil she had done could never be remedied. She had released Narahdarn into the world, and from that day onwards he became the symbol of the death that afflicts all the descendants of Ber-rook-boorn. It was the end of the golden age for Ber-rook-boorn and his wife.[20]

Jesus Christ, God's reconciliation in the face of humankind's rejection of the Creator, is the only truth that can set men and women of every culture, technology, people group, or color truly free (John 8:32; 14:6). Thus, the answer to racism is to believe and apply the history of the human race as given in Scripture. If every person were to accept that

- they are all equal before God,
- all humans are descendants of Adam,
- all people are sinners in need of salvation,
- everyone needs to receive Jesus Christ as Savior and Lord of his or her life,
- each person must build his or her thinking on God's Word,
- all behaviors, attitudes, beliefs, etc. should be judged against the absolutes of God's Word, no matter what culture one is from, then the problem of racism would be solved.

Postscript

More than half a century has passed since the Nazi extermination camps shocked a disbelieving world. Yet racial prejudice remains one of the burning issues of our time. Ken Ham's groundbreaking book, *One Blood: The Biblical Answer to Racism*, explains the root causes of racism and gives the biblical solution. You will read, perhaps for the first time, about racism's evolutionary connections, including the origin of the idea of multiple races. In contrast to modern prejudices, the Bible says that God has "made of one blood all nations of men for to dwell on all the face of the earth" (Acts 17:26, KJV). *One Blood* gives irrefutable biblical and scientific evidence that there is only one race—the human race. For a whole new light on the debate over racism, read *One Blood*. This powerful book is only one of many antiracism resources produced by Answers in Genesis, a Bible-upholding ministry that gives answers to today's issues. *One Blood,* only $10.99. Call 1-800-778-3390 or visit www.AnswersInGenesis.org.

Discussion Questions

1. Have you ever heard someone either directly or indirectly question interracial marriages because of the supposed biological differences between the races? How would you deal with such concerns?
2. What do you think about the author's contention that Noah's family was probably middle brown? What race have you traditionally thought Noah's family to be? What are the implications of a "brown" Noah?

3. Many have criticized Christianity as a racist belief system. Can evolution also be a racist belief system? How? What does this imply about sin and the nature of racism?

4. The authors talk about how our missionary endeavors would change if we were to recognize that those of other races are our cousins. What other aspects of Christian life might change if we take seriously the fact that all races are genetically related to each other?

5. How do the legends of other people groups that are similar to biblical accounts demonstrate a spiritual kinship that transcends the racist attempts that have been made to promote racial separation?

Notes

1. *However, people inhabiting the Indian subcontinent are mainly Caucasian, and their skin color ranges from light brown to quite dark. Even within Europe, skin color ranges from very pale to brown.*

2. *Other substances can in minor ways affect skin shading, such as the colored fibers of the protein elastin and the pigment carotene. However, once again we all share these same compounds, and the principles governing their inheritance are similar to those outlined here. Factors other than pigment in the skin may influence the shade perceived by the observer in subtle ways, such as the thickness of the overlying (clear) skin layers, the density and positioning of the blood capillary networks, etc. In fact, "melanin," which is produced by cells in the body called melanocytes, consists of two pigments, which also account for hair color. Eumelanin is very dark brown; phaeomelanin is more reddish. People tan when sunlight stimulates eumelanin production. Redheads, who are often unable to develop a protective tan, have a high proportion of phaeomelanin. They have probably inherited a defective gene that makes their pigment cells "unable to respond to normal signals that stimulate eumelanin production." See P. Cohen, "Redheads Come Out of the Shade," New Scientist 147 (September 30, 1995): 18.*

3. *Most of this DNA is in the nucleus of each cell, but some is contained in mitochondria, which are outside the nucleus in the cytoplasm. Sperm contribute only nuclear DNA when the egg is fertilized, so mitochondrial DNA is generally inherited only from the mother, via the egg.*

4. *Werner Gitt, "Dazzling Design in Miniature," Creation 20, no. 1 (December 1998–February 1999): 6.*

5. *Incredibly, sometimes the same stretch of DNA can be "read" differently, to have more than one function. The creative intelligence behind such a thing is mind-boggling.*

6. *This simplification is not done to help our case—the more genes there are, the easier*

it is to have a huge range of "different" colors. The principle involved can be understood from using two as an example.

7. *For more about the so-called curse of Ham, see chapter six in Ken Ham et al.'s* One Blood *(Green Forest, Ark.: Master.*

8. *For a detailed examination and refutation of the so-called "ape-men," see Marvin Lubenow,* Bones of Contention *(Grand Rapids, Mich.: Baker, 1992).*

9. *A. W. Reed,* Aboriginal Fables and Legendary Tales *(Sydney: Reed Pty., 1965); idem,* Aboriginal Legends: Animal Tales *(Frenchs Forest, NSW, Australia: Reed Pty., 1980); idem,* Aboriginal Myths: Tales of the Dreamtime *(Chatswood, NSW, Australia: Reed Pty., 1980); idem,* Aboriginal Stories of Australia *(Frenchs Forest, NSW, Australia: Reed Pty., 1980); idem,* More Aboriginal Stories of Australia *(Sydney: Reed Pty., 1980).*

10. *Reed,* Aboriginal Fables and Legendary Tales, *34–35.*

11. *Reed,* Aboriginal Myths, *70.*

12. *"We're All the Same," www.abcnews.com, science page, September 10, 1998.*

13. *Ken Ham,* The Lie: Evolution *(Green Forest, Ark.: Master, 1987).*

14. *Of course, racism predated Darwinian evolution: "The heart is deceitful above all things, and desperately wicked" (Jeremiah 17:9, KJV). But first, there were evolutionary theories around long before Darwin, and second, Darwinism gave a seeming scientific respectability to racism. The bottom line is that pre-Darwinian racism was equally contradicted by the biblical history of humankind.*

15. *Arthur H. J. Keane, "Anthropological Curiosities: The Pygmies of the World,"* Scientific American, *supplement 1650, 64, no. 99 (1907): 107–8.*

16. *Ernst Haeckel,* The History of Creation: Or the Development of the Earth and Its Inhabitants by the Action of Natural Causes, *trans. E. Ray Lankester (London: Henry S. King, 1876), 2:362–3.*

17. *A. S. Brown, "Missing Links with Mankind in Early Dawn of History,"* New York Tribune, *February 10, 1924, 11.*

18. *Ali Gripper, "Blacks Slain for Science's White Superiority Theory,"* The Daily Telegraph Mirror, *Sydney, Australia, April 26, 1994, 32; Carl Wieland, "Evolutionary Racism,"* Creation 20, *no. 4 (September–November 1998): 14–16.*

19. *Don Richardson,* Eternity in Their Hearts *(Ventura, Calif.: Regal, 1986).*

20. *Reed,* Aboriginal Fables and Legendary Tales, *21–22.*

❦ FIVE ❦

Interracial Sexual Relations in
Early American History
Sherelyn Whittum Yancey

MY HUSBAND AND I MARRIED IN THE HISTORIC LITTLE CHURCH of La Villita in the heart of San Antonio's romantic River Walk district in 1995. If we had married in Texas thirty years earlier, we would have committed a crime. Instead of spending our honeymoon in the British Virgin Islands, we would have been sentenced to prison for two to five years. What crime could we commit worthy of such a sentence? The crime of interracial marriage: my husband is black, and I am white. We would have faced the same paradox as many before us: Do we marry, commit a crime, and willingly go to prison? Or do we live in sin without legal marriage because the state of Texas criminalizes our interracial union?

This paradox was legally settled in 1967 when the U.S. Supreme Court abolished all state laws against interracial marriage in the landmark *Loving vs. Virginia* case. Yet this issue has not been spiritually or socially settled. The aftermath of forbidding interracial marriage still lingers in some families and churches, with a haunting legacy of shame attached to couples who are judged as betraying their own race by marrying a believer of another race. Pressure is placed on multiracial children who do not want to be forced to identify with only one parent's race. Mixed-race families still often have to choose which race of congregation to attend or whether to quit church attendance altogether due to disapproval by same-race congregations.

The purpose of this historical chapter is to inform Christians, especially white believers, of how race-based slavery defined, shaped, and corrupted the formation of families and churches by criminalizing interracial marriage and denying legitimacy to multiracial children from the time of English settlement in the New World to the American Civil War. This essay explores how interracial sexual relations challenged three building blocks of American society: slavery, the traditional family, and churches. Free multiracial children and interracial marriages threatened the institutions of race-based slavery, families, and churches by their very existence. Legal interracial marriages and children embody racial unity and equality by defying the notion of racial superiority—the faulty foundation upon which American Christian society, north and south, was built. Slavery was conceived in self-serving economic sin, giving birth to an unrighteous racial hierarchy, which used laws against interracial marriage to sustain it.

Since this is an essay with historical references, please note that the use of racial language is constantly changing. Out-of-date terms, such as *mulatto* or *Negro,* are not intended to insult readers but to use the terminology of the time described. By *racial hierarchy,* I mean the value or importance of a person based on skin color, with whites at the top and blacks at the bottom. *Antimiscegenation* comes from the Latin meaning "to not mix the race," referring to white and nonwhite sexual mixing, either within or outside marriage. Previous to the Civil War, the term *amalgamation* (Latin meaning "to blend diverse elements") was used to describe interracial sexual liaisons. The terms *interracial children, mixed-race children,* and *multiracial children* are used interchangeably. Various terms have been used to refer to mixed-race children, such as *mulatto* (Euro-African), *mestizo* (Euro-Indian), and *mustee* (African-Indian). Latinos were exempted from formal antimiscegenation laws since they were classified as white by treaty protections with Spain and Mexico, yet many faced local discrimination from white supremacists.[1]

Interracial Marriage and Multiracial Children Challenge the Rise of Slavery Laws

When life was a difficult struggle to survive in the New World, interracial marriages and illicit liaisons created a new race of multiracial children. The question of what to do about these children led to the rise of the first slavery laws written in America in an attempt to control sex and marriage among Europeans, Africans, and American Indians. The extent of this amalgamation is unknown, but it was so common for four centuries that ethnohistorians may have cause to consider revising the simplistic view that American slaves were full-blooded Africans. The time line in table 1 may help demonstrate how interracial sexual relations have always been with us, ranging from legal marriages and concubinage to illicit liaisons, fornication, adultery, and rape.

Native Americans, Africans, Spanish, and Portuguese participated in interracial sex, producing multiracial children for over one hundred years before English settlement. This situation in the New World during the first century of European immigration created social structures that tended to be fairly

TABLE 1: Time Line of Interracial Sexual Relations

1492 Columbus and his men enslave, rape, and cohabit with Taino Indians, taking more than three thousand slaves to Spain, where Indians and Africans create interracial slave children.

1502 The first Africans arrive in the Caribbean to intermix with and gradually supplant Indian slaves.

1500s Spanish conquistadors enslave Indian women as concubines or wives. They also rape African women slaves en route to the Caribbean islands and Central and South America, producing mulatto children.

1500s Portuguese form a multitiered racial society in Brazil with Indian and African women, enslaving but also often legally claiming their offspring.

1526 Africans and Indians successfully overthrow Spanish colony in South Carolina. Spanish abandon their outpost and slaves. Africans freely cohabit with local Indian nations.

1534 French intermarry and establish a fur trade with North American Indians.

1607 Jamestown colony is founded in Virginia for commerce and Christian conversion.

1613 Pocahontas is kidnapped by English persons expecting a ransom. Her interracial marriage with John Rolfe follows in 1614, with a mestizo son born of the union. Subsequent descendants are classified as white, not Indian, under the "Pocahontas Exception" to ensure privileges of whiteness.

1619 Africans arrive in Jamestown, traded by the crew of a Dutch ship to obtain food supplies. Some Africans intermarry with white servants and eventually rise to the top of the planter society. Mulattos form a new race in the English colonies.

1637 Puritans enter the slave trade by exiling Pequot prisoners of war to the West Indies, where the Pequot mate with Africans. Their offspring are traded back as slaves to the colonial mainland.

1660 Virginia statute states that baptized Indians or freed Negroes may not purchase Christian (white) servants but may purchase slaves of their own nation.[2]

1661 Maryland becomes the first colony to enact a statute against interracial marriage.

1661 Virginia writes the first slavery law in response to a large number of mulatto children born to white and black women. This law reverses English tradition by declaring a child's inheritance (status, name, property) would be derived from the mother, not the father. Mulatto children of English women are born with free status regardless of father's race.

1664 Maryland enacts a slavery law aimed at punishing free/white/English/Christian women who marry slave/black/African/heathen men by enslaving these white wives during the lifetime of their black husbands and enslaving their mixed-race children for life.

1679 Virginia law permits enslavement of Native Americans and their offspring.

1681 Maryland changes the law of 1664 because white masters coerced English women servants into interracial marriages to gain more slaves. The new law states that freeborn English or white women married to slave men would be released from forced service and that their children would be born free.

1691   Virginia law banishes white women within three months of wedding if they are interracially married to black, Indian, or mulatto men. If an unmarried white woman bears a mulatto child, she is punished with five years of labor and her child with thirty years of forced labor.

1700s   Runaway Africans and the Creek Nation amalgamate to form the Black Seminole Nation in Spanish-held Florida, building independent villages and forts to repel slave hunters.

1705   Virginia law imprisons a white spouse for six months when he or she marries a black or mulatto person.

1705   Virginia law defines as mulatto the child of an Indian or the child, grandchild, or great-grandchild of a Negro. Whites later convert the lightest-skinned mulattos into blacks with the "one drop of African blood rule," thereby depriving them of any white heritage or privilege.

1715   North Carolina passes an act to punish any white for marrying a Negro, mulatto, or Indian. The act also punishes any minister for performing an interracial wedding.

1723   Virginia free mulattos lose their previous rights to vote and carry a gun.

1760   Biracial and triracial descendants of Indian mothers sue and win freedom from slavery regardless of their father's African or European admixture.

1765   Virginia changes its punishment regarding mulatto grandchildren of free white women, reducing involuntary servitude from thirty years to twenty-one years for men, eighteen years for women.

1782   Virginia law allows slave owners to free their slaves. Many free their mixedrace children, setting them up in mulatto communities in Ohio.

1806   Virginia exiles slaves within one year of manumission or they will forfeit their freedom.

1830   Indian Removal Act breaks treaties, exiles Indian nations west of the Mississippi River, thereby giving whites legal but fraudulent claims to Indian lands.

1835   Virginian mulatto slave appears so white at a public auction that men refuse to bid on him for fear he will easily walk away from slavery, posing as a free white man.[3]

1843   White Virginians petition to exile Pamunkey-Black Indians from tax-exempt reservation for fear of uprising and use of land as refuge for runaway slaves or home for free blacks.

1857   Wisconsin pastor is fired for marrying a Negro to a white woman.

1865   Race-based slavery is abolished in the United States.

1967   U.S. Supreme Court federal ruling overturns state laws criminalizing interracial marriage.

2000   U.S. Census application instructs Americans to check all categories that apply to racial identity instead of choosing only one classification.

lenient toward mixed-race unions and children. For example, although slavery and a color hierarchy operated in Mexico, the Spanish-Indian formation of Mexican people is widely acknowledged. The focus of this chapter, though, will be with the English, since more than three hundred years of American antimiscegenation laws began with them.

During early English settlement in Virginia in 1607, the Powhatan Confederacy was willing to trade but not be enslaved as a labor supply. The English soon learned that their dream of forcing the Indians to mine for gold, replicating the Spanish conquest of the Aztecs and Incas, could not be fulfilled. Religious justification to take the land without permission of the native inhabitants can be found in the king's charter to bring Christianity to the Indians. Yet Captain John Smith recorded in his diary that religious interests cloaked the primary goal—to acquire wealth. In reality, the English depended on the Indians to supply them with food when they were sick and starving. A stormy relationship developed after some English settlers killed local Indians and stole their food supplies. Other English indentured servants found conditions too harsh under gentry masters; many defected to intermix with the Indians.[4]

Eventually, tobacco would thrive as a single cash crop, but it would need intensive manual labor. Investors eyed England's vast surplus of landless, unemployed, poor, single men and convicts who could escape their lot by contracting out their labor in Virginia. In exchange for paid ship passage, food, clothing, shelter, and their freedom, after serving from four to seven years, these dregs of England had an opportunity to become landowners. In 1619, three important events occurred in Jamestown: (1) male colonists elected their first representatives to govern themselves; (2) the first boatload of single English women arrived to boost morale and create families; and (3) the first boatload of Africans arrived. The appearance of black men and white women amidst white men and Indian women interwove the first generation of multiracial Virginians. In spite of this hopeful beginning, the establishment of the power of white males to govern themselves and everybody else would backfire for blacks, women, and Indians for centuries to come.

Indentured servants saw their dreams turned into nightmares. Away from the mother country, English servants had no rights to protect them; they were the personal property of their owners, who auctioned them off to the highest bidder at the dockside. Many did not live to see their freedom; they were broken, whipped, worked to death, or died of malaria—essentially, they were white slaves for a limited time. Blacks and whites lived, worked, suffered, and ran away together. European male indentured servants arrived alone and outnumbered white females about four to one. Indentured women could not marry or have children during their term of service (in contrast to the New England family units, who arrived together to reconstruct English religious communities). English, Irish, Africans, and Indians were bound closely together as indentured servants for whom life was fast, difficult, and uncertain. These living conditions contributed to interracial sex and escalating unwed pregnancies, with 20 percent of births producing mixed-race children in the days before institutionalized slavery.[5]

Many Africans participated in the full life of the community with the same rights and responsibilities as Europeans. They attended church services, had legal access to sue and be sued, and could buy and sell goods as well as servants or slaves.[6] Historian Martha Hodes documents numerous accounts of sexual liaisons, including marriages, between white women and black men in the antebellum South that were socially tolerated.[7] Mulatto children born to these white women were viewed as second-class citizens, but they experienced relatively more freedom compared to multiracial children born to black women.

Some historians assert that interracial sexual relations were more prevalent during the colonial era than during any subsequent time in American history.[8] The evidence can be found sparingly in the written record but can be easily seen in the faces of many African American families and the rapid rise of the mulatto population. A few examples, however, are found in court documents. For instance, historian Paul Spickard reports that white men were named as fathers to numerous illegitimate children born to black slave women in New England. Hester, a white woman servant, married James Tate, a black slave in Virginia during the 1680s. An interracial marriage in Massachusetts produced a biracial son who became a noted preacher and married a white woman. An Irish woman, Peggy Kerry, and her black lover, Caesar, were among those executed for supposedly conspiring to burn down New York City to overthrow the white upper class.[9] Another historian searched colonial records for evidence of interracial sexual liaisons and discovered a few directly identified by marriage certificates, such as Irish Nell Butler and Negro Charles, who married in 1681. Yet numerous accounts of interracial sexuality can be found indirectly under charges for bastardy, fornication, adultery, divorce, and freedom from slavery suits filed by mulatto children of white women.[10]

Interracial marriage and inheritance laws offered a number of social and economic advantages. Multiracial children of married couples typically enjoyed economic opportunities via family connections, property inheritance protection, and legitimate standing in the community. Interracial marriages challenged notions of white superiority and black inferiority because marital mates are usually considered social equals. Intermarriage also compromised the effort to solidify a legal color line between black and white, slave and free, heathen and Christian, African and English. For a few generations, interracial marriage was legal and socially acknowledged.

In 1662, Christian Englishmen devised a brilliant self-serving plan to elevate their own socioeconomic status. They reversed English common law by declaring that a child's inheritance (status, name, property) would be derived from the mother, not the father. This reversal allowed paternalistic slave owners to decrease the number of free mulattos born to legally married white women and black men while simultaneously increasing the number of enslaved mulattos born by sexual exploitation to black and mulatto women slaves. Masters, their sons, and overseers could now procreate their own children as slaves rather than spend money to buy new slaves. In addition, slave masters and overseers could keep this sexual exploitation a family secret within the confines of secluded plantation communities. The responsibility for raising these biracial children fell to the slave mother, with no hope of the white father's financial provision or legal inheritance.[11] This shift in inheritance laws was extremely clever, cruel, and economically advantageous. The majority of mulattos born to black women slaves and white men would no longer be free to threaten white social control or the racial hierarchy with their white ancestry.

Drawing and maintaining a color line defining whites as free and blacks as slaves was most easily accomplished by outlawing interracial sex and marriage. For race-based slavery to succeed, whites could not marry nonwhites and produce legal interracial heirs. This was the essential first step to keep the color line distinct. Notions of white superiority and racially-pure legal bloodlines were written into American laws. These notions were justified by stereotyping interracial marriage and sexual relations as deviant, lascivious, and immoral—especially for "good" Christians. Interracial lovers did not commit indecent crimes; rather, a deceitful crime was committed against them by outlawing interracial marriage. Criminalizing interracial marriage allowed patriarchal white masters to pressure white women into producing only white heirs while they continued to have illicit interracial sex for pleasure and procreation of slave children for their own economic gain. Conveniently, a white man could legally own, but not marry, his black sexual partners. He could have interracial children, but not acknowledge them socially.

Slavery was not just an economic system of forced labor; it was also a social and sexual system that led to the rise of biracial human beings who yearned for freedom. Historian Edmund Morgan argues that American freedom for whites was made possible by justifying American slavery for blacks. A common bond of whiteness joined the ruling class of planters and lower-class farmers when they enslaved Africans as a poor, landless underclass. English/American rights were purchased at the expense of wrongs done to Africans and Indians.[12] One of these wrongs was to deny interracial couples and their offspring the sanctity of legal, Christian marriage. If legal interracial marriage had continued, I contend, race-based slavery might not have succeeded, because slave status could not have been equated with skin color.

Interracial Sexual Relations Challenge Traditional Family Formation

At one point in my life, I did not understand how the institution of slavery, not marriage, defined legitimate family members. Who belonged in white families, and who did not, was based on a socially constructed color line, not a biological bloodline. For example, a biological daughter could be a mulatto slave, but a mulatto slave could not be acknowledged as a daughter in the house of her father, a white master. Even today, a white woman can give birth to a black child, but a black woman cannot give birth to a white child. This paradox is the result of the one-drop rule: a fiction created by slave masters that branded interracial children as black slaves if they inherited "one drop" of African blood. The Christian ideal of a white man and white woman creating white children as heirs became the traditional family standard by which all other family structures were judged. Therefore, interracial marriages were eventually outlawed in most colonies, slave marriages were not binding, and Indian marriages were generally viewed as heathen rituals.

Yet under slavery, many single and married white men fashioned other kinds of nontraditional family groupings as a way around antimiscegenation laws via voluntary cohabitation, concubinage, slave wives, rape, and brief illicit sexual encounters resulting in illegitimate, multiracial children. For example, I am confronted with our interracial Yancey family tree. It reveals the history of how slavery, not marriage, was the legal institution that inspired sexual unions between the white men and black, mulatto, or Indian women who would become my husband's ancestors. My legal name is

Yancey, inherited from a white slave owner four generations ago who had sexual relations with an unknown black slave woman. The fact that this black grandmother is unknown and was not married to the white slave owner is a result of slavery. I now bear the name of that white slave owner even though all my Yancey relatives are African American. As I research our family tree, I cannot find records of George's great-grandfather, the child born of that illicit sexual liaison. Did the white man and black woman love each other? Was she raped? Was she kept as his concubine because he could own her but not legally honor her with marriage?

George's great-great-grandmother Kitty Harrison was born in 1850. She was the daughter of a slave master's son and a black-Pamunkee Indian woman slave. Kitty was the triracial granddaughter of William Byrd Harrison, master of the Upper Brandon Plantation on the James River in Virginia, who had a reputation for being an earnest and devout Christian.[13] Kitty's father may or may not have raped her mother, but he certainly did not marry her nor did he acknowledge Kitty as family with a right to inheritance. When Kitty was thirteen years old, she was among the 105 slaves at Upper Brandon who were valued at $62,400.[14] My black mother-in-law and I plan to visit this same plantation to check the property lists and see if her great-grandmother's name is listed—not as family, but as property. Slavery clearly shaped the formation of our interracial Yancey family because white Christian fathers sexually exploited women to produce biracial children whom they valued as slaves yet abandoned as heirs.

By the 1700s, in the eyes of the law as well as social custom, only white children produced from marriages between white men and white women were considered legitimate heirs, thereby securing access to family wealth and property inheritance. By adopting the one-drop rule, whites kept their multiracial slave children from transmitting special privileges to their children. This served to prohibit these children or grandchildren from claiming their partial white ancestry. For example, if a biracial slave was only one-sixteenth "black," with all the features of a white person, he or she was denied marriage, professional work, public accommodations, freedom to travel, or other privileges whites took for granted. Multiracial children were known as "step-asides" because, after their conception, many white men stepped aside from their responsibilities to claim, financially support, or raise them.[15] Today we call such fathers "dead-beat dads."

Yet, some white fathers lived as bachelors with their enslaved mixed-race children. A few freed their mistresses and children or willed them property.[16]

A notable exception to the general rule was made in the case of Amanda Dickson, an enslaved mulatto daughter of a wealthy Georgia planter. She and her children were acknowledged as family and heirs to his half-million-dollar fortune—although her white relatives contested the will in three separate trials.[17] Ultimately, Amanda prevailed.

Generational concubinage was another challenge to nontraditional family formation, as illustrated by the extended members of Thomas Jefferson's family. In a newspaper interview in 1873, Madison Hemings described how his African great-grandmother became pregnant by Captain Hemings en route to Virginia, where John Wales purchased her. Captain Hemings attempted to buy his biracial child, Betty, and her mother, but Mr. Wales refused due to his curious fascination with the outcome of this amalgamated child. Mr. Wales must have been very intrigued with Betty, because she became his concubine after his wife's death. She bore him seven slave children, one of whom was Sally Hemings. When John Wales died in 1774, his daughter, Martha, and her husband, Thomas Jefferson, inherited Sally, her mother, and her grandmother. Jefferson had two surviving daughters at the time of his wife's death. Following in his father-in-law's footsteps, Jefferson took Sally, his wife's half sister, as his concubine at Monticello, where she reportedly bore him six children. Each new generation brought about lighter-complexioned slaves. Sally's daughter, Harriet, escaped concubinage by passing as white after she left Monticello with her brother in 1822.[18] After his death in 1826, most of Jefferson's two hundred slaves were sold, except for the Hemings slaves, who were freed according to his will. But not Sally. Jefferson's daughter, Martha, made special provision for Sally by unofficially freeing her so that she would not have to leave Virginia within one year in accordance with state law.[19] Sally lived with her two sons in Charlottesville until her death in 1835. Census takers in 1830 recorded Sally Hemings as white, while others listed Sally as a free person of color, demonstrating how socially fickle the color line could be to enslave people by racial classification.[20] Historians continue to debate the veracity of the Hemings' claim of their descent from Thomas Jefferson, yet DNA results revealed to the public in 1998 appear to validate their oral family history and genealogy.[21]

The practice of *placage* is another example of the formation of nontraditional interracial families. *Placage* was an intricate French system of setting up cohabitation between free women of color and wealthy white men who signed contracts that obligated them to provide exquisite homes, clothing, and food for their concubines for a certain amount of time. When the contract expired, the women were promised money to live on and an education for any biracial children they might bear. This arrangement could occur before, during, or after a man established a traditional white family.[22]

Other family patterns developed in various parts of the Deep South, where slave auctions held a "fancy trade," selling multiracial women for twice the price of a male field slave. The lighter the skin color, the higher the price. White men bought or hired these women as concubines or prostitutes; other masters actually brought their concubines into their own homes, where their white wives were humiliated by having to endure their husband's adultery.[23] This practice was socially accepted under a conspiracy of silence. Yet one Southern white wife confided to her diary that other wives lived under the same roof with patriarchal husbands and their concubines. These wives were quick to identify slave masters as the fathers of the many biracial children at other plantations but believed the mixed-race children at their own plantations dropped out of the sky.[24]

Because of antimiscegenation laws, an unusual family arrangement arose among Louisiana's Catholic Creoles of Color, who intermarried and created close-knit family alliances that consolidated wealth and social status. These French-speaking free persons of color fostered an elitism that garnered most of the same legal rights as whites, distancing themselves from their own darker-colored slaves. They formed the middle ground between whites and blacks in a three-tiered society. Church and legal records have only recently been unlocked, revealing the great extent of amalgamation between Creoles of Color and white plantation owners. These influential, free families of color frequently used the legal system to protect their property. For example, numerous white men, such as Jacques Fontenette, gave his last name and tracts of land to his mulatto children and great sums of money to his common-law Creole wife four years after he married a white woman to establish white heirs.[25] This practice often angered the white family when money or property was willed to the interracial family of polygamous patriarchs, but it was upheld in court until the later antebellum period, when jealous white family members passed laws to invalidate wills that would endow concubines and their children. These distinct, sophisticated interracial communities were devastated after the Civil War when whites applied the one-drop rule to them. After that, Creoles of Color suffered the same discrimination as the black folk whom they had once held in contempt.[26]

The French also tended to create nontraditional interracial families by adapting to Native American lifestyles, purchasing slave wives, and migrating with them to develop fur trades. French Canadian mountain men lived as tribal members whose multiracial children later became important cultural brokers. For example, the 1804–06 Lewis and Clark expedition employed a number of mixed-blood Indians. Sacajawea, the Shoshone slave wife of a French Canadian, served as an interpreter. The presence of her mestizo baby, Jean Baptiste Charbonneau, conveyed to Western Indians they encountered that the expedition was not a war party.[27] Jean later lived with and was tutored by William Clark and his slave, York. Under black, white, and Indian influences, Jean became a gifted multilingual and multicultural interpreter.

Other nontraditional families included blacks and Indians who intermarried despite extreme efforts of whites to keep the two races apart. For instance, Indians of the Southeast were frequently paid bounty money to bring runaway slaves back, dead or alive, while black slaves were armed by white militia to put down Indian uprisings. When possible, the "divide and conquer" strategy was used. Whites rightly feared an alliance between blacks and Indians might overthrow white domination. For example, as early as 1502 the first Africans arrived in Hispaniola—just ten years after Columbus's initial voyage. Immediately the Africans escaped to live with the Indians, never to be recaptured. In 1526 the Spanish tried to colonize South Carolina only to be overthrown by their African slaves and local Indians. The Black Seminoles of Spanish Florida were famous for their mixed-blood origin of African and Creek runaways who built interracial families and independent villages in the relative safety of the swamplands. The term Black Indians was coined by William Katz to describe these multiracial people whose vast unwritten history is greatly underresearched.[28]

Triracial isolate groups also challenged traditional white families. This little-known phenomena began when many Europeans and free blacks left English settlements and intermarried with American Indians who reorganized their tribal networks after being decimated by death and disease. Outside the authority of English antimiscegenation laws, these isolated, multiracial families were scattered from New England throughout the Middle Colonies to Louisiana. Dr. Virginia DeMarce published her findings after interviewing a large number of triracial descendants who defied white American racial classification systems.[29] What is remarkable about these families, clans, tribes, or Indian nations is that they chose to live for centuries as triracial family groups safely isolated from the emerging racial hierarchy of American society. They did not allow interference from outsiders, whether they were census takers or slave catchers. An interesting map published in 1953 identifies multitudes of triracial families, such as the Louisiana Redbones, Tennessee Goins, and the New England Jackson Whites, who moved frequently in order to intermarry with other known triracial family groups.[30]

In summary, American Indians, Europeans, and Africans each held sacred traditions of how to build family ties. By legalizing slavery of Africans and Indians while criminalizing interracial marriages in the emerging colonies, Englishmen gradually institutionalized slavery and deinstitutionalized legal marriage for everyone except themselves and white women. This became the basis of the institution of the traditional (white) family. Jesus condemned the Pharisees for creating laws and then devising ways to get around those laws. If the love of money is indeed the root of all evil (1 Timothy 6:10), perhaps we can understand why many white men preferred to own women they could breed and sell their own offspring for a profit rather than limit their sexual activity to honoring one woman with marriage and raising their biracial children as heirs. Despite the white master's attempt to control the sexuality of black men and women, many did create unofficial marriages with a very strong devotion to their children. Conforming to white society, some Indians enslaved blacks, yet many other runaway slaves found refuge and forged family ties within Indian communities.

Interracial Sexual Relations Challenge Churches

As American slave society developed, many theologians and pastors taught that the institution of slavery was ordained by God and took priority over the institution of marriage. This meant slave marriages were invalid; husbands, wives, and children belonged to the master, not each other.[31] Christian slave owners could then break up slave families by selling a spouse or child, with no compunction, despite Jesus' teaching that whom God had brought together, no one should separate (Matthew 19:6). Defending race-based slavery became an overarching structure that infiltrated and corrupted white churches.[32] The focus of this section will be limited to how the issue of amalgamation tended to divide Christians into two camps: proslavery churches, such as Southern Baptists, and the antislavery (abolitionist) churches, like the Quakers.

During the Great Awakening of the 1740s, the authority of churches, especially the Anglicans and the Congregationalists, was challenged by evangelical male and female, black and white, itinerant preachers. They drew thousands to outdoor camp meetings. This spiritual awakening manifested itself by evangelical Baptists and Methodists calling for egalitarian interracial fellowship with black slaves. While actively evangelizing slaves, these radical white evangelicals were whipped, beaten, and driven off, yet they were able to win converts who in turn evangelized other slaves. Mixed-race congregations grew where blacks and whites were discipled, baptized, and shared their testimonies. Black preachers were chosen to lead mixed or white congregations. In such congregations, interracial couples were gladly received. Unfortunately, segregation of multiracial churches became more common after 1810.[33]

The word *amalgamation* conjured up emotionally charged fears that proslavery Christians used to justify separation and slavery of blacks. In 1852 Josiah Priest taught that the very thought of interracial marriage or amalgamation was repulsive because it was unchristian. He hypothesized that when the two races came into contact and the thought of amalgamation crossed the mind of a white, it was accompanied with a chill of the soul, that chill being the very voice of God.[34] Apparently many Christian slave masters paid no heed to that chill when sexually exploiting their women slaves. Perhaps that chill of the soul only crossed Preacher Priest's mind.

The rhetoric of amalgamation sharply divided Christians. Those invested in domestic breeding of slaves as a profitable business *practiced* amalgamation (white men with black women) while they *condemned* amalgamation (black men with white women) if it would inflame public sentiment against abolitionists. For example, the 1838 Anti-Slavery Convention of American Women in Philadelphia gathered black, biracial, and white speakers to conduct a conference at Pennsylvania Hall. This crossing of color and gender lines to express religious convictions experienced a backlash of white violence culminating in the burning down of the hall. City officials blamed the abolitionist speakers for the violent incident. Political cartoons, printed and distributed to the public, renamed Pennsylvania Hall as "Abolition Hall" and described it as an "amalgamation brothel" for black men to fondle white women. Other racist propaganda newspapers printed grotesque pictures of blacks and whites caressing one another as proof of the horrific amalgamating tendencies of abolitionists. These cartoons were intended to sway public opinion in the north and south against antislavery activists.[35]

In 1839 another popular political cartoon vilifying amalgamation pictured a Christian women's antislavery group in Massachusetts lusting after the black Haitian ambassador who was being introduced to them by John Quincy Adams. This abolitionist group of five hundred women was accused of wanting to marry black husbands because they signed a petition, along with several thousand other signatories, to abolish the ban against interracial marriage. Many Christian women abolitionists did not support amalgamation in principle, yet they risked their reputations by being maligned in the press when speaking in public or signing petitions to end racial discrimination and slavery. Ironically, Puritan Massachusetts was the first English colony to sanction slavery as a legal institution in 1641, but it was also the first state to nullify its antimiscegenation law in 1843.

Numerous Christian slave masters endowed themselves with "biblical," patriarchal power. They justified adultery and concubinage of black or mulatto women by making references to Abraham, Sarah, and Hagar, or David and his harem, not to mention Solomon. Slaveholding was a noble ambition even for pastors, deacons, elders, and churchmen. For example, Frederick Douglass described his former master as a pious, but poor, Methodist deacon who bought a female slave *"as a breeder."*[34] The deacon rented a male slave to fornicate with his female slave. The birth of twins resulted—a double economic bonus for the deacon and his wife. They considered it a sure sign of God's blessing.[35] Later, Douglass was ordained by the African Methodist Episcopal Church. He skillfully exposed the influence slavery held upon white Christians, who in turn deprived couples and children of the dignity of sanctified marriage and family life. One of Douglass's prophetic rebukes of proslavery churches follows:

> I am filled with unutterable loathing when I contemplate the religious pomp and show, together with the horrible inconsistencies, which every where surround me. We have men-stealers for ministers, women-whippers for missionaries, and cradle-plunderers for church members. He who sells my sister, for purposes of prostitution, stands forth as the pious advocate of purity. He who is the religious advocate of marriage robs whole millions of its sacred influence, and leaves them to the ravages of wholesale pollution. The warm defender of the sacredness of the family relations is the same that scatters whole families, —sundering husbands and wives, parents and children, sisters and brothers, —leaving the hut vacant, and the hearth desolate. We see the thief preaching against theft, and the adulterer against adultery. We have men sold to build churches, women sold to support the gospel, and babes sold to purchase Bibles for the *poor heathen! All for the glory of God and the good of souls!*[36]

Having broken free from the mentality of slavery, Frederick Douglass's keen intellect and study of human nature emerged from his experience as a man of mixed African, Indian, and white ancestry. His first wife, Anna Murray, was black, and his second wife, Helen Pitts, was white. Interracial marriage in his later life hit a raw nerve in some of his black and white followers, although the Douglasses were continually invited to the White House for social functions and treated with respect. Douglass commented on how odd it was for some to condemn him for marrying a woman just a few shades lighter than him while nothing would have been said if she were just a few shades darker than him. Even this icon of black freedom and dignity was labeled a traitor to his race for interracially marrying the wife of his choice.

Conclusion

During slavery, the very presence of legal and voluntary interracial sexual relations and multiracial children testifies to the strength of their love and commitment that transcended the laws and prejudices of families and churches in early American history. This essay has demonstrated how interracial sexual relations challenged three institutional building blocks of American society: slavery, traditional families, and churches. By criminalizing interracial marriage and depriving multiracial children of a legitimate place in society, white men were able to gain an economic upper hand by gradually associating race with slavery.

First, interracial marriage and multiracial children challenged the rise of slavery laws because of their very existence. Slavery laws first came about by struggling to define the legal status of a child born with both European and African ancestry. A rapid increase of free mulattos alarmed the ruling class, who devised an ingenious self-serving economic plan by overturning English common law to declare that a child's inheritance would follow that of the mother's station in life, not the father's. This strategic reversal of English law resolved the master's racial dilemma of how to breed African slave children with partial English descent. Unrighteous laws governing interracial sexual liaisons and marriage continued to harden with each new generation, reinforcing a color line that equated blacks with slavery and whites with freedom and full citizenship.

Second, interracial sexual relations challenged traditional family formation because interracial mixing continued to flourish despite laws and penalties. These sexual restrictions were intended to punish white women, coercing them into marrying only white men and procreating white heirs. Still, historical research is uncovering increasing accounts of white women who did interracially marry, cohabit, or give birth. Conversely, white men formed nontraditional interracial family lineages with women of color whom they could legally own but not marry. The spectrum of sexual slavery included concubinage, brief illicit sexual encounters, rape, and voluntary cohabitation. One can debate whether some of these interracial unions were voluntary, given the power differential in race and gender status, yet as the Creoles of Color demonstrate, legal contracts sometimes were negotiated and they were binding. Several slave families declared that God had married them even if whites would not allow it.[37] Where Native American control of land predominated, many white men married or bought Indian women to forge kinship and economic alliances. Whites attempted to prevent the amalgamation of blacks and Indians but were generally unsuccessful.

Third, as Christian churches split over the issue of slavery, multiracial children continued to be born. Christian slave masters and their sons *practiced* amalgamation but *condemned* interracial sex between white women and men of color. After the American Revolution, major debates in churches questioned the hypocrisy of slavery in a newly formed nation dedicated to ideals of freedom and equality. Antislavery churches were maligned as "amalgamation brothels" where lustful black men ravished compliant white women. Proslavery churches were denounced as religious rapists and greedy kidnappers. There was very little middle ground, since both sides appealed to Scripture to defend their positions and religious convictions ran deep. The Civil War put an end to race-based slavery but not to racism. Interracial marriage would continue to be illegal in many Southern states for another hundred years until the civil rights movement of the 1960s.

When it comes to race relations, we white Christians seem to have historical amnesia over past interracial sexual relations and resulting multiracial children. Perhaps it is because the brutal treatment of Africans and Indians was not written into American history until the 1960s. What can we do about historical racial injustice? Many of us might complain, "I wasn't there. I can't help it if my family owned slaves or killed Indians." No, we are not responsible for others' behavior, but we are accountable for how we use our social and economic inheritance. For instance, sexual slavery is still a painful, historical wound that festers while most whites ignore it and many blacks are embittered by it. I believe that racial healing might begin if descendants of white slave owners would own the past and locate descendants of their families' slaves to admit the damage of slavery and acknowledge any interracial family connections. Whites who have done this shared historical family documents that shed light on the unknown origins of interracial, Indian, and black families, especially when they have a property list from a will.[38] These journeys into the past involve risks of rejection, yet they also bring about a measure of truth, justice, and reconciliation.

There is a need for racial healing in our families, churches, and nation that will not go away. It begins by searching for the truth and admitting that truth if we are to be set free from racial mistrust and alienation. In the midst of all this past racial confusion, there is a truth we have not yet heard. Interracial marriage was illegal for over three hundred years of American history. Interracial marriage continued to be illegal for more than one hundred years after race-based slavery was abolished. So much of slavery and segregation in America was prompted by the fear of interracial love, marriage, and multiracial children. That legacy lives on in monoracial churches where interracial couples and their children are not welcome. In many families and churches, the prejudice of racial superiority manifests itself when it comes to interracial dating and marriage. We repeat our sinful history when we pass on unwritten rules: "Yes, you can play together and go to school together. You can even be friends. But ... just don't marry one."

Discussion Questions

1. How did race-based slavery define, shape, and corrupt families and churches?
2. How did interracial marriage and multiracial children challenge the development of race-based slavery?
3. What effect did interracial sex (marriage, cohabitation, concubinage, rape) or multiracial children have on the formation of traditional white families?
4. Explain amalgamation and how it affected churches splitting over the slavery issue.
5. How has the racism of white Christians using the fear of interracial mating justified slavery and segregated churches? How has this fear damaged our efforts at racial reconciliation?

Notes

1. *Rachel F. Moran*, Interracial Intimacy: The Regulation of Race and Romance *(Chicago: University of Chicago Press, 2001), 17.*

2. *See this website for more changes that developed as slavery laws became racialized:* http://jefferson.village.virginia.edu/vcdh/jamestown/servlaws.html#2

3. *Moran,* Interracial Intimacy, 20.

4. *Gary B. Nash,* Red, White, and Black: The Peoples of Early America *(Englewood Cliffs, N.J.: Prentice-Hall, 1982), 50–57.*

5. *Ibid.,* 20.

6. *Edmund S. Morgan, "Slavery and Freedom: The American Paradox,"* Journal of American History 59, *no. 1 (1972): 17.*

7. *For specific case studies, see Martha E. Hodes,* White Women, Black Men *(New York: Yale University, 1997).*

8. *Winthrop D. Jordan,* White over Black *(Chapel Hill: University of North Carolina Press, 1968), 137.*

9. *Paul R. Spickard,* Mixed Blood: Intermarriage and Ethnic Identity in Twentieth-Century America *(Madison: University of Wisconsin Press, 1989), 237.*

10. *Hodes,* White Women, Black Men, 2–3.

11. *Ibid.,* 30.

12. *Morgan, "Slavery and Freedom," 29.*

13. *Robert P. Hilldrup,* Upper Brandon *(Richmond, Va.: James River, 1987), 83.*

14. *Prince George County Tax Records, 1861 and 1863, Virginia State Library.*

15. *Edward Ball,* Slaves in the Family *(New York: Ballantine, 1998), 294.*

16. *Kent A. Leslie,* Woman of Color, Daughter of Privilege: Amanda America Dickson, 1849–1893 *(Athens, Ga.: University of Georgia Press, 1995), 11.*

17. *Ibid.,* 96–97.

18. *John W. Blassingame,* Slave Testimony *(Baton Rouge: Louisiana State University Press, 1977), 474–80.*

19. *See this official website for the facts concerning Sally Hemings' ambiguous slave status after Thomas Jefferson's death:* http://www.monticello.org/plantation/appendixh.html

20. *Blassingame,* Slave Testimony, 480.

21. *See this website for more documentation concerning the Hemings-Jefferson DNA debate:* http://www.people.virginia.edu/~rjh9u/tomsally.html

22. *Spickard,* Mixed Blood, 243.

23. *Moran,* Interracial Intimacy, 24.

24. *Hodes,* White Women, Black Men, 3.

25. *Carl A. Brasseaux,* Creoles of Color in the Bayou Country *(Jackson: University Press of Mississippi, 1994), 10–11.*

26. *Ibid.,* xiii.

27. *Stephen E. Ambrose,* Undaunted Courage: Meriwether Lewis, Thomas Jefferson,

offspring and guidance for biracial parenting. But at the time, what I could say for sure (and perhaps in the end it is what matters most) was that having biracial children, and what those children would face in this life, should definitely not be the reason *not* to get married.

Almost a decade later, I am much more reflective about what being biracial has meant for my life than I was when my friends asked for help with their question. I have read more, I have interviewed other multiracials, I have written a book; my thinking about the issues involved has broadened and deepened. A movement of multiracial consciousness has swelled as more people have spoken out, creating language that describes our experience and validates our existence. Ten years ago, I did not even *know* the term *multiracial*, at least not as a title for myself. Now I would say that the possibility of having multiracial children should not only not prevent people from tying the knot; it should be considered one of the greatest "pros" to marrying interracially.

There are some real challenges to being multiracial in this world, but there are also incomparable benefits and joys. In the end, it has turned out that my greatest difficulties have resulted in the deepest benefits: understanding, truth, character, compassion, awareness of what is real and what matters. There is a Christian principle at work here: suffering leads to glory. I have had suffering as a result of being biracial (because of how our society deals with race), but I have also tasted the glory that is available now and that is to come.

God's glory is revealed in the growing numbers of multiracial people and in the greater freedom to identify ourselves fully. God's Spirit brings liberty (2 Corinthians 3:17), and through the multiracial movement, the Spirit is liberating us to claim all of our races and ethnic groups proudly instead of hiding certain parts of ourselves or having parts denied because of shame, fear, and racism.

The 2000 Census reported that 6.83 million people in the U.S. (2.4 percent of the population) identified themselves as belonging to more than one race. Among those under eighteen, the proportion was almost 4 percent, reflecting a growing multiracial population and perhaps a growing desire to identify more broadly.

California, where I live, is the state that has the largest number of multiracial people. In the 2000 Census 1.6 million (4.5 percent of the population) chose more than one race. Out of the ten U.S. cities with the highest proportions of multiracial individuals, six were in California. In Los Angeles County, one out of five generation X-ers has married someone of a different race.[1]

As I have traveled and met mixed-race young adults around the country, I have heard a fierce pride in being multiracial and have observed a striving after self-acceptance (which we all have more or less success at, depending on a variety of factors, including personality, parental input, friendships, and our view of God). I have also seen them yearning for others' acceptance. We want others to acknowledge that it is okay, even good, to be multiracial.

In this chapter, I will describe how it has been good for me to be biracial, particularly as I have been helped to know God's nature, love, grace, and truth, and I will offer some suggestions for adults in the lives of multiracial youth. Through this, I hope to provide a helpful response to that ever-present question: *What about the children?*

The Benefits of Being Biracial

I love being biracial. Growing up seeing black and white people loving, celebrating, even eating together gave my heart a taste of the heavenly togetherness that will one day be reality. I have been raised to enjoy cultural differences and am comfortable in diverse settings. I connect with two distinct racial groups and can say about both blacks and whites that they are "my people." I feel like I have been given a great honor: God chose a biracial body to house my soul and an interracial family to nurture it. As my dad would tell my brother and me, we have gotten "the best of both worlds."

At the same time, we are sometimes privy to the worst of both worlds. Those of us who gladly belong to more than one racial group and present ourselves to the world as such have experienced being misunderstood, misinterpreted, even punished for our makeup. I know of a black-white girl who was sent to a counselor for the sole reason that she was of mixed race, as if she would have more psychological problems than the next middle school student. She resented the assumption. Or there is the 1994 example of black-white biracial Revonda Bowen, whose high school principal outlawed interracial couples at a school dance. She asked with whom she was supposed to attend the event. He told her that she was a mistake, and the story became national news. We have been the butt of jokes, called names, and mistreated, even by our own.

Being biracial can be a lonely experience, but loneliness is a human reality. Each person has his or her own struggles that must be weathered alone. Multiracial people, however, often confront this reality earlier and more frequently than those with full membership in a single racial community. We feel the isolation inherent in being human because of our society's emphasis on race as a primary source of identity and racial membership as a primary place of belonging. Disdain between two races becomes a personal and alienating issue for those of us who belong to both.

Our society's collective investment in maintaining separate races is a formidable barrier to the person who knows she is more than one race and wants to live peacefully so. I have gotten around this barrier by seeking out those who enjoy cross-cultural relationships: black, white, and other friends who like to hang out with each other. My closest friends are interracially married, interracial families through transracial adoption, or multiracial individuals. With them, I can be myself completely without worrying about my racial status.

God redeems all things, and God has used our country's racial situation to teach me, as God's multiracial daughter, a number of important lessons regarding the source of my value and the depth of God's desire to make people one.

Our source of value, belonging, and wholeness. Racial labels, like standards of beauty, are highly subjective because they are based on appearances. As a biracial person, my race (and subsequently my appearance) has been focused on to such a degree that ultimately I have been driven to search deeper for the source of my value and identity. Fortunately, as with many African Americans, I have found my value and identity in being a child of God, a reflection of God's likeness. I have also gained a high appreciation for the unseen, for the souls of myself and others.

I have come to understand that people are, at a basic level, the same. We are human beings first. (I cringe when people, well meaning but oblivious to racial realities in the U.S., use this line to insist that they do not see color and are not racist or to avoid racial topics. This is not my intention. I realize that we are different and that these differences are beautiful but have also been used as reasons to oppress and discriminate.)

I have a particular affinity for African Americans because that is the minority ethnic group to which I belong and relate. Being a minority forges a particular pride in one's identity that is not anti-Christian but rather serves as a guardian of the image of God in that group that would otherwise not be affirmed. Because of my racial mixture, however, I experience being on the borders of both races, though I know objectively that I am a member of both. The positive outcome of this sometimes difficult position is that I have always related to being a "global citizen" whose ultimate citizenship is not of this earth but is of God's kingdom.

My primary place of belonging is within the family of God, which is not circumscribed by race, and my loyalty is to God's agenda, not to a particular race's agenda (though I recognize that our view and understanding of God's agenda is inevitably racially and culturally influenced). I have been given a hunger for the kingdom of heaven, which when it comes in its fullness will be a place where the divisions between races will be no more and I will have a sense of total belonging no matter where I go.

Because our world remains racially divided, I have had to think consciously about what it means to be a whole person versus half this and half that, to be integrated internally regardless of external schisms. God is the source of my wholeness—the one who knit me together in my mother's womb, exactly as I was meant to be. And God does not create half people but whole human beings.

Yearning for reconciliation. The scorning of interracial marriage is an affront to those of us who are multiracial. I take people's objections to interracial dating and marriage personally when the motives are rooted in personal prejudice and racism (which they usually are). Objectors are basically saying that my existence is invalid; I should not have been. Whenever I hear stories of Christian parents rejecting their children's choice of spouse on the basis of race, or churches rebuffing an interracial couple, I have to run to Jesus' cross to be able to forgive. And to remember the truth in spite of people's rebellion: the two have been made one (Ephesians 2:14).

Jews and Gentiles (Paul's subjects in Ephesians 2) were as far removed from each other as blacks and whites are in the U.S., socially, culturally, and in their attitudes toward one another. Being biracial is an honor because I reflect the truth that the dividing wall of hostility has been removed, even if it does not always seem like it in the world or inside of me. The two have been made one—literally, in the case of biracial individuals—and I think God is pleased with our existence as a symbol of this great truth that Jesus made possible.

Interracial families and multiracial people reflect a change in racial attitudes approaching the Bible's view that "there is no longer Jew or Greek" (Galatians 3:28). Ethnicity was never meant to be the basis of salvation or of prohibitions against marriage. In the grace-filled atmosphere of God's family of believers, ethnicity does not bar intimate relationships but points us to the beauty and creativity of our Creator. Multiethnic people reflect that beauty and creativity as well.

We are emblematic of the beauty, vitality, and strength that result when people work together and love one another across racial lines. The existence of healthy, smart, contributing multiracial people through whom the Creator is working to fulfill divine purposes exposes the lie that interracial unions are ungodly or cause degeneration. The church needs to be reeducated in this matter because this lie was propagated for so long.

When it comes to church, self-segregation is again the rule and not the exception. It is painful for me to see the glaring sins of commission and omission that have resulted in such separation and contentment with separation. While I recognize that there is a place for ethnic-specific gatherings of Christians and that the segregated state of neighborhoods makes the development of multiethnic churches difficult, I cannot help but regret the deep lack of ethnic diversity with which the vast majority of Christian children are being raised.

To grow up thinking it is all right to live life completely separate from and unaware of the experience of other races and cultures is a travesty. Separation at best creates naive curiosity; more commonly, it fuels suspicion, fear, and misinformation. It perpetuates ignorance about material inequities in the body of Christ. Ultimately, it stunts one's understanding of the multifaceted nature of God and God's desire for a multiethnic and reconciled people.

Since multiracial churches are hard to find, my husband and I have chosen to belong to predominantly black churches because we have experienced much more openness to multiracialism and to speaking out against racism in these churches. Black churches attract nonblacks who are interested in pursuing relationships across racial lines. Plus, I appreciate the chance to have my black cultural ways affirmed.

This segregation, in churches and elsewhere, is comfortable for most. For me, it is understandable yet intolerable. I feel angry when a white person complains that blacks are overreacting to an injustice and when I see a black person snubbing someone who is white. I hear and see things differently as a biracial person, and I long for the two sides—so long estranged—to be reconciled, to be brought together in just and merciful circumstances. I am much less comfortable with the separation than most monoracial people are, and I have accepted this discomfort as part of my existence. It motivates me to do whatever I can to bring the two sides together, because the Bible indicates that unity, not division, is God's aim.

In my experience, most children who are raised in interracial households are taught to appreciate cultural differences and to respect all people, including (not regardless of) their ethnic background. Because of who they are, my parents welcomed people with racial and ethnic diversity into our home, including Japanese and African international students who lived with us for a time. This exposure to interracial interaction, as par for the course, produces more than a tolerant attitude. Biracial children are often raised with a value for intercultural exchange and an awareness that we have much to learn from one another across ethnic lines. It is this kind of openness that will characterize the leaders of a new, more globally minded generation eager for and equipped to facilitate racial reconciliation.

Being biracial is an honor and a joy. God has taught me important lessons through how I was made: ethnic heritage is God-given and valuable, but my value does not come from my race, and my primary place of belonging is not racially based. God desires racial hierarchies to be destroyed, racial hostility to be ended, and racial divisions to be mended. My multiracial makeup causes me to yearn and strive for this too.

What We Need from You

Through listening to other multiracial people, examining sociological studies, and reflecting on my own experience, I have discovered certain themes regarding what children with multiple racial and cultural heritages need from the adults in their lives. In this section I will quote a number of people of whom I asked the question "What were the most and least helpful things your parents and other adults did for your ethnic identity?"

I will discuss five aspects of the parent-child relationship and interracial family dynamics that came up repeatedly in interviews and studies that impacted the development and adjustment of multiracial children: providing diverse social settings; talking about race and cultural differences; passing on a multicultural history and legacy; affirming the heritage that likely will not be affirmed outside the home; and letting children choose their own identities.

Where you live matters. One of the decisions you will make that will impact your children the most is where you situate your family and with whom they are then able to interact. Giving your children the opportunity to relate to a racially diverse set of peers will help them to see themselves not as different or wrong but as one of many possibilities. One Asian-white woman shared:

> My parents were intentional about fostering an appreciation for all ethnic groups in us kids. They chose to raise us in multicultural environments, and they instilled in us a deep commitment to justice, tolerance, and respect for all people and cultures. Among

other benefits, I believe this helped us to see ourselves within the context of a larger ethnic "picture." ... We were not the "other" in an otherwise white world—rather, we possessed one of many possible ethnic identities, ... none of which was seen as being inherently superior to any of the others.

Being in a racially diverse setting increases the probability that your child will meet other multiracial children. Many biracial adults I have spoken with wish they had known others like themselves when they were younger. For biracial people, seeing reflections of ourselves decreases the sense of isolation and validates our existence. As we grow older, we need friends with whom we can laugh about the difficulties, and share the joys, of being of more than one race.

Your choices of places to live, worship, and educate your children are crucial because we learn culture through social interaction. If your child's races are not represented in the place where you live, a hole will be created in his or her identity that will have to be filled in later, with much greater turmoil and pain.

Living in environments with higher percentages of black youth would not necessarily have been easier for me as a biracial person, because of potential taunts, tests of my loyalty, or my physical appearance. I believe, however, it would have taught me cultural norms and ways of relating that would have assured me of my membership in the black community and increased my comfort with myself as a black person much earlier. As it turned out, I had to struggle to gain this in my adult life, which I did through participating in black student groups, conferences for black Christians, and predominantly black churches.

Making sure your children have access to their extended family members will also increase their sense of confidence in their racial and ethnic identity. "Probably the [most helpful] thing ... was the way my whole family got along, the way people from both sides of the family would gather for holidays, for example. That, above all else, gave me a sense of wholeness, that all the parts of me fit together," said one black-Jewish woman.

Another woman whose white-Jewish father and black mother split after ten years said that even though her dad moved to another state, her paternal grandparents continued to relate to her sister and her, having them over every other Sunday for dinner. "Having a consistent relationship with relatives on both sides of my family was an essential part of my identity development," she says.

A young man of Belgian-Palestinian heritage said that his mom and Belgian grandmother, who speaks only French, made sure he and his sister learned French fluently. This was crucial to his current closeness with his grandmother and to his ability to learn from her about his Belgian grandfather and great-grandfather. She taught him the history of Belgium and of his family, and as a result, he feels connected to being Belgian. At the same time, he was raised five minutes from his Palestinian aunt and uncle, who speak Arabic around his parents. He did not learn as much of this language but still feels connected to his Arabic culture, which values family highly.

Unfortunately, some family members are inaccessible due to their unwillingness to accept the interracial marriages of their sons, daughters, or siblings. Others are not emotionally but geographically distant. Having contact with my grandparents and other relatives, however, was one of the greatest gifts my parents and family gave me in terms of confidence about my identity. I am both black and white, and my black and white relatives formed the foundation of this identity and reinforced it throughout my life.

A thirty-year-old man of Navajo and Dutch descent sums up well our need for relationships with our extended family:

> As a child, I grew up knowing my extended family very well. My parents did a great job of showing me that my family and my identity were much larger than my immediate family. We would travel regularly (long distances, if necessary) to visit aunts, uncles, cousins, grandparents. Culture and ethnic identity comes from a sense of belonging and knowing who you are and where you came from. When I went off to college, I was amazed at how many of my Anglo friends barely knew their extended family.... Culture is a shared value, and the knowledge of it comes from people, not books or study. This makes a large extended family incredibly important in the lives of multiracial children. We need to know well our grandparents, aunts, uncles, and cousins.

Do not avoid the topic. I did not consciously know it as a child, but I felt it: race was a topic of anguish and discomfort for my parents. They had been threatened and rejected because of race. Most likely, my mom, having been raised without any contact with black people, was completely unprepared to have children whom society would consider black, even if we did not look it. This lack of exposure and preparation made it difficult for her to know what to talk about, let alone how. My dad, having experienced racism firsthand, was more aware of race dynamics. Yet how could he know what it would feel and be like to have a white parent?

Though I have a lot of sympathy for my parents, still, talking more about what my brother and I were experiencing as we interacted with our mostly white world would have been helpful. I do not think I needed them to have all the right answers as much as I needed to be heard and reassured.

Dr. Maria P. P. Root, in her *Biracial Sibling Project* from 1997 to 1998, interviewed more than sixty people—adult siblings from interracial homes. She asked them, "Is there anything that you wish could have been different growing up, that would have made your life easier, happier, or better?" At the top of the race-related wishes was wanting parents to have talked more about race, about why people acted the way they did, and about how they might respond.[2]

Her findings suggest that biracial children do want parents to provide some answers. Why do certain people shun me? Why are we stared at? Why do others assume I am not your child? Why do I get called names by people who are of my same race?

In her book, Root presents a litany of questions directed at interracial couples that go straight to the heart of the most crucial issues I faced as a biracial child and adolescent. Some I continue to wrestle with to this day. You may want to consider how to talk to your children about these things. Even your adult children may be served by your initiating a conversation; sometimes later is better than never. Root provides the following questions:

> Are parents aware that their child may be put through the social ritual of hazing to prove allegiance to an in-group? Are they aware that acutely sensitive children dealing with the usual adolescent angst need extra help in working through the sense of isolation that comes from being mixed and misunderstood by one's peers? Or the hurt that comes from being a popular girl or boy, but one who has a difficult time dating because of peers' perceptions of their racial ambiguity? … Does a parent understand the depth of problem solving a child engages in when she or he goes through a phase of not wanting to be seen with a particular parent? Does the parent know that this is not only about being a teenager but may also be about the child's awareness of how that parent's race marks her or him racially (much as partner choice marks the mixed-race person)? … Does the parent of color know that mixed children are no longer automatically accepted by their peers of color, Asian, black, Latino? Do parents know that

siblings in the same family may identify themselves differently? Do parents know that a child does not always identify himself racially in the way a parent thinks the child ought to, or even in the way that other people interpret the child's physical appearance? ... Do parents know that biracial kids and adults may fret more about their physical appearance than other people because of the questions and comments they have received?[3]

Studies show that children begin noticing racial differences between two and four years of age. It is a myth that color or race does not matter or that spiritual people do not see color or race. This attitude discourages discussion and may prevent children from asking their questions or sharing how race is affecting them outside the home. It will certainly leave them unprepared for the real world, where race matters a lot when it comes to how people interact and are treated.

At the same time, do not feel you need to confront your children with their multiracial status or make them deal with issues before they are ready. One woman told me, "We knew from an early age that we had both white and Chinese heritage, but it was never presented as an 'issue' for us to deal with. It was just who we were. This foundation of normalcy was helpful, not just when I was young, but also when as an adult I became interested in exploring my biracial identity further.... The ethnic exploration I did was just part of coming to a more mature understanding of who God created me to be."

In a study of black-white biracial adolescents, factors that were associated with positive pyschosocial adjustment in the children included being a part of intact families, having a higher socioeconomic status, living in integrated neighborhoods, attending integrated schools, and having open, warm relationships with parents. In the families where both parents and adolescents dealt with issues of biracial identity, teens appeared to be better adjusted. These families endorsed and participated in a multicultural lifestyle, allowing their children to explore both sides of their racial heritage while they exposed them to a variety of ethnic activities, institutions, and role models.[4]

Perhaps the best thing adults can do when it comes to talking about race with biracial children is to let them know that being biracial is something to be celebrated. One black-Jewish woman mentioned that her esteem received a boost whenever her black Sunday school teacher would refer to her Jewish heritage as something special.

Pass on your cultural legacy, whatever it is. We biracials want to know where we come from, perhaps even more so than those with single-race or ethnic group membership. When I asked people what adults had done that was most or least helpful to the development of their multiracial identity, being taught about their cultures was repeatedly mentioned among the most helpful; not being taught about their cultures was among the least.

Those who were pleased with how they had learned about their cultural legacy talked about how their parents partnered to educate the children, held up both cultures as equally valuable, and even embraced each other's culture as their own.

> My mother [white] really took on my father's Japanese culture. When I was young, she explained traditions like Boy's Day and Girl's Day in Japan. We had origami paper in the house for crafts. I had no idea other little kids were probably used to just construction paper for crafts. As she spoke of Japanese cultural dynamics, she would jokingly say, "We Japanese ..." (as a six-foot-tall Caucasian of Irish-German descent) and my father would chuckle.

A Mexican-white man noted how his parents embraced one another's cultures by accepting one another's families.

> Growing up, I never had the picture of having two different families with two different sets of cultural views and ideas. I just had one big family, the individual nucleic units of which were different from one another just like any two families from the same culture will be different. The differences were never directly attributed to ethnicity and thereby dismissed as barriers to full inclusion.
>
> An easy example is display of affection. I think that if I grew up being told that we kissed our maternal [Mexican] grandparents in greeting but not our paternal grandparents because of ethnicity, we wouldn't have thought to kiss our dad, because he's white. Now, however, I do kiss my dad in greeting ... because that's part of our family culture, which blends both families' cultures.

Culture is more than history and holidays. Culture influences our most dearly held convictions. These convictions often become the source of greatest conflict between spouses. That is why it is crucial to be as self-aware as possible about our cultural values; your level of awareness and ability to articulate and negotiate differences matters not only to your marriage but also to your children.

An Arabic-white young woman mentioned how her parents' unawareness of their differences created turmoil for her and her brother.

> A lot of times they ignored the fact that they had very different

cultural backgrounds, which caused internal conflicts for my brother and me. We couldn't deny that we were being raised under two different cultural traditions, but it was never talked about, so we were sort of left to figure it out for ourselves.... Each parent had different values about how to handle the situations involving us, which could tend to cause conflict. I am not sure that they ever discussed how their different traditions could cause them to deal with us differently, or that they even realized that their difference in opinion could be cultural.

She went on to say that what helped her most as a biracial person was the time her parents took to tell her and her brother about their cultures. "I love hearing about both of my cultures," she said, "and knowing how I am a part of both of these rich traditions." Her words echo the sentiments of most multiracial people I know.

Affirm the unaffirmed. For children of ethnic heritages that are shrouded by racist stereotypes, such as about intelligence, morality, and overall competence, extra affirmation of those heritages will be necessary. One family I know intentionally emphasized their children's African American identity during their formative elementary years because they recognized how little positive reinforcement of blackness there is in the U.S. This emphasis did not keep their children from being aware of and proud that they are biracial. Rather, it seemed that emphasizing the identity that was in danger of being degraded gave these children stronger overall self-esteem and confidence. When I met their eldest son, he told me that he stood to be counted as both black and white when his teacher required a racial count of her classroom—to the surprise of the teacher, who assumed he was black only.

One teen I spoke with said she credited her parents with moving their family, when she was five, from a predominantly white church to a predominantly black one. Without that positive reinforcement of black culture, she and her siblings would "be very narrow minded, and possibly not willing to know the black culture."

The degrading of black and Latino identities, in particular, remains a serious issue in spite of civil rights advances and the higher visibility of these groups in the media as entertainers and fashion trendsetters. Children pick up messages about societal perceptions of their racial groups early on. One Chinese-Mexican person I spoke with said that as a teenager, before he came to appreciate his Mexican heritage, he and a white-Mexican friend would sometimes joke that they had gotten the "Chinese and white brains," and not the Mexican one, because they did well academically.

The Palestinian-Belgian young man mentioned earlier said that, growing up in the 1980s and 1990s, he experienced the unpopularity of being Palestinian. He loved his culture at home, but outside the home, he would try not to reveal his identity. A friend's Italian grandfather, having had his own struggles growing up, could see that the boy was ashamed and afraid of others knowing his ethnicity. "I never said it to him; he could just read me. He sat me down when I was in junior high and said, 'When I grew up here, it wasn't very popular to be Italian. People made fun of me and said all sorts of nasty things. But I made it, and I love my people. Don't worry about what other people will think.' " The wise man's words sunk in over time, and now the biracial man he encouraged loves being Palestinian.

For one of the black-Jewish women I interviewed, her Jewish grandfather's pointing to an ad for a trip to Israel for Jewish youth and suggesting that she should go communicated to her that he accepted her, in some sense, as a Jew. This affirmation was instrumental for her self-view, since Jewish heritage traditionally is considered matrilineal and it is her father who is Jewish.

It is important to recognize that it is normal for biracial children to show ambivalence toward their races, usually the ethnic minority side before the white one. A study of black-white children showed that these feelings usually increase at around four years of age and gradually decrease until about eight years of age. The study concluded that ambivalence is dealt with primarily by the influence of the parents' supportive interest in the child's racial feelings and secondarily by the racially supportive environment outside of the family.[5] Suppressing this process, on the other hand, may stop children from further exploration of their racial identity. Ambivalence is simply one stage of the exploration.

Though affirming the ethnic minority heritage of biracial children is crucial to their self-esteem, helping them know something about their white heritage is also important. "Whiteness" does not need to be reinforced (the child's environment will most likely do that), but the white parent's heritage needs to be explored, shared, and celebrated for the sake of defining for the child what this heritage brings to his or her identity. In the U.S., being white is an abstract concept that carries a freight load of meaning. Making white heritage concrete without elevating it above other heritages gives children a stronger sense of who they are and what they bring to our country's developing multicultural dialogue.[6]

Let children choose. Though parents play a crucial role in the development of their child's self-esteem, including the child's acceptance of his or her racial self, they cannot control the experiences and factors that finally form the child's identity. Ultimately, we need to decide how we will think of ourselves and present ourselves to the world around us.

It is frustrating and potentially damaging when people insist on labeling and seeing us as something other than how we see ourselves. One person shared with me, "The least helpful thing was when adults ... would overrule my descriptions of my ethnic identity. My earliest self-identification was black and white. I put that on a standardized test, and when I got the form back, I saw my answer had been changed to just black. Similar things happened other times as well. No one ever really discussed it with me; they just decided I was wrong."

Multiracial children who are raised in an environment that affirms each of their racial backgrounds (or their multiracial heritage) will have less psychological turmoil and less trouble coming to conclusions about their identity. Lack of affirmation of one of a child's races, even unwittingly, has the potential to breed confusion and feelings of shame or even of nonmembership.

The Arabic-white young woman I mentioned earlier told me that the most unhelpful thing her adult family members did was to joke that her brother was the "Arab" and she was the "white child," based on their respective appearances. As a child, she took their words literally and thought she must not be Arabic, because that is what the adults in her life said. "Although I know differently now ... , it is still hard for me to believe sometimes that I am really Arabic. Even though I have a lot of the culture inside of me, and I feel at home with other Arabs and within my own Arabic family, some part of me refuses to believe that I am Arabic, beyond what my brain can logically conclude."

Letting your children choose does not preclude offering them a racial label that they can use in responding to the myriad of questions they are likely to get from peers and others. One person I interviewed said that she wished her parents could have helped her to identify as biracial earlier in her life.

I was not given the language to help form my identity as a biracial person. I never liked when I heard people call me "mixed" or "half black and half white." It always seemed like a technical description.... Now I confidently call myself biracial but am very comfortable when people refer to me as black, Hispanic, and occasionally white.... I realize that [my parents] did not know this word [biracial] or the importance of having a racial/ethnic *title*. But it would have been nice if I had been prepared with an answer to all those times people asked me, "What are you?" I would love to hear a little six-year-old respond "I'm biracial," and know that is a legitimate thing to be.

Suggesting options that include both or all of children's races will reinforce that they can be proud of who they are regardless of how others respond to them. Some may still choose a single race as the totality of their public identity, because that is the way they feel or how the world sees them or for some other reason, but they will have the strong foundation of knowing that they do not need to be ashamed of their racial mixture.

More Helpful Ideas for Multiracial Parenting

- Help your children find multiracial heroes to give them a sense of pride, community, legitimacy, and historical precedence.
- Expose children to appropriate films, books, television programs, and adult models to serve as positive reinforcement of their various ethnic heritages.[8]
- Give them resources that affirm and normalize mixed-race heritage, such as *Mavin* magazine or *What Are You?* by Pearl Fuyo Gaskins.
- Celebrate your children's multiracial heritage, without putting down other cultures.
- Get rid of your own racial biases—toward others' races or your own; be comfortable with who you are.[9]
- Help children to learn both your and your spouse's language; consider learning your spouse's language as well.
- Acknowledge conflicts, particularly cultural ones, between you and your spouse so that children will know what the tension is about and not think they are its source.[10]
- Be as reconciled as possible with a divorced spouse; children "act out" in destructive (including self-destructive) ways as long as they sense discord between their parents.
- Help teens distinguish between their personal interests and abilities and those that have been adopted from a stereotyped notion of their racial identity.[11]

Glad to Be Alive

In this life there are many troubles. Jesus did not try to sugarcoat this truth for his followers. Regardless of whether a child is mono- or multiracial, he or she will have difficulties.

Multiracial children do not have it worse off than others; our troubles are not quantitatively greater simply because we are multiracial. In some cases, the benefits we gain from being bi- or multiculturally socialized actually outweigh the difficulties. Sociological studies are beginning to shed light on this truth.[7]

Racial dynamics in our world, however, make some of our troubles qualitatively different. Forming a racial identity as a multiracial person is complex. Fortunately, I have found that these challenges have made me a stronger, richer person.

Hopefully, my experiences and those of others mentioned in this chapter have assured you that multiracial children grow up to be healthy, insightful, contributing adults. I am grateful for my life and for my parents' strength in the face of society's anti-interracial marriage atmosphere.

I also salute my friends, Sacha and Eric, who asked for my advice about having and raising biracial children as they decided whether to marry. They did get married and now have two vivacious, unique, wonderful biracial children, Kyle and Emma.

Discussion Questions

1. Of all the benefits the author noted that biracial individuals enjoy, which do you think is the most valuable?
2. Of all the potential problems that biracial individuals may face in our society, which do you think is the most difficult to overcome?
3. Which of the five aspects of parent-child relationships and interracial family dynamics do you think most impacts the psychological health of biracial children? Why?
4. How should a parent change his or her child-rearing practices or lifestyle to accommodate having a biracial child as opposed to a same-race child?
5. Which of the ideas in the section "More Helpful Ideas for Multiracial Parenting" do you think is most insightful for interracial couples with children? Why?

Notes

1. Maria P. P. Root, Love's Revolution: Interracial Marriage (Philadelphia: Temple University Press, 2001), 26.

2. *Ibid., 157.*

3. *Ibid., 149, 152. Used by permission.*

4. *Maria P. P. Root,* Racially Mixed People in America *(Newbury Park, Calif.: Sage, 1992), 237.*

5. *Ibid., 205.*

6. *For more help on this topic, see the Web site of the Center for the Study of White American Culture, www.euroamerican.org.*

7. *For example, see Root,* Racially Mixed People, *60–61, 217–20.*

8. *Paul C. Rosenblatt, Terri A. Karis, and Richard D. Powell,* Multiracial Couples: Black and White Voices *(Thousand Oaks, Calif.: Sage, 1995), 204.*

9. *Reger C. Smith,* Two Cultures, One Marriage: Premarital Counseling for Mixed Marriages *(Berrien Springs, Mich.: Andrews University Press, 1996), 60.*

10. *Susan W. Schneider,* Intermarriage *(New York: Free Press, 1989), 146.*

11. *Smith,* Two Cultures, One Marriage, *60.*

SEVEN

"What about My Family?" and Other Premarital Questions

David T. Tatlock

IN DECEMBER OF 1998 MY WIFE, EDITH, AND I WERE RELAXING IN a hotel lobby in Atlanta while attending a large, predominantly African American Christian conference. Our children were wrestling with each other on the carpet while we enjoyed a brief rest period between seminars. There were over two thousand young people at this conference, and we loved being in the midst of their energy and passion. Many of the students were congregating in the lobby. As we started to converse, the looks started out subtly, but as time went on, grew longer and more intense. We call this the "pre-interracial relationship question" stares, which precede someone approaching us to say something cute to our kids. It is the cover an individual uses to lay groundwork before asking deeper questions. We are always amazed at how much of our ministry starts with our little girls giving each other "noogies" and head butts.

"What's yooooour name, little giiiiirl?" asks a young African American woman in a sweet voice. Ahhh, the first victim has made her move.

My African American wife handles the "pre-interracial relationship" conversation. She is more of a pro than I. "Tell her your names, girls," Edith says just as sweetly.

My oldest daughter, who is three and a half, knows the routine and politely says, "Hannnnnnah." Mary-Catherine has not quite got the routine down, even though we have worked with her. She immediately runs from the young woman and buries her head in her mom's armpit while staring at the young lady with one eye.

Seeing that the young lady does not understand two-year-old symbolism, I add, "Her name is Mary; she's a little shy."

The young lady smiles and proceeds to take the bait. "Your children are so pretty. I think mixed children are sooooo beautiful." She is not wasting any time. She must have a seminar that starts in another ten minutes or so.

"We think they're beautiful, but of course we're a little biased," says my wife.

"How did you two meet?" the young lady says. Now she realizes that her cover is completely blown, because she has not even told us her name. She quickly calculates her next course of action. She decides on the polite, apologetic strategy. "Oooooh, I'm sorry. I have not even told you my name. My name is Renee."[1]

"My name is Edith and my husband's name is David," my wife politely says, putting the young woman at ease. "Perhaps you'd like to sit down and talk a little before your next session." Man, my wife is good. While saying this and before the young lady looks at me, she shoots me a one-millisecond look that says, "Why don't you take the kids for a walk?"

I have to pause for a second and admire a true master of her craft before I say, "Hey, girls, let's go see if there's some candy at that table over there!"

"HoooooRRRRRAAAAAAYYYYY!" my kids shout as we saunter off, leaving my wife and young Renee to talk about many of the issues and difficulties facing her as she enters into a dating relationship with a white guy and how she should handle her family, her friends, etc....

Although not every situation is the same, Renee is an example of the many people we encounter who are looking for guidance on the topic of interracial relationships and marriage.[2] Looking back, I wish there had been a Christian resource or someone who could have talked to me when my wife and I met back in 1992. I had so many questions and no one to give me any answers. Quite frankly, if I had listened to the nonbiblical advice of many Christians, I might not have married Edith and would be missing the wonderful blessing she has been. I am thankful that God led me to seek my own answers from His Word with "eyes that see and ears that hear."

Can We Talk?

You probably would not be reading this article if you did not have some of the same questions Edith and I had. You may be getting ready to marry interracially, thinking of dating interracially, or giving counsel to someone in this type of relationship. Whatever your reason, you are interested in this issue and in the perspective of someone in this type of relationship. Most importantly, my desire is that you receive a biblical perspective on many of the questions about these relationships.

So, get comfortable, because we are going to have a good conversation. I have a couple hours for us to spend some time together. Let us suppose that you and I are in my living room relaxing on the couch. It is a nice 70 degrees outside and the windows are open, with a breeze wafting through the house. Our kids are at the neighbors' house and my wife is getting ready to make her world-famous chicken enchiladas and rice along with some homemade lemonade. (I do not know what you like, but this is what I like, and I am making up this scenario.) I want to spend some quality time with you as we explore this issue.

Our Background

As you sit down on my couch and take a sip of lemonade, you begin to wonder about the background of this guy and why you should take advice from him. I would feel the same way. The fact that I am white and my wife is black makes me a little qualified experientially. Furthermore, my wife and I have spent many hours talking about this issue with college students, parents, teachers, coaches, etc., and there seem to be some common questions and biblical interpretation problems that continue to pop up. Let us start with some background information about me first and then my wife.

Where I Come From. I was born in a little town called Seymour, Indiana, which is located south of Indianapolis. Most of what I saw growing up was farmland, corn, countryside, and rural America. I was brought up in a divorced home and lived with my mom. However, I spent most of my days with my grandparents. They provided tremendously for me, emotionally and physically, modeling my only idea of a family. Most of my memories of being cared about are with my grandparents. Southern Indiana is an interesting place since, until you get to Evansville, it is mostly small towns with little turnover in the population. Minorities are a very small percentage in the towns in southern Indiana, and most of the blacks I know avoid the southern half of the state. When we told Edith's parents we were getting married in Greenwood, her grandparents' reply was "We're not coming down there to get lynched!" They were not joking. I played three varsity sports and almost never remember playing a team with a black person on it. When I was a kid, my friends and I told "nigger" jokes regularly, and I remember some of those jokes today. I even remember my grandma's warning to me when I went off to college, "Don't get mixed up with those coloreds when you go up there to college."

When I went to Purdue University, I realized that there were many more types of people than I was used to, including black people. I remember being scared of blacks because of all the things that I had been told about them while I was growing up. Yet I was getting into rap and dance music at the time, which brought me into contact with blacks. My last two years at Purdue, I lived in a fraternity that was across the street from the Baptist Student Union. I would usually go to church on Sunday from 10:00 A.M. to noon, eat some lunch, then come home to my room in the fraternity. One Sunday when I was opening the door to my fraternity, I could faintly hear some singing from across the street. It was 2:15, and I thought it was quite late for a church service. I went across the street, sat down on the steps outside the building, and listened. It was the most awesome singing and worship I had ever heard. It was so emotional that I just started crying right there. In fact, I was bawling. The singing reached down deep in my soul and captured the emotional pain of my past (my alcoholic father, my estranged mother, etc.). Since then, I have seen the same sort of thing happen to many other white people the first time they hear gospel music.

I probably would have sat there a little while longer and then gone back to my fraternity. However, a black woman was taking her little boy to the bathroom and saw me on the steps. She opened the door and said, "Why don't you come in?"

As sweat started pooling on my body, I stuttered, "I c-c-c-can't g-g-go in there."

"Why not?" she asked.

"Because I just can't," I said. I could not tell her that I had never been around a group of black people and that I was petrified. I thought all black people were mad at me for everything in the past, and if I ever got alone in a room with some of them, I was going to be beaten to death. (This was 1989—is that not ridiculous to you? It is to me.)

She said, "Come on in here and quit being silly. It's all right."

I do not know what made me go in that building with her, but when I went in, there were about twenty-five rows of chairs. About twenty-five people, all of them black, were packed into the first three rows. Which row did I sit in? You guessed it, row twenty-five! I was scared to death, and it was the first time I realized what it must feel like to be the minority.

I started attending every Sunday, and the people were some of the warmest, kindest people I had ever met. I had sung in choir in my high school, but I was not prepared for the choir that they asked me to join. I remember going home after rehearsal so hoarse that I could not talk. I had never sung with that kind of power and volume.

After a month or two of singing with the church choir, the choir director (Virginia) made an interesting statement. "You're ready now," she said.

"Ready for what?" I replied.

"You're ready to go to tryouts with me for BVOI. It stands for Black Voices of Inspiration."

I was short for words as I looked at my skin and said, "Virginia, I know this comes as a surprise to you, but I'm not black!"

She laughed and said it would be all right. Singing with Purdue's gospel choir called "Black Voices of Inspiration" helped prepare me to meet Edith in Indianapolis at Indiana University–Purdue University, Indianapolis.

Where Edith Came From. Edith grew up in Gary, Indiana, as the youngest of three kids. Her dad was a full-time steelworker and pastor of her home church. Her mom is the oldest of twelve children, so she was often surrounded by lots of family members, including many cousins, aunts, and uncles. In 1906 U.S. Steel, the largest steel mill in the U.S., opened in Gary, and people flocked to work there. Gary boomed from the 1930s through the 1960s as its economy and populations exploded. A popular musical, *The Music Man,* had a song about Gary being "just one place that can light my face."

Starting in the 1970s, Gary's economy and population dramatically shifted. The same city that was supposed to "light" the face of people was joked about in 1975 on the sitcom *That's My Mama:* "Be sure you're getting the world on a silver platter and not Gary, Indiana, on a paper plate." The combination of white flight, political agendas, and other social problems that started plaguing all urban centers led to Gary's becoming one of the crime and murder capitals of the United States in the late 1980s and 1990s.

The other major influence on my wife's background is her love for Chicago, where she was exposed to many different cultures through art, cuisine, and entertainment. She loves being in large crowds attending festivals like the "Taste of Chicago" and other big events with lots of people. She attended a school for fine arts in fourth through seventh grade and came to college a very cultured and cosmopolitan individual—the opposite of me.

Our Relationship Together. Edith and I met in college. I was in physical therapy school, and she was trying to get into that school. The school started a minority mentorship program, and I volunteered to be a mentor. Can you guess who was my protégée? Yep, Edith.

We could not stand each other for the first three or four months. She seemed very unmotivated, shy, and uncommitted. I was required by the program to contact her weekly, and that is the only reason I continued to talk to her. I realized later that I was really turning her off to our friendship by always trying to let her know how "down" I was with black people. A lot of white people who are getting familiar with black culture go through this stage. My conversation went something like this when I met her: "My name is David. I go to an all-black church in the city, and I really can relate to black people … in fact … black … black … and I really like black people … black … church … black … black … you know … black."

As we got to know each other better, a tremendous friendship developed. We were best friends for a year and a half, then dated. We married eight months later. Before we got married, and even before we were dating, Edith had feelings of selling out. When we were in the company of other black people, she would sometimes stand a little farther away from me and not give the impression that we were an item.

I was dealing with my own difficulties. My mother was quoting Bible verses completely out of context when I would talk to her on the phone, and she always ended with the biggie: "The Bible says to obey your parents." This was despite the fact that she had hardly been involved in my life since I was eight, was not a Christian, and did not care that I was a twenty-two-year-old man. However, my grandparents were the big blow because they considered me a son and were my closest family members. It completely broke their hearts when I told them that I was marrying a black person. I cannot remember crying so much as I did after that phone call.

I tried for two or three months to work with my family, but they did not want to know whether this marriage was right in a biblical sense. It was wrong to them, and that was all that mattered. My dad and stepmom came to the wedding, as did most of my other family. However, my mother and grandparents did not come to the wedding, and I was disowned as a family member. They also said that my children would never be claimed as family. (Ouch!)

Not only did my mom and grandparents say I was disobedient to God, but in addition I often had well-meaning Christians tell me how I was going to die at a young age for disobeying the commandment "Honor thy father and mother." They also said that I should never have gotten married unless I had my mother's and grandparents' blessing. I felt so condemned that I thought a trapdoor was going to open up on my way to the grocery store and I would slide down a chute straight to hell.

Well, I can see that you have finished your lemonade. I hope this background helps you understand where I am coming from. I'm sure you have a lot of questions, so ask them now.

Frequently Asked Questions

1. Am I being a "sellout" if I date or marry outside my race and culture?

If you are asking this question, you are telling me that you have trouble standing up for your own convictions in the midst of your peers. If you know that all people are created in the image of God, then you have only one concern if you are interested in a relationship with someone: Does this person have saving faith in Jesus Christ, have a deep commitment to God, and love me biblically? Our faith is always called to rise above the level of our culture.

This does not mean that you disown your culture. It is a part of your identity, and so your relationship partner should care about it. It is healthy to consider some of these differences before marriage. For example, I love the country and my wife loves the city. When I first started visiting her family, I had to tell myself, "This is my wife's home; this is part of who she is, no matter how uncomfortable I feel in an urban environment." It was a hard adjustment, but I cannot ask her to avoid her family or always send her to them by herself. I love her family immensely, and they have become a significant part of our lives, but there was an initial discomfort period for me. I have learned that her people are my people, and my people are her people. It is all part of being one.

2. Is it wrong to date someone from another culture and race just out of curiosity?

Yes! Do not date anyone out of curiosity like he or she is a plaything. You should have a firm grasp on a person's character before you have any romantic interest. Next question.

3. What about the children? People tell me that our biracial children will suffer.

This is a common statement made by family members when people are considering interracial marriage. I love a quote by Lee Chanult, cited in the book *Mixed Messages:* "What white people are saying with that statement is that they think racial prejudice is awful, especially when it affects children, and they sure are glad their kids are white!"[3] The only reason biracial children suffer is because they live in a racist society conditioned to make character judgments based on someone's amount of melanin. Unfortunately, the church has been a big proponent of racism in America's history.[4]

I often think of the irony of the same people who make statements of concern for children of interracial marriage clapping and rejoicing when a white couple adopts a child from another country. I recently read an article in a prominent local "Christian" newspaper that celebrated the naturalization of numerous foreign-born children who had been adopted by couples in the state of Ohio. I read intently to see if anyone asked the question "What about the children?" since all of the children were taken directly from their countries and cultures and placed into American households.[5] A child who is internationally adopted has more adjustments than a child who is raised and loved by his biological mother and father in his or her land of origin and who might be a shade lighter or darker than a parent.

What is important for children is that they are loved and given a chance to embrace all they culturally are, in spite of what society will tell them. In our society, if a child has "one drop" of African American blood, he or she is determined to be black. It is up to loving parents to teach children that their identity is much deeper than their skin color. Our daughter Hannah already is interested in her color compared to Mommy's and Daddy's colors. She calls herself "golden" and seems fine with this simplistic comparison. As she gets older, "golden" will not answer all her questions about herself and our color-crazed society. We often listen to a song about an interracial family called "Black, White, Tan" by Nicole Mullen. It says, "You are not a color and the color is not you." My child is not black or white or any other color. She is an individual created in the image of God who happens to have a certain skin color.

I am amazed when people think that the color of a child's skin is the only thing that will target him or her for malicious teasing from other children. I remember catcalls of "four eyes" for having glasses, "runt" and "shrimp" for being short, and "loser" when I was kicked off the basketball team. Kids are going to make fun of other kids because kids are sinful. Whether it is for their nose, their eyes, their glasses, their teeth, their "momma," their clothes, their music, or their skin color, they are going to deal with teasing and cruelty from other children. What is important is the amount of love and godly self-worth parents infuse into their children.

Yes, biracial children will go through a process of discovering who they are, like everyone else. A child with godly self-worth can endure societal torment and taunts. Besides, the Bible teaches that my children will have to endure tremendous hatred and be considered social outcasts—just for being Christian! I have never heard a believer ask a Christian couple through tear-soaked eyes, "Have you thought of the implications of having godly offspring? It says in the Bible that if you have children who follow Christ, they will be hated. What about the children?"

If the world hates you, keep in mind that it hated me first. If you belonged to the world, it would love you as its own. As it is, you do not belong to the world, but I have chosen you out of the world. That is why the world hates you. (John 15:18–19, NIV)

In this world you will have trouble. But take heart! I have overcome the world. (John 16:33, NIV)

4. Some people tell me that marriage is hard enough already, so why would I want to make it more difficult than it already is?

Most of the time, the people who pose this question reluctantly agree that there is nothing wrong with interracial marriage. But their thinking goes something like this: (1) It is not biblically wrong; (2) it is hard to do the right thing—stay married; (3) do not make doing the right thing any tougher than it already is. In fact, make it as painless as possible in order to decrease the failure rate.

I wonder why the same people do not take the same approach to their children when it comes to being a Christian. "Johnny, it is so hard to be a Christian. I do not want you to be teased, so do not tell anyone about Jesus. Do not take a Bible where your friends might see you, and do not wear any Christian T-shirts, as surely this will target you for undue suffering. Johnny, your mom and I do not even tell our neighbors that we go to church, and in fact we rent a Ryder truck so that other people do not see our car in the church parking lot."

Is this ridiculous to you? I hope so, and so is this question. I pray for the day when racism and prejudice are eliminated from America and from the Christian church. But if God has called you into an interracial relationship, then be a ready soldier to endure mockery and scorn that come when you testify against a racist society and church.

The reason an interracial relationship is harder in our society is because of the sin of society, not the sin of the people in the relationship. No parent should tell his or her children to alter their course of action because a sinful society cannot tolerate their biblical actions. Evangelicals are called to stand up and be counted for righteousness and endure scorn as Christ did. However, the motive for your relationship should be your desire and commitment to biblically love each other, not a desire to make a social statement.

5. My parents ask me, "Why not find a good mate with one of your 'own' people?"

Sometimes people pose this question out of a flawed understanding of the command by God to the Israelites not to intermarry with other people groups around them. Any critical examination of those particular passages shows that the command came because of the neighboring groups' idolatry, not their specific physical characteristics (Deuteronomy 7:1–4).

If you are a Christian, this question is easy to answer. People are really asking why you cannot find a mate within your own cultural group. But if you are a believer in Christ, then your "people" includes any Christian person on the face of the earth.

> We were all baptized by one Spirit into one body—whether Jews or Greeks, slave or free—and we were all given the one Spirit to drink. (1 Corinthians 12:13, NIV)

> There is neither Jew nor Greek, slave nor free, male nor female, for you are all one in Christ Jesus. If you belong to Christ, then you are Abraham's seed, and heirs according to the promise. (Galatians 3:28–29, NIV)

If you are in Christ, then you are part of the family of God with everyone who belongs to Christ. "Your people" for marriage partners are other believers. Have enough faith in your convictions to talk openly with your friends and family about the character of your possible mate being much more important than outward appearance. Discern the heart of the person you seek to date and possibly marry. Do not let your cultural bias define you; rather, let your identity be rooted and grounded in Christ and in his love. Just remember that the further apart you and your mate are culturally, the more effort that will be required to transcend the sinful hindrances erected by different cultural groups. If you biblically love that person, then this should not be considered too much to endure for the relationship to flourish.

6. How do I deal with my family members who disapprove of my relationship? What biblical role does my dad, my mom, my aunt, etc., play in the decision process of who I should date or marry?

Ah, you are finally ready to tackle the biggie. This is the toughest question to deal with because it is complex, and so I will spend the most time on it. It is a tough question because I have to spend some time debunking bad teaching that many evangelicals have offered about the scope of parental involvement in a child's life and decision making. Some Christians say that when you are in an interracial relationship and someone in your family disagrees with it, then you should wait until that person gives his or her blessing before getting married. Other evangelicals suggest that you are violating the commandment of honoring your father and mother. Much of this bad teaching comes from the ministry of Bill Gothard. Christians are still using some of the bad theology that emerged from his teaching. In the end, I hope you understand healthy scriptural principles to use in your situation.

We will start with where the concept of honoring our father and mother begins—Exodus 20:12: "Honour thy father and thy mother: that thy days may be long upon the land which the LORD thy God giveth thee" (KJV). I have been told all my life the meaning of this verse, from Sunday school teachers all the way to pastors of large churches. Do you want to know what I was always told this verse means? I will spell it out: O-B-E-Y! Do not argue or question but obey. I have never heard any other implication attached to this verse or any conditions given for obedience. My mother constantly used this verse when disagreeing with my marriage to Edith.

Prominent evangelicals seem to emphasize this commandment regardless of the age of the offspring. For example, Matthew Henry's *Commentary on the Bible Entire* explains this verse about unquestionable obedience to parents as "a decent respect to their persons, an inward esteem of them outwardly expressed upon *all* occasions in our conduct towards them" (emphasis mine). He says further that honoring one's parents incorporates "submission to their rebukes, instructions, and corrections; not only to the good and gentle, but also to the *froward* [disobedient or willful], out of conscience towards God" (emphasis mine). Henry implies that disobedience to one's parents is not an option in any of the children's decisions.[6]

I remember struggling with several questions during my premarital relationship with Edith: Is it ever right to choose a course of action different than your family's commands? If so, when is it allowed? Why and at what age? If my family disagrees with interracial marriage, shall I break up with Edith and call off the wedding? What if my grandparents or other extended family members disapprove? These are some of the dilemmas created when these passages are not studied in context with the rest of the Scriptures.

A. Honoring Your Parents Implies That Their Opinion Has Extra Weight
The Hebrew word for "honor" is *kabed,* meaning to "be heavy."[7] What the text is saying is that parents should be esteemed and that their opinion has a lot of weight.

We understand words by knowing their opposite meaning. In Leviticus 20:9 the Bible commands, "If anyone *curses* his father or mother, he must be put to death" (NIV, emphasis added). The Hebrew word for "curse" is *qalal,* which gives the idea of "making light or small" or means to "lightly esteem, curse, or revile."[8] This is the opposite of "honor," in the Hebrew sense, as one indicates heavy and the other is light.

Thus, we can see that, biblically, in the concept of "honor" there is the idea of giving proper weight to your parents' opinions.

B. Honoring Your Parents Implies Taking Care of Their Physical Needs as They Grow Older

When talking to the Pharisees about how their traditions were contrary to God's teaching about honoring your father and mother, Jesus probed,

> Why do you break the command of God for the sake of your tradition? For God said, "Honor your father and mother" and "Anyone who curses his father or mother must be put to death." But you say that if a man says to his father or mother, "Whatever *help* [provision] you might otherwise have received from me is a gift devoted to God," he is not to "honor his father" with it. Thus you nullify the word of God for the sake of your tradition. (Matthew 15:3–6, NIV, emphasis added)

Jesus exposes the hypocrisy of the Pharisees who were teaching children that whatever money they were going to use to take care of their parents they could just donate to the temple as a vow to God. (Guess who that helped?)

This implication is further reinforced by Paul's instruction to Timothy: "Honour widows that are widows indeed" (1 Timothy 5:3, KJV). Dr. Greg Couser, professor of New Testament at Cedarville College, states that "here Paul reprimands believers who are failing to take care of their widowed mothers and speaks of it in terms of a failure to keep the command to 'honor' their parents" (1 Timothy 5:3–8).[9]

C. Honoring Your Parents Does Not *Mean Obedience to Them in All Situations*

The idea of a blind obedience is often taken from Deuteronomy 21:18–21.

> If a man have a stubborn and rebellious son, which will not obey the voice of his father, or the voice of his mother, and that, when they have chastened him, will not hearken unto them: then shall his father and his mother lay hold on him, and bring him out unto the elders of his city, and unto the gate of his place; and they shall say unto the elders of his city, This our son is stubborn and rebellious, he will not obey our voice; he is a glutton, and a drunkard. And all the men of his city shall stone him with stones, that he die. (KJV)

The Hebrew word for "stubborn" means "to turn away *morally*" (emphasis mine).[10] What this verse is indicating is that the son is turning away from his parents' morally right instruction to do what he wants to do, which is morally wrong.

This idea is further supported in Colossians 3:20–21, where the directive of Paul is "Children, obey your parents in everything, for this pleases the

Lord." Many people stop their interpretation of child-parent relationship here and fail to include the next verse, which states, "Fathers, do not embitter [provoke] your children, or they will become discouraged" (NIV). Paul indicates that there is a two-way relationship when talking about parents and children. Parents have a responsibility for proper, scriptural instruction, and children (that is kids, not adult children) have a responsibility to obey their parents' scriptural instruction. Sound scriptural and moral instruction is assumed in this passage, since Paul was writing to the families in the saved church. Paul seems to be saying that children should obey their parents and that parents must admonish their children toward morally correct instruction.

Let us bring this back to the issue of interracial dating. The ethnicity of your partner matters but does not influence your biblical morality. Nevertheless, nowhere in the Old or New Testament is an age stipulated as to when a child becomes independent and able to make his or her own decisions. We can, however, assert that whomever we consider to be an adult should be allowed to make a marital decision without having to obtain the blessing of their parents, even though the parents' involvement and blessing is preferred. I am grateful for Dr. Couser's explanation based on the Book of Proverbs (6:20–35):

> There we find parents giving advice to their adult son and the advice consists of wise direction, i.e. biblically based approaches to living, that is somewhat general in nature. They tell the son what kind of wife to look for, but not which particular wife to marry. This suggests a change in what it means to honor one's parents from the type of relationship that would pertain to a small child. To honor your parents as an adult would be to *base your life and choices on scriptural principles, not necessarily to do what your parents told you to do.* The parents do not seem to operate with that type of authority in relationship to their adult child (emphasis mine).[11]

WWJD?

Did Jesus always obey his parents? Jesus' mother and brothers decided to visit him in Capernaum. Their motive is made more clear in Mark 3:21, where the Bible tells us, "When his family heard about this, they went to take charge of him, for they said, 'He is out of his mind' " (NIV). Jesus' mother had come to take him back home because she thought he was losing it. She thought he was a wacko, cuckoo, a crazy man! The people told

Jesus that his mom was outside calling him to come back with her to Nazareth. What did he say? "Who is my mother, and who are my brothers?" Pointing to his disciples, he said, "Here are my mother and my brothers. For whoever does the will of my Father in heaven is my brother and sister and mother" (Matthew 12:48).

Jesus tells the whole crowd that he is not listening to his family because they did not understand that he was doing God's will. This is in spite of the fact that Jesus' mother was a devout follower of God (Luke 1:28). This adult son was sure of his choices being God's will in spite of his loving, God-fearing family's objections. It is important to note that Jesus did not use disrespectful language to his mother, but he knew that she really did not understand what God's will for him was. Sometimes family members can misunderstand and misinterpret God's Word and try to hold their adult children hostage to their interpretation. This is what I see in many interracial dating and marriage situations.

What Honoring Your Father and Mother Does Not Imply

We have seen what the command to honor one's parents implies. Here is what that command does not imply:

1. That you always obey your parents 100 percent of the time, no matter what.
2. That you always agree with your parents and extended family.
3. That you follow a parent's immoral and unscriptural advice.
4. That you always make decisions that your parents agree with.
5. That your parent's interpretation of Scripture is absolute and infallible.

When you interracially date or marry, you are saying that you realize the Bible teaches that all men and women are related to each other through two common ancestors. You are also agreeing with the Bible that there is no prohibition against marriage between people of different ethnic or cultural backgrounds. The only marriage the Bible prohibits is that of a believer with an unbeliever (2 Corinthians 6:14). If your family disagrees with an interracial relationship, they are saying that they do not believe the Bible teaches these things. This is in spite of the many such marriages in the Bible: Moses was married to an African woman (Numbers 12:1) and God punished Aaron's wife for saying something negative about it; Rahab (a descendant of Ham) married an Israelite and is part of the lineage of Christ (Matthew 1:5); Ruth (a Moabite) married an Israelite and is part of the lineage of Christ (Matthew 1:5).

As we conclude the difficult issue of how to deal with family, I want you to be sure that you do not hear me saying that interracial dating and marriage is

"God's mission" for you. Your motive for marrying should not be skin color—or any other physical trait, for that matter. However, it is important to know that you have the freedom to interracially marry.

Now I move closer to you and look into your eyes. You can see I am very serious about what we are getting ready to talk about.

The Really Big Question

Now that I have answered your questions, I need to ask you about your interracial dating or marriage relationship. I think the really big question for you is this: "How do you prepare to react when you are teased, stared at, questioned, called immoral, called un-Christian, told you are responsible for Grandma's heart attack, accused of splitting up the family, etc.?" Such questions and comments are going to happen to you in America, which legally allowed interracial marriage in every state only thirty years ago![12] How are you going to handle these issues? Are you going to handle nonbiblical criticism as Christ would or with hostility? This is the key question for every person considering or in an interracial relationship or marriage.

You must decide ahead of time if you will approach unexpected situations as a representative of Christ in people's lives. You have to be an agent of redemption in a fallen world, including a world polluted by the sins of prejudice and racism. If you have no desire to model a loving relationship of Christ and his church across racial lines, end your relationship now! If you are already married, then ask God to give you the heart of Christ to minister peace to your family, friends, enemies, skeptics, etc.

> If you suffer for doing good and you endure it, this is commendable before God. To this you were called, because Christ suffered for you, leaving you an example, that you should follow in his steps.
>> *"He committed no sin,*
>>> *and no deceit was found in his mouth."*
> When they hurled their insults at him, he did not retaliate; when he suffered, he made no threats. Instead, he entrusted himself to him who judges justly. (1 Peter 2:20–23, NIV)
> I tell you who hear me: Love your enemies, do good to those who hate you, bless those who curse you, pray for those who mistreat you. If someone strikes you on one cheek, turn to him the other also....
> If you love those who love you, what credit is that to you? Even "sinners" love those who love them. And if you do good to those

who are good to you, what credit is that to you? Even "sinners" do that…. But love your enemies, do good to them, and lend to them without expecting to get anything back. Then your reward will be great, and you will be sons of the Most High, because he is kind to the ungrateful and wicked. Be merciful, just as your Father is merciful. (Luke 6:27–29,32–33,35–36, NIV)

What should you do when people ask you ignorant questions? Answer them with patience and love. What should you do when everyone at the mall or church stares at you? Smile at them and say, "Hello." Treat them as if you cannot tell their mouths have been open so long that drool is pooling on their sweater. What should you do when family members disown you? Love them and continue to pursue your relationship with them. People should know that no matter how they treat you or your mate, your love for them is unconditional, irrepressible, and unstoppable because that is the way God loves the wicked as well as the just (Luke 6:35–36). Use your relationship to demonstrate a ministry of reconciliation to the world and to raise godly offspring who will do the same. The entire New Testament is full of verses on forgiveness and loving people who hurt, mistreat, and injure us (Good Samaritan, the cross, etc.). If you and your potential mate have an "us against the world" mentality, then please reevaluate your relationship and get on your knees before God. Ask God to give you the kind of love that can forgive others, no matter how big the offense.

Let me share with you an example of how God used hurt and pain by others to advance God's kingdom. In 1994 Edith and I were regular attendees of a church in Indiana where we were actively doing evangelism every week. I had been discipled for three years in this church as a college student during the summer, and as Edith and I began to date, she attended with me. She was the only black person in the congregation of about eight hundred or nine hundred. We knew the pastor and many leaders in the church well. We were actively involved in Sunday school and outreach. On many of our outreach visits, we would tell prospective visitors how much we loved the church and how wonderful it was to be involved there. Our pastor unreservedly agreed to marry us. We reserved the church and a reception hall. We made invitations and even worked through Edith's grandparents' fear of being lynched if they came to the wedding. All the preparations were done and we were about two months away from being husband and wife.

Then we received an unexpected phone call from our pastor. He had just come from a deacons' meeting in which a heated discussion about our marriage had occurred. He asked us to not get married at this church because they were not ready for us to be married there yet. He said he tried to show the deacons that what they were saying was not biblical, but they were not convinced.

I was tremendously hurt by that phone call. I told Edith, and we just started crying. We could not believe that the very church we were representing every week in outreach would not even recognize or participate in our union in the eyes of God. We were hurt, frustrated, and angry, but the Lord spoke to my spirit. I knew what had happened was wrong and that the pastor should have had enough biblical conviction to act accordingly, but the Lord clearly led me to not "pick up my toys" and leave the church. Edith and I prayed about it and both felt the Lord wanted us to stay there in spite of all that had happened. We made a covenant with each other not to tell anyone in the church, even our friends, about our hurt. There were many leaders at that meeting, and word got around to some of our classmates. Many of them came to us and said they were leaving the church. We asked them why they should leave if the Lord had not even released us to leave.

It was difficult to tell everyone that we needed to move the wedding without explaining why, but we did the best we could. It was sad to see what that episode did to the church's witness. We attended for another five months before moving to Alabama. Many times the pastor came up to us and said how much it meant to him to see us continuing to try to help the church change through love. Five years later we visited this same church. They had voted to approve their first interracial marriage just five months previous to our visit. One of their most prominent families was African American, and their worship style was very much like Brooklyn Tabernacle Choir music, with electric guitar, bass guitar, drums, and an orchestra, in stark contrast to the style of music when we had attended. The Lord led me to write a long letter before this visit to ask for the pastor's forgiveness for continuing to hold bitterness toward him about our wedding incident. He met with my wife and me, telling us that the Lord had continued to show him many things after we had left. Today that church has two interracially married couples, has about fifteen hundred people at Sunday worship, and is impacting their community for Christ. What a neat story! This was a very painful episode in our relationship, but Christ gave us the strength to react in a way totally opposite of how we initially wanted to.

By the way, do you remember that I told you my grandparents disowned me when I married my wife? My wife and I continued loving them the best we knew how, and about four and a half years ago, they both invited us to spend the night with them so they could meet Edith. I have seen God tremendously change these sincere Christians' hearts to the point of outright love for my wife and me. To give you an idea of how far the relationship has grown, our youngest daughter, Mary-Catherine, is named after my grandmother (Mary) and my wife's grandmother (Catherine). My grandmother often asks, "When are you guys coming to visit?" (My grandfather passed away in December 2000, but he had developed a special fondness for my wife.) That only happened because my family and I always operated with my grandparents out of God's love and not our response to hurt. Praise God!

I do not have time to get into all the other goodies like death threat letters, family reunion denials, etc., but the important thing is that you decide how you are going to react before such things happen. You must decide to react like Christ in your relationship.

I Enjoyed Talking with You

"Come and get it," my wife says as she comes over to give me a hug and some "sugar." "Yeah, we've been through a lot of bad stuff together," I say to you as I rise to go to the dinner table. "But our relationship is well worth it. We have also been used by God to help the world understand a lot about God's Son. I'm crazy about that girl."

Do not go looking for an interracial relationship just to "suffer for Jesus." Look for a mate who is a redeemed individual who expresses godly character, no matter what hue he or she is. If that person happens to be a different shade, then realize that this society has set rules that certain shades are more acceptable to be with than others. As you encounter this racist society and the racism within the church, be a representative of Christ who seeks to transform individuals and institutions. If you are not ready to pray for the very individuals who hurt you, do not enter into an interracial relationship. Christ compels us to hope that these very people are part of our next family reunion at the marriage feast in heaven. I have no idea if you will ever experience problems or persecution because of your interracial relationship, but you must decide ahead of time how you will deal with these potential encounters.

Let's just go eat, because you have a lot to think about after our little talk. The couch will be here again when you need to talk, and maybe next time we'll eat what you like. God bless and keep you in your journey of relationships.

Discussion Questions

1. What are good reasons for getting into an interracial relationship? What are improper reasons for getting into such a relationship? If you are in an interracial relationship, what are your reasons for being in that relationship?
2. How did Tatlock's personal background help him prepare for an interracial relationship? What in your personal background helps prepare you for a possible or a current interracial relationship?
3. How important is it to obtain the permission of your parents so that you can marry someone of another race? At what point do you go ahead and marry your partner despite your parents' disapproval?
4. If you are in an interracial relationship, are there opportunities for you to use that relationship to further the Kingdom of God? If so, what are they?
5. Are there questions about entering into interracial relationships that are not covered in the chapter? If so how would you answer those questions?

Notes

1. *A pseudonym.*
2. *I disagree with the term "interracial" from a biblical and biological basis, but I understand the term's usage of race as a social construct.*
3. *Fred and Anita Prinzing,* Mixed Messages *(Chicago: Moody Press, 1991), 12.*
4. *I do have to qualify by saying that there were some people in the church who fought this, but their voices were few and far between.*
5. *Diane K. Schultz, "Children Naturalized in Ohio under the Children Citizenship Act of 2000," Christian Citizen, April 2001, 1.*
6. *Matthew Henry,* Matthew Henry's Commentary on the Whole Bible *(Peabody, Mass.: Hendrickson, 1991), 125, emphasis added.*
7. *Spiros Zodhiates, ed.,* The Hebrew-Greek Key Study Bible, *5th ed. (Iowa Falls, Iowa: World Bible Publishers, 1988), 3513.*
8. *Ibid., 1634.*
9. *Dr. Greg Couser, electronic mail response to interview questions, April 4, 2001.*
10. *Zodhiates,* Hebrew-Greek Key Study Bible, *1619, emphasis added.*
11. *Dr. Greg Couser, electronic mail response to interview questions, April 4, 2001, emphasis added.*
12. *Phillip Koslow, ed.,* The New York Public Library African-American Desk Reference *(New York: Wiley, 1999), Table 12.2, 312.*

❧ EIGHT ❧

And Two Shall Become One: Merging Two Racial Cultures in Christian Love

Art and Debbie Lucero

IN 1994 AS MY SON TONY FILLED OUT AN APPLICATION FOR SCHOOL, he asked, "Dad, what do I mark on this application for my ethnic identification?" The options at that time were white, Hispanic, African American, Native American, and Asian. I told him, partially in jest, "Check them all, son."

The confusion my son had in filling out his application was not uncommon for the time, nor was my suggestion that he mark more than one racial category. The 1990 Census witnessed "a mild act of civil disobedience" when half a million people marked more than the requested one race.[1] Subsequently, for the first time, the 2000 Census permitted individuals to mark more than one racial category. Demographer Sharon M. Lee writes, "The option of choosing more than one race provides a more accurate, if complex, portrait of diversity in America. Although the people identifying themselves as multiracial were just 2.4% of the U.S. population, their numbers may grow faster than the total population as interracial marriages increase and more people acknowledge their multiracial backgrounds."[2]

Our marriage was not the first multiethnic marriage for either Debbie's family or my own. Debbie's father is Anglo and her mother is Japanese. My parents are both Mexican, but they are each descendants of multiethnic parents. I learned that to get an understanding of prospective mates' cultural programming, values, and behavior, it's important to understand some of their family history. The purpose of this essay is to look at how we dealt with the different racial cultures we brought into our marriage.

Art's Family

Hispanics, unlike the other racial categories identified by the federal government, are not a racial group. My Mexican heritage reflects a tapestry of

---

Editor's note: While this chapter is written in the first person from Art Lucero's perspective, Art and Debbie Lucero are coauthors of this contribution.

interracial weaving. Hispanics can be of any race. Kanellos and Ryan explain:

In 1492 with the discovery of the new world by Christopher Columbus, began three centuries of Spanish exploration, conquest, and colonization in the Americas. In the Spanish Empire that grew, the Old World–Europeans and Africans came together and mixed with the New World–Native Americans. These people of Spanish America created the cultures and traditions that we now see in the United States among Hispanic Americans.[3]

My paternal grandmother, Ramona Lucero, didn't like to talk about her ancestors, but the nappy hair of my uncles made it very clear that there was an African in the family tree. We believe my maternal grandmother, Monica Polanco, was a Native American or a mestizo (Native American and Spanish mix), heavy on the Native American genes, with dark skin, long, straight jet-black hair, and high cheekbones. She married Eutimio Polanco, a white Mexican national, fair skinned, with sandy blond hair and blue eyes. It is this combination of the red, brown, yellow, black, and white bloodlines that run through the veins of my children and that caused me to respond like I did to Tony's question.

One would think that after five hundred years of racial blending among Hispanics in Latin America, racism would not exist. Unfortunately, it is as alive today as it was the day Spain began its colonization of the New World. There are three major categories of Hispanic racial mixes: the *European,* those of pure Spanish blood, of which there are few in Latin America; the *mestizos,* those of mixed Native American and European blood; and the *mulattos,* those of mixed African and European blood. Those of European ancestry, because of the fair skin and light brown to sandy blond hair, are usually referred to as *guerros* (blondies). The mestizos tend to have various shades of brown skin with either European or Native American facial features. Mestizos make up the largest segment of the Hispanic population in Latin America. Mulattos are predominantly found in the Caribbean and Central American countries. Those at the bottom rung of the social ladder are the Native Americans of Central and South America.

While the mulatto strain was evident in the Luceros, I personally never sensed any racist attitudes or experienced any racist treatment in Mexico. However, any feelings of inferiority I had as a child in Mexico were due to my dark complexion, especially after weeks of playing baseball in the blazing sun of Ciudad Juarez. My complexion would get so dark that my uncles called me *"bola de humo"* (ball of smoke) and *"pinacate"* (stink bug). In the case of the latter, I am certain the nickname was for the jet-black coloring of the insect and not its pungent odor, although I could be wrong.

I was the firstborn of all my cousins. The next two, Jorge and Chuya, were "little blondies." I once asked my aunt why my cousins were white while I was dark skinned. She jokingly replied, "It's because I bathe them in Clorox bleach." I took her words literally. When I got home that night and prepared for my evening bath, I started pouring Clorox in the bathwater. When I told my mother what I was doing, she drained the tub and gave my aunt an earful.

Debbie's Family

The transition from a feudal to a modern government in Japan took a toll on the peasants. They suffered the brunt of financing the new government with heavy taxes. Thousands lost their farms and homes. America offered them employment in the labor-intensive industries of railroad construction, logging, mining, fish processing, and agriculture. Debbie's great-grandfather was among the hopeful who sought a new life in America.

The events that followed the "day of infamy" on December 7, 1941, changed the lives of Japanese Americans. "Banks refused to cash their checks; insurance companies canceled their policies; milkmen and grocers refused to sell to them. 'A Jap's a Jap!' declared Lieutenant General John L. DeWitt, charged with the West Coast's defense. 'It makes no difference whether he's an American or not.' "[4]

Debbie's maternal grandmother, Koko Sasaki, was born in Winslow, Arizona, in 1919, the daughter of immigrant parents whose father worked for the Southern Pacific Railroad. Koko returned to Japan in 1922 with her mother, only to return to the United States in 1938, at her father's request, to study nursing. When she arrived in the U.S., she was met by a man she did not know, who had arranged with her father for Koko to be his bride. Her father's story of sending her to America to study nursing was a lie. Not wanting to shame her family, Koko married Takeo Otsubo and bore him two daughters: Sachiko (my mother-in law) in 1939 and Yoshiko in 1940. By 1941, it was evident to Koko that the marriage was not going to work. She left Takeo and, with the aftermath of Pearl Harbor, found herself a resident of the Heart Mountain Japanese internment camp in Wyoming with her two- and three-year-old daughters.

Grandma Koko's second husband, Grandpa Komatsu, was in the U.S. Army on December 7, 1941. He was removed from his regular duties for fear of sabotage. When the Army discovered that he was bilingual, he was transferred to a signal battalion, where he served his country by translating intercepted Japanese messages. His brother, Harry Komatsu, served in the highly decorated Japanese American unit, the 442nd Regimental Combat Team.

At the end of WWII Grandma Koko Otsubo returned to California, where she met Grandpa Kim Komatsu. They were married in 1949.

An Allied victory may have ended the war overseas, but it did not end the prejudice many Americans held toward Japanese Americans. Debbie's mom, Sachiko, recalls being chased home by rock-throwing students because she was Japanese.

Debbie's parents, Norman Lee and Sachiko Otsubo, met in high school. Like most dating couples, Norman and Sachiko could be seen walking hand in hand down the school corridor. Their romance did not go unnoticed. Sachiko was called into the principal's office, where she was asked, "Don't you have any other friends?" to which Sachiko innocently responded "Yes, I have a lot of friends." As the conversation developed, it became obvious to her that the principal's question referred to her having any nonwhite "other friends" she could date.

Being descendants of interracial marriages ourselves, Debbie and I did not face the resentment of family or society. We had other prejudices to deal with, not from the outside world but from within our own hearts.

Art and Debbie's Story

My mother was instrumental in developing my respect for people of other races. She always reminded me that all people are the same and that nobody is better than anyone else. However, for decades I was very prejudiced. Not against other races, but against my own people. My earliest recollection regarding coming to the United States from Mexico was of the advice my Aunt Mague had given me when I was four years old. She said, "Arturo, when you go to America, please do not become like those Chicanos." I had no idea what a Chicano (Mexican American) was, but judging from my aunt's facial expression and her vocal intonations, it had to be bad. She went on to say, "If you're going to speak English, then speak English; if you're going to speak Spanish, then speak Spanish. Please don't mix the two languages, and learn to speak them both properly."

After a few years in the United States, I began to understand the advice my aunt had given me, and it developed within my own heart the resentment she obviously held for Chicanos. When I was growing up in East Los Angeles, the "Spanglish" spoken in Ramona Gardens, the government housing projects in which we lived, not to mention the barrio accents of so many Mexican Americans, hurt even my little ears. To prevent my falling into the same speech patterns, I, while still a child, would listen to the news on television and mimic the newscasters. This is a habit I still practice, although I now do it more with Spanish-speaking broadcasters.

My aunt's simple advice not only bred in me a desire to speak both English and Spanish properly and without an accent; it also developed in me a strong sense of prejudice toward Hispanics who did not. While I had several male Hispanic friends throughout my school years, I was twenty-one before I dated a Hispanic girl. Most of my girlfriends were white, blonde, blue-eyed, and at least an inch taller than me. I never thought that I would marry a Hispanic. While I found many attractive Hispanic American young ladies to date, all they had to do was begin speaking and I was immediately turned off.

It was not until I came to a saving knowledge of Christ that my attitudes began to change. Under the ministry of Pastor Harry Wilson, a white who loved Hispanics and was himself married to a Mexican American, I learned that I needed to love my neighbor as myself and not to think so highly of myself. The Lord dealt swiftly with my pride and feelings of superiority.

Debbie had her own prejudices with which to deal. They were aimed at no one but herself. Debbie's family lived in an all-white middle-class neighborhood. The elementary school she attended had one Chinese and a couple of Hispanic students. Anti-Japanese feelings were still strong in the 1960s. Debbie's Japanese features made her stand out in a predominately white school. Her classmates often called her a Jap. Reflecting on her youth, Debbie said, "I recall being chased home from school almost every day for a whole year by a girl who didn't like me because I was Japanese. She never caught me. Honestly, I don't know what she would have done if she had."

Debbie's desire growing up was that she would marry a white man with dominant genes to wash out any physical traits of her Japanese roots. It was not until her high school years in the mid 1970s that the demographics of her community changed significantly. A large number of Hispanics were now part of the student population. As Debbie affectionately likes to say, it was at that time that she "began having a preference for dark meat." Eventually Debbie's original desire was fulfilled, much to my disappointment. None of our biological children has Japanese features. Only our daughter Sachiko, who is adopted, has eyes that reflect the Asian thread of her mixed ancestry.

Cultural Adjustments

The union of a man and a woman in holy matrimony can lead to a virtual minefield of cultural issues. Adjusting to the racial culture of your partner is important in an interracial marriage. Debbie's exposure to Hispanics as a child was valuable in helping her anticipate the demands of my culture. But I did not have early exposure to Asian culture, and I had a lot of learning to do. Among these cultural adjustments were the use of names, expectations, machismo, mother-son bonding, and emotional expressions.

Names. First impressions are important for the development of any relationship, especially when the individual you are meeting is a key figure. Debbie and I had recently announced our engagement, and I was on tour, meeting extended family. On this particular day, we traveled to City Terrace, a community in the heart of East Los Angeles. As we got out of the car, I could hear the ferocious barking of a dog. Debbie was excited to introduce me to the Komatsus and was not thinking about the dog. She said, "Oh, good. Koko is here."

Being the dog lover that I am, and because my parents owned a pet dog named Cocoa, I immediately assumed that Debbie was referring to the barking dog. As we approached the front door, the dog barked uncontrollably, throwing itself against the screen door in an effort to attack the unwelcome visitors. In an attempt to make peace with the protective spaniel, I bent down and placed the back of my hand up against the screen door so he could smell my scent. In a soothing voice I said, "It's OK, Cocoa. It's OK, Cocoa." At that moment, as Grandma unlocked the screen door, she said in her broken English, "Nooo . . . dog Sumi . . . me Koko." I wanted to crawl in a hole. It is in moments like these that I thank God for my dark complexion, for no one could see the agonizing embarrassment in my face as the blood rushed to it.

Expectations. In the first year of our marriage I took Debbie to Ciudad Juarez, Mexico, and El Paso, Texas, to meet my relatives. Debbie was a little nervous, in part because she did not speak much Spanish. However, Debbie actually could understand quite a bit.

As my aunts, uncles, and cousins gathered around, Debbie sat close to me. They peppered me with questions about how we met, how long we had been dating, and our recent wedding. Debbie sat patiently as I responded to their questions. They would look at Debbie, smile, and turn and talk to one another. Then they asked the one question that really mattered to them, *"Habla español?"* (Does she speak Spanish?). I said, "No," to which they responded, *"Pobrecita"* (Poor little thing). Unknown to them, Debbie understood not only the term *"pobrecita,"* but she also picked up on the complete sense of pity they expressed for her lack of Spanish language proficiency. Most Hispanics to whom I introduce Debbie expect her to speak Spanish, probably because I am Spanish-speaking. On several occasions when I am asked if she speaks Spanish and I say, "No," their typical response has been *"Pobrecita."*

A major source of conflict in any relationship is unfulfilled expectations. It is tough enough trying to live up to the expectations of our mate. Adding the cultural expectations of our mate's family can significantly strain the marital relationship. New multiracial couples contemplating marriage, or those already in multiracial marriages, should seriously consider a response, one that is mutually agreeable, to deal with key cultural expectations of extended family members.

Machismo. My cousin Jaime (Mexican) and his wife, Mati (Cuban), were visiting us from Texas. Debbie was pregnant with our first child. Jaime and Mati had a three-month-old son, Adrian. As the men visited in the living room, the women visited in the kitchen. Jaime reached down for Adrian and noticed that his diaper was soiled. He called out to Mati to change the baby's diaper. From the kitchen Mati said, "Jaime, you change him. I really would like some help in this area." Jaime, in a firm voice, lectured Mati on the man's and woman's roles in child rearing, of which changing diapers was definitely a woman's sole duty. Mati arose from the table, complaining under her breath, while Jaime passionately restated his position.

I watched this exchange with great interest because our son Tony was due to be born soon, and I did not want to change diapers. A few days after Jaime and Mati's visit, I summoned up the courage to face off with Debbie regarding the diaper-changing issue. She was nine months pregnant, feeling miserable and edgy. Talk about bad timing. I had not finished making my case when Debbie locked and loaded both barrels and pulled the trigger. The lesson we learned on that occasion was that cultural values are much easier to enforce when both husband and wife are from the same culture.

Male-female roles in America have become fuzzy. The woman's entrance into the workforce has impacted the traditional roles of men and women. But that is not the case among many first- and second-generation immigrants from Asia, Africa, and Latin America. Cultures from these regions still tend to hold to strict gender roles. The tendency of the woman will be to feel that she is nothing more than a servant, and the feelings of the man will be that his manhood is being attacked by efforts to force him to perform women's duties.

As a convert to diaper changing, let me add that some of my most enjoyable times with my five children occurred when I was changing their diapers. For Debbie, diaper changing was a chore that needed to be done quickly. For me, it was an experience, a brief moment in time that allowed me to bond with my children. Unlike Debbie, who shocked the child with cold wipes, I warmed them up in my hands. I would not trade those precious moments for anything.

The bond between mother and son. Debbie and I had been married a little over a year when we rented our first home. Conveniently, the rental home was directly across the street from my parents. It is a well-known fact that Hispanic males are very attached to their mothers, sometimes to the detriment of their own marriages. It became my custom to pull my car into the driveway and walk across the street to visit with my mom (your assumption is correct—I had not yet greeted my wife). As soon as I walked into the house, my mom would serve me a *bocadito* (a small serving of food). As the conversation continued and the *bocadito* was consumed, it was not untypical for mom to give me a second serving. Becoming aware of the fleeting of time, I would hurry home to greet my lovely bride.

Striving to fulfill her role as a dutiful wife, Debbie always made dinner and had it ready for me when I walked through the front door. As she served my plate, I forced myself to display an appetite and eat the entire serving. After a few days, I was bloated to the point of painful discomfort. I couldn't take it anymore! One day after visiting with Mom, as Debbie prepared to serve me dinner, I told her that I was not hungry. My delusion was that she would accept that simple response without question. That was not to be the case; she wanted to know *why* I was not hungry. Different scenarios raced through my mind about her possible responses. I was concerned about how she might respond to the truth, but I bit the bullet and told it to her anyway. An animated lecture ensued. "You do not respect my hard work! All you think about is yourself!" And finally, the proverbial "If you like it so much at your mom's, then maybe you should go live with her!"

This incident had positive side effects. I learned the value of cutting the umbilical cord (at age thirty-three). Debbie, in recounting this story, says, "I came to the realization that if I wanted to keep Art home for dinner, I was going to have to learn how to prepare Mexican food." She did learn and does it very well.

Emotional expressions. Japanese consider emotional expressions in public inappropriate, whereas Hispanics are a very emotionally expressive people. This has not been an issue in our marriage. But I did notice it at the funeral service for Grandpa Komatsu.

It is interesting how we can observe the behavior of people from a different culture and not really see it. When family and friends were given the opportunity to pay their final respects to Grandpa Komatsu, they approached the coffin as family units and stood four to five feet away from the coffin. The heartache was obvious in their faces, and the tears flowed freely and silently. Then they would bow at the waist and move on. When it was our turn, Debbie and I walked up to the appropriate spot. I felt an overwhelming need to stand over Grandpa Kim, caress his head, and whisper my goodbyes. As I took one step forward away from the appropriate spot, I felt Debbie's firm grasp upon my left wrist. Immediately I knew that such an act was not appropriate. I restrained myself and stepped back. Like those who had gone before me, I, too, bowed at the waist and said my goodbyes from a distance.

Conclusion

Debbie and I were not the first multiracial marriage in our respective families, nor will we be the last. The growing ethnic population in America will surely reflect an increasing number of multiracial marriages. While adjustments are important in all marriages, in interracial marriages it is critical to learn how to adapt to the racial culture of your spouse. The stories of our lives in this chapter are not just entertaining; they illustrate how valuable it is to learn as much as you can about your spouse's culture and to be ready to accept his or her culture as much as possible.

As a pastor, I see the tremendous value of premarital counseling. However, I believe that we must change our approach to it. Current training for this ministry skill has been within the context of a monocultural couple. Pastors need to be equipped to understand multiracial relationships. We need to help couples get beyond the perceived physical differences between races that many outside the marriage focus on so that they can start making adjustments on important cultural issues, such as gender roles, finances, continuing education, parenting, extended family activities, etc. We need to help them understand the cultural programming that drives the behavior and beliefs of their prospective mate. Only in this way will they be able to reach compromises that are mutually agreeable.

Discussion Questions

1. Art's confusion about the name of Debbie's grandmother shows that we all can make mistakes when we get involved in someone else's culture. How can we handle such mistakes when we make them? How can we handle our mates when they make such mistakes?

2. What gender roles have you been taught in your culture? How might those gender expectations differ from those in other cultures? How would you handle these differences in an interracial marriage?

3. How has your culture affected your relationship with your parents? How might these expectations differ from those in other cultures? How would you handle these differences in an interracial marriage?

4. What are your cultural expectations concerning the expression of emotions? How might these expectations differ from those of other cultures? Can you marry someone who has a very different way of handling his or her emotions? Why or why not?

5. What are other potential cultural differences that can arise in an interracial marriage? Are there cultural differences that you cannot tolerate in a marriage? What are they?

Notes

1. *Sharon M. Lee*, Using the New Racial Categories in the 2000 Census *(Baltimore: The Annie E. Casey Foundation, 2001).*

2. *Ibid.*

3. *Nicolas Kanellos and Bryan Ryan, eds.,* Hispanic American Chronology *(New York: UXL, 1996), p. xiii.*

4. *"Heroes Abroad, Interned at Home," in* Time-Life Books History of the Second World War, *ed. Kenneth Winchester (New York: Prentice-Hall, 1989), 238.*

NINE

Mixed Blood:
I Am a Bridge

Randy Woodley

MIXED-BLOOD PEOPLE COME IN ALL SHADES, CULTURES, AND blood degrees. In my case, I am a mixed-blood Native American/European American. Whatever the combination of race, ethnicity, or nationality that comes together to create us mixed-blood folks, each has its own set of circumstances and brings with it different issues for us to experience. What all these combinations have in common is that they create people who may experience a great deal of difficulty knowing where to fit in. Sometimes even the most basic issues of life, like trying to figure out what to call yourself, can take many years to figure out. Here is my story.

I am Randy Woodley—or Ani-keetoowagi, to give you my Keetoowah (Cherokee) name. I received many traits from my forebears. Perhaps it was a genetic trait such as a wrinkle when I smile that was passed down from a fourth great-grandmother. Or perhaps it was some predilection to kindness, descended from a great-grandfather, a minister who asked God's blessings on all his generations. Of course, maybe I was handed down some bad things as well. Everything and everyone who went before me affects me today to some degree.

That may be a silly notion to some non-Indian Americans but not to most Native Americans. We do not make time distinctions about our identity. I have noticed that very few Americans really take stock of their lineage, regardless of whether it be traditions, cultural practices, or ethnic inheritances. Many Americans tend to believe that they can reinvent themselves in every new generation without regard to their past. But I am proud of my past, even though that kind of healthy pride did not come without a struggle.

I am a blend of Cherokee, Scottish, Irish, and English from both parents, and I know most of my family lines. This is the way God made me, and anything God makes is very good. Long ago, before the age of nine, I accepted my Cherokee identity as primary. Thinking of myself as primarily Cherokee

139

does not diminish my other bloodlines or relatives but rather it enhances them. This thinking is in sharp contrast to Christians who, in order to keep a bloodline "pure," have accepted that it was sinful to mix the races. Somewhere in our history, God's design of unity within diversity was lost. Yet Jesus himself was a prime example, for not only was his blood mixed with divinity and humanity; he had Jewish and Gentile progenitors. Many more of us are of mixed blood origin than we may realize.

In God's design, each race offers its own special beauty. Each culture brings new meaning to life. Each ethnic group displays the wonderful gifts with which the Creator has endowed them. Not that there is anything inherently wrong with homogenization or "sameness" in its rightful place. Yet homogenization can (and has) engendered efforts to dehumanize other people groups, which has eventually lead to genocide. This is what happened to my Keetoowah (Cherokee) people. It happened to my ancestors at the hands of the British, then the Americans, and it affects me directly.

Maternally, I am a descendent of Big Acorn, a Chickamaugan war chief who fought the Americans and was cited as one of the forty-two chiefs and leading men of the Cherokee Nation. Big Acorn (Gule-equah) signed the peace treaty of Holston in 1791 with the Americans. He was my third great-grandfather. Chief Big Acorn was a full-blood traditional who later became an Old Settler in Oklahoma, Indian Territory. His father, also a chief, was killed by the Americans in 1776 while defending his homeland from tyranny. But it has been a few generations on either side of my family since we had any full-blood traditionals. I pretty much look like a white guy—but I am not. I'm a mixed-blood Cherokee, and that is a good thing also.

People sometimes say things to me to me like "You don't really look like an Indian." When I hear this, I always wonder what might be an appropriate response. My gut reaction when I hear such statements is always the same. I think, *Is he calling my honesty into question?* or *Should I ask her if she wants to see my tribal identification?* I have also thought to myself, *Maybe it would provide shock therapy to tell them my grandma was raped by a white guy* (which is not true). But I usually say something like "I got my mom's lighter genes, but her two brothers are dark featured" or I just say nothing at all.

When we move outside of our comfortable circles, those of us who have light skin and more European features, and yet who still identify ourselves as Native Americans, are often made by the dominant society to feel that we have some explaining to do. We just do not seem to fit people's stereotypes of Indians. It has always been a wonder to me that after European Americans imposed 350 years of intentional assimilation, they are still surprised when every Indian does not match their Hollywood image of "Native American"!

Once a woman said to me, "That's funny, you don't look Indian." Before I could stop myself, I replied, "Yeah, genetics can be cruel." I fear she was terribly offended.

We should just be happy to be who God made us. If we try to hide it, we only deny the uniqueness that the Creator has bestowed upon each one of us. There are no accidents when it comes to our ethnicity (see Ephesians 2:10). On the other hand, we can choose how we will relate to the world. As Native Americans, we have very different values and traditions than does the dominant society.

Regardless of the shade of color an Indian may be, we generally have a very different worldview than the majority white culture. We process things differently. For example, whites tend to be more analytical, while Indians tend to accept the circumstances as they are at the moment. Native Americans are less time conscious than European Americans. In the dominant society, things are often divided into many categories, whereas First Nations folk tend to think more wholistically. To many white people, "the facts" seem to be very important, but Indians generally rely more on experience.

These are just a couple of examples, and I realize it is dangerous to generalize without long explanations, but from my perspective, I see hundreds of differences like these between my two people groups. I only mention them because it is especially easy for those in the majority culture to assume that the rest of society is like them. This is a common misconception that is applied often to Native Americans. Because we wear Levi jeans and live in stick frame homes, we are assumed to be like everyone else. Being surrounded by the dominant white culture, we understand this mistaken belief and we always have the option of trying to blend in or hold to our Indian ways.

Even in many mixed-blood families different siblings identify culturally in various ways. In my own birth family there are four siblings. All of us grew up in the same house, hearing the same stories from elders, sharing many of the same experiences, but only two of us strongly identify as Cherokee. I hear similar stories everywhere I go.

Will Rogers, the great American statesman and humorist (also a mixed-blood Cherokee), was once addressed by a statement similar to my experience, "But you look like a white man." With his unceasing wit, he replied, "I am an Indian, but I have enough white blood in me for you to question my honesty." Sometimes Will had a wit that stung like a bee through honey, yet one really does get tired of explaining oneself.

From a little child on, I have held within me a lot of anxiety about being a mixed-blood Cherokee/European. I was always proud of my heritage, but at the same time I sensed that I was supposed to be ashamed as well. (Most mixed bloods will understand that statement.) This type of social rejection can set a person up in life to have a chip on his or her shoulder or to express an inward self-hatred—or both.

I lived much of my early life in fear of rejection. I believe most Native Americans do to one degree or another, but rejection is especially an issue with mixed bloods. The expectancy to be rejected, formed through the history of European American men taking Indian women as domestic comforters and then rejecting their own progeny, is somehow woven deep into our DNA. Call it, if you will, the sins of the fathers passed on through the generations. But it is there and it is real and it hurts.

Rejection coming from the dominant society was one with which I was familiar, and I learned to live with it. Rejection from my own Native people—because I might not be "Indian enough" for them—was something I learned to handle much later. Even worse, being dubbed a "wannabe" is the highest form of insult. ("Wannabe" is a derogatory term applied to people who have no Indian blood but want to be thought of as truly Indian.) It took many years of exposing these hurts to Jesus through prayer, and waiting for confidence in him, before I could continue to pursue the path our Creator had laid out for me in my life and in my marriage.

I was a single dad when I married for the second time, following a divorce that most Christians would consider biblically valid. My first wife is Puerto Rican, and we have a beautiful Puerto Rican/Cherokee/white daughter, Leanna, who attends college in Chicago. After our divorce, I met my second wife, Edith.

In the fall of 1989 I began to hear about a woman in eastern Oklahoma who was the relative of a friend. As it turned out, she was not interested in dating anyone. She had just been through a Christian recovery program and was only interested in having a time of hearing from God alone. She assumed that a man was not a part of this picture.

Edith Engavo was raised on the Wind River Indian Reservation in central Wyoming. She was an enrolled Eastern Shoshone Indian, but her mother was a mixed-blood half Choctaw and half white from southeastern

Oklahoma. Edith had been attending an Indian college in eastern Oklahoma and had fallen on hard times. Like many young people on the reservation, she had been exposed to drugs and alcohol at an early age, and beyond that, she had experienced the pain of other traumas that no young girl should ever have to go through.

Things seemed only to become worse for her while she was away at college. One day she realized that she had become everything as an Indian that she hated. She decided to end it all and quietly locked herself in her dorm room and then slit her wrists. Fortunately, a concerned dorm worker decided to check on her and found her unconscious in a pool of blood. She was rushed to the hospital. She awoke strapped to a bed in the observation unit. Again, at the first chance, she tried to end it, using a lightbulb in the bathroom.

Following the advice of concerned friends, she finally agreed to go to a Teen Challenge program in Missouri. In her final week of the program, she accepted God's love for her in Jesus Christ. As she relates it, she kept telling God all the reasons why God should not love her, and God yet persistently and gently continued to whisper, "I made you and I love you." That meant that for the first time in her life she could feel God's love for her as an Indian. What freedom!

With her program nearly at an end and a new life ahead of her, she and the staff felt it was time for her to be discipled. She was given the option of attending the Walter Hoving Home for Girls in New York. For the next two years, Edith learned about God's Word and God's deep love for her, just as she was. God also gave her a desire to work with her Native American people in some capacity, though she did not know exactly in what form this might occur.

It was late September when I was given the word by one of Edith's cousins that she was coming to town to attend the State Fair in Oklahoma City. Knowing she was not interested in dating (neither was I at that time, for that matter), I asked her to go to church with me. Afterward, we stopped for a short coffee and ended up talking for about three hours. We found that we had much in common. That was the start of a good friendship.

Over the next several weeks, things developed. She was on one side of Oklahoma and I was on the other. It was obvious to both of us that God had arranged our meeting and had more plans for us together than either one of us had thought we might be ready for. I decided to take her to meet my uncle and aunt, who lived less than an hour from her in southeastern Oklahoma.

While we were driving around with my uncle, viewing his cattle and land, I stepped out to open and close a cattle gate. It was then that my Uncle Leonard popped the question for me. Trying to convince Edith on the merits of his nephew, he asked her if she were going to marry me. Later, when she shared the details of the conversation with me, I made the statement "That sounds like a good idea to me. How about you?" We were married December 23, 1989.

Along with Leanna, we now have another daughter, Skye, and two sons, Young and Redbird. We have a marriage built on love and trust, and God has blessed us beyond our dreams. I thank God for my little family every day as I pray for them. God truly gave to me much more than I had ever expected to receive. As a mixed-blood family, we have some interesting conversations, especially since one of my children and I have lighter skin color.

Outsiders asks questions to find out which ones in our family are the "real" Indians. Perhaps it is overcompensation or maybe just DNA, but it has also been noted by those who know us well that my light-skinned child and I in many ways take our "Indianness" more to heart. At any rate, we often have to think about our identity, whereas perhaps other Indians do not.

Not long after we were married, Edith and I began to minister together. Through the years, we have formed a number of ministries that have reached into the Indian community. One of Edith's favorite ministries was to young Indian mothers, teaching a class on parenting skills from a Christian perspective and making available baby items, such as diapers or formula. Each year, before Christmas, Edith would organize "Baby Day" in our community, and dozens of young mothers (many unwed) would come to get a bundle for their little ones.

Because of our inclusion of Indian culture in our ministry, we had to withstand much opposition from many of the established Indian churches. Basically, past missionaries had declared that most everything Indian was evil and could have no place in the church. Thus, the drum was replaced by the organ, the circle and arbor were replaced by square church buildings with steeples, and European-based Christian culture became the standard for Native Americans who chose to follow Christ. This is just one more thing we have to deal with concerning the church's racist past.

The kind of racism that our Native American people have had to suffer from the dominant culture is multilayered, like an onion. At first contact, we were considered "filthy savages." The now-famous military slogan "Nits make lice" was propagated by ranking army officers over whether or not they should also kill our women and children in military campaigns. In the "progressive" era of the last decade of the nineteenth century and into the twentieth century, the slogan that many Christians embraced was "Kill the Indian, save the man."

During all our history, Native women have been considered by many in the white society to be good enough for mating purposes. As a result, the first Indian/white mixed-blood generations began. The term "half-breed" was coined to refer to someone who was neither white nor Indian and who was not good enough for either society. At least this was the commonly held view among European Americans. Among most of our tribes, the mixing was of little concern, and many of the most powerful Indian leaders of the eighteenth and nineteenth centuries were considerably mixed in their bloodlines.

In all of this ugly history, the church has perhaps been even more culpable than the U.S. government. I have often defended the work of the missionaries as being "people of their time." But in my most honest thoughts, after having read the few missionary reformers among our people who tried to do it right, I recognize the fact that evangelical Christians acted toward my people as racists and allowed their hearts to be hardened against the leading of God's Holy Spirit and their ears to be closed to the voices of the prophets of their day.

Because of this particular history, Christian Indians were taught by missionaries not to question why they needed to reject their own sin-stained culture just to take on the white race's sin-stained culture. As a result, Edith was skeptical of the cultural aspects of our ministry when we were first married. She was eventually won over to contextual methods of ministry, in her words, "by the fruit of the ministry."[1]

The twist about all this was the role reversal. Edith had been raised on the reservation, and I was raised in both urban and rural areas. Yet her shame at being an Indian was much greater than mine. This shame drove her to want to be white in every way. For me, it was the opposite. I learned from every Indian elder I could how to be "more Indian," even from an early age.

My spiritual life began to blossom greatly after we were married. Through our identity as a mixed/Indian couple, the Creator began to show us many things about ourselves and others. God had always given me big dreams, but my own sense of inadequacy often blocked the way. Finally, I lived among traditional Indian culture. I arrived at a place that had been in my heart since childhood. This was a sacred place because I had always longed for it, and now my dream had become a living reality. Edith and I spent the first five years of our marriage in Oklahoma and then the following seven years pastoring a Native church in Nevada.

One of the greatest events that took place in our ministry in Nevada came out of a vision that God gave me concerning racial healing in our community, particularly between whites and Indians. It took place on October 31, 1997, and was called "Colors of the Kingdom: A Festival for Racial Reconciliation for Carson City and Beyond." A great number of people assisted in making the event a success, including staffers from Kings Kids, Youth With A Mission, and Larry Norman, the father of Christian rock. The event drew about eight hundred people and proved to be the largest interchurch gathering of its kind in our city's history. It was at this time that Edith and I began to realize that just by virtue of who God made us, we could have a natural role in reconciling people groups to one another. This was exciting, and in many ways it all made sense. This was perhaps God's intention all along.

Restoration is beginning to take place between Native and non-Native people in America. It is slow and awkward. But it is happening. One of the things that makes it so difficult is the humbling that is necessary if people are to really hear one another's stories. White people, who are generally more verbal and analytical, often have a hard time just listening. I have learned that until an oppressed people can direct their story to the right listening ears, they will continue to be frustrated.

To the European mind, knowledge is often perceived as power, and it is used to gain entrance into whatever arena you are dealing with. But most Indians are not interested in using knowledge in this way. It is covenant relationship that we are looking for. Our whole basis of thinking sometimes seems opposite to that of the European mind. Still, forgiveness is necessary for God to heal the breach. Being a mixed blood helps me be a bridge because I can cross over to understand both worlds.

Of the many reconciliation efforts Edith and I have experienced, perhaps the one that taught me the most about my identity as a mixed-blood person was the Cherokee Prayer Initiative (CPI).

As a follower of Jesus, I know we all have a responsibility to be reconcilers, but I could not forgive Gene Brooks that dreary day in late October. Gene, the leader of the CPI, had decided we should walk a mile and pray on Tatum Gap Road in North Carolina. This road was built by the U.S. government to force-march my Cherokee people to a concentration camp at Fort Butler in Andrews, North Carolina. After months in holding, they would be forced to walk to Oklahoma.

This road is the beginning of what has been called "The Trail of Tears" or "The Trail Where They Cried." I had a bad feeling about the whole thing. As I began to walk, taking the lead, my anger immediately began to rise against Gene for making us do this. As I walked ahead of everyone else in an effort to get this thing over with, I observed the sheer rock walls to my right and the steep drop-off on my left side. Although I kept a hurried pace, my steps continued to feel heavier.

I began to imagine the sense of hopelessness that those first Cherokees must have felt after being roused from their sleep, thinking that they were secure in their own homes. Whole families forced at bayonet point to start walking down this road, made to abandon everything they had. I thought of how I would feel, being made to walk this road in those conditions, with my wife and children. I am sure I would have considered trying to escape. Perhaps a man could have survived throwing himself down the mountainside, dodging all the bullets, and successfully making his escape. But no real man would abandon his family to an unknown fate. I contemplated the resolve it must have taken to stay, uncertain of what might lie ahead, feeling powerless, hopeless. I began to weep.

My weeping turned into deep sobs as I considered the fate of my people on this nearly abandoned road. I was walking in the very place where my ancestors may have trod. My sobs turned into cries of anguish, then into uncontrollable bellows of pain. Anger toward the CPI leader returned, and eventually I felt the full impact of hatred toward the whites for their cruelty.

As I neared the end of this agonizing walk, I saw the van and I tried to calm myself. The driver was a fellow team member, Edd Stovall. We had met only days prior but had immediately connected, and I had known somehow that we would become good friends. Edd was much older than me, and a genuinely nice fellow, but at that time I could not look him in the eye as my emotions continued to rage, because Edd was white.

I searched for a place to sit where hopefully I could be alone. Only then did I notice that somehow Edd had slipped into my hand a packet of peanut butter crackers. As I sat there, devoid of all feelings, my hands slowly fed the crackers into my mouth. I really did not even know if I were hungry or not, but I remembered that we had skipped lunch that day, so I ate.

Eventually the whole team completed the one-mile walk, and they began to gather for prayer. I stayed at the back of the group purposely, so that I would not be noticed and called on to pray. How could I pray? The last emotion I had felt was hatred. Everything after that was just numb. However, for all my efforts to remain inconspicuous, Gene called me forward to identify with the Cherokees in an act of reconciliation. Then he called a white man forward to stand in the gap and repent for this atrocity; it was Edd.

As Edd recounted the sins of his forebears against my ancestors and against me, I vowed to God, "I will not be hypocritical! I will not say that I forgive their sins, because I can't!" After Edd finished, there was silence as the group waited for me to speak, but I could not. I could not forgive. As we all just stood there in the quiet, I silently begged God to release me from the responsibility that had been thrust upon me. Even as a mixed blood, I wondered how I could be a bridge of reconciliation with this inability to forgive.

Then a simple thought rushed through my mind—*the crackers*. I realized that Edd had seen my pain as I was coming down the road, and he had offered the only thing he had: a packet of crackers. Then I began to remember some of the stories I had heard about the Trail of Tears. It was not called the Trail Where *We* Cried but rather the Trail Where *They* Cried.

Reports from non-Indian doctors, missionaries, and soldiers all confirm that our people suffered with great dignity as we buried our loved ones along that trail. Sometimes a man would have to carry his dead mother, wife, or child for half a day before he would be allowed to stop and bury his dead. In all this, the reports indicate that the Cherokees remained resolute in their vow to remain unbroken, and few tears were shed—on the outside.

Stories are also told of how in cities like Hopkinsville, Kentucky, white people lined the streets, screaming for the soldiers to stop the march. They tried to give Cherokee families clothing and food as we were marched through their streets. They cried for us, en masse, along the trail. Our death march was the trail where *they*—the white people—cried for *us*!

As I remembered all this, I looked into Edd's eyes and saw that same grief that many whites have felt before—grief for all that was done to our people. I recalled again how he had slipped the food into my hand, not expecting any thanks. I thought of how much Jesus had done for me and how I offend him daily. Only then was I able to look at Edd and see his heart. Only then was I able to finally forgive him and his ancestors and, yes, my own ancestors as well. Next, I asked for *his* forgiveness, for my hatred toward him and all whites. Inside I was able to release some of the old hatred I had stored up toward myself for having a mixed-blood identity. Finally, we joined hands and together petitioned God to forgive us all.

I learned much through that experience, but mostly I learned that true love and friendship, forgiveness, and even restitution can come through a simple pack of crackers if a person is willing to be a reconciler. Though I may not always welcome it, I am a mixed blood and, based on my understanding of Scripture, I am a bridge.[2]

Discussion Questions

1. Based on your reading, do you think it is healthy for a mixed-blood people to think of themselves as having a primary identity? Why or why not?

2. What are some of the identity issues for a mixed-blood person? How do these issues differ among siblings with darker and lighter skin colors?

3. How did you feel when you read the author's description of differences between Native American thinking and European American thinking?

4. Given the poor history between Native Americans and Christianity, do you believe the church has any kind of responsibility to help heal the wounds of Native Americans now? If so, how might this be done? If not, why not?

5. Do you agree with the author's argument that white people have a hard time listening to oppressed people? State your reasons why or why not.

Notes

1. *Contextual methods of ministry means the presentation of the gospel within the cultural context of the intended listener. This helps Christians to avoid the implication that the gospel pushes the cultural trappings of European Americans onto Native Americans.*

2. *For a more in-depth understanding of the issues explored in this chapter, see Randy Woodley,* Living in Color: Embracing God's Passion for Diversity *(Grand Rapids, Mich.: Chosen Books, 2001).*

❧ TEN ❧

Interracial Marriage:
An Asian American Christian Perspective
Bob and Jean Chin

WHY IS IT THAT IN THE CONTINENTAL UNITED STATES, ESPECIALLY among Christians, interracial marriages are frowned upon? How is it that in Hawaii interracial marriages are not only accepted but are the norm? Of course, a distaste for interracial marriage is not unique to stateside Christians. Still, it is amazing that Christians would have difficulty in this area, especially when the Bible records interracial marriages among God's people from Moses onward.

Asians, especially new immigrant Asians, consciously try to keep their ethnic identity and culture the same as they were in the country from which they came. For some Asians there is even resistance toward marrying someone from another Asian group, although this sort of marriage is generally preferred to marrying a non-Asian. The more generations that pass, the more willingness there is to allow marriage outside a person's own ethnic identity, especially if the potential partner is another Asian. Asians still like to be with other Asians because there is commonality in physical appearance, although there are differences in customs from one Asian ethnicity to another. Nevertheless, there is still, among new immigrant Asians, a pecking order as to which Asian ethnic group is superior to the others and a preference as to which of the Asian ethnic groups are best to marry.

What we will be doing in this chapter is making some observations from an Asian American perspective and looking at some of the dynamics that came into play with the marriage of Bob, a Chinese American, and Jean, his Anglo wife.

Bob and Jean's Story
I (Bob) was born and raised in the continental United States in a Chinese family. I was made very aware from an early age of my heritage and my part in carrying on that heritage. My upbringing, on a family and social level, centered on associating primarily with Chinese. The area we lived in was

150

primarily inhabited by Chinese people, so I began my education surrounded by other Chinese. In my early years, the only other large ethnic group nearby was Italian Americans. This changed, however, when our family moved just as I started high school. I then attended a large school with great racial diversity. I primarily associated with Asians as my best friends, and my study partners were Asians. I received Christ at an Asian church, where I socialized primarily with Asians. Because I participated in athletics, as well as various other school functions, I interacted with members of other ethnic groups and began to develop friendships with them as well.

When it came to opposite-sex relationships, I was made very aware that if I were to develop any special ties, they should be with Chinese girls. Therefore, all of my early dating was with Chinese girls. In fact, I had a Chinese girlfriend off and on for over seven years. I even planned on asking her to marry me, but I chickened out. Now it happened that on the day I was going to ask this Chinese girl to marry me, I met Jean, my bride-to-be. I met Jean at a streetcar stop while we were both waiting for a streetcar. I noticed that she was a new student at the college I was attending, and I started a conversation with her. What began as a friendship later developed into a romance. The only issue for Jean was my faith. Did I know Christ as my Lord and Savior?

I happened to meet my former Chinese girlfriend some time later. I told her about my feelings for Jean and said that I wanted to marry her. She responded by saying that if she dated outside her own ethnicity, her father would "kill" her. Such a response indicates the importance some Asian Americans place on maintaining one's ethnic identity.

Asian Americans are not unique in their desire to maintain their own ethnic culture. Yet there are elements in Asian culture that create unique challenges for those who enter into an interracial marriage that includes an Asian American. The purpose of this essay is to explore some of these challenges.

Han

As with my former girlfriend's parents, it was important to my family that I marry a Chinese girl. They wanted grandchildren who were *"Han,"* or pure Chinese. Han can be seen as the desire to maintain biological purity. The value of Han was communicated to me as a child when it was emphasized that social interactions that lead to close friendships should mostly be with other Chinese. At this point, let us recognize that every ethnicity believes its way is superior to any other. So it is with Asians as well. In fact, in my family's dialect, the Chinese are called the "golden people." There appears to be a similar type of ideology within most other Asian cultures as well. White notions of racial purity have led to violence and hatred for those who interracially marry. Han does not bring about such violence, yet pressure to maintain racial purity is often created by shame-based sanctions and the fear that one will dishonor his or her family.

Every culture has a way of measuring success, whether it is economic, educational, or social status. For Chinese specifically, and Asians in general, Han helps to shape how success can be measured. Han affects our understanding of success by making marriage, especially to the right person, an indicator of success—that right person being another Chinese or at least an Asian. This means that to the members of their families, Chinese in interracial marriages will be seen as less successful than other Chinese.

Fear of Mixed Children

I knew from the beginning that my parents would not be open to my marrying outside of our Chinese ethnicity. For a long time, I was even afraid to bring up the subject. Jean and I had been dating for several months, and still I did not tell my parents. I had a lot of mixed emotions as to when and how I might tell my parents of my intentions. I decided to have Jean meet my parents by asking them if she could come to dinner. I remember my two younger sisters watching every move Jean made at our dinner. I think they were surprised that she could use chopsticks. My parents were impressed by the fact that Jean ate what was served. However, it was not many days after her visit that my parents shared their thoughts and feelings regarding Jean. Initially, my parents reacted negatively to the idea of my marrying anyone who was not Chinese. It was not that they disliked Jean as a person (they thought she was a fine person); it was just that her "eyes did not slant the right way." I recall my mother saying that if I were to marry Jean, she would always introduce her as my wife and not as her daughter-in-law. They were also fearful that children born in this type of marriage would be considered "half-breeds" by society. My parents cited people they knew who were in mixed-marriage situations and had received discriminatory treatment. This kind of response is not unique to Asian culture; it applies to all monoethnic thinking. I believe that because of what my parents had experienced in their lives, they wanted to save me from any pain and social stigma that might follow. I also believe they wanted to "save face." They did not want to be embarrassed by having a daughter-in-law who was not

Chinese. Jean's parents had a similar viewpoint and concerns. Her mom stated that she "did not believe in the 'mixing' of the races."

Honoring Your Elders

Another value in Asian culture is that of honoring your elders. Often an elder of the family makes the decision for the whole family. This happened in my family. My maternal grandmother felt that Jean was a fine woman and that it would be okay for me to marry her. This broke the ice. My parents struggled over her approval because it set a precedent for the other children who would follow me. They wanted to keep our family's culture ethnically and socially intact.

In Asian culture, education is highly valued as well. Parents expect their children to go to college. Therefore, my father extracted the promise from me that I would graduate from college before getting married. As a "good" son, I honored my parent's request. I learned sometime later why my father had extracted this promise from me. My parents believed that between the time of this promise and the graduation date, Jean and I would break up. Nevertheless, when I received this conditional approval, I looked for the fastest way of graduating from college. I recall looking at my coursework, how many credits I had, and how many credits I needed to graduate. I graduated six months earlier than the time I had originally estimated for my father. Because I honored my father's request, my parents honored my decision. Because Jean honored my father's request, my parents accepted her as part of the family. My mother always introduces Jean as her daughter-in-law.

My parents came to love and respect Jean as a member of our family. When our two girls were teenagers, my grandmother from my father's side, Abak, came to live with us. She lived with us six and a half years until she died at 101 years old. Jean's loving care of Abak during that time really sealed her relationship with my parents as well as my entire family.

Blending Two Cultures

Deciding to marry is one thing, but living out that marriage together is another. As in all marriages, in an interracial marriage two people come together and they have differences. Being of different ethnicities adds to those differences. It is even more difficult if the two people have been raised in different countries. While Jean and I were both born and raised in the continental United States, we still learned early in our marriage how "Chinese" I was in my thinking and how much adapting we would both have to do to accommodate our respective cultures. Asians are raised in strict, often rigid and inflexible, homes. There are very clear guidelines as to behavior and expectations. Of course, this carried over into our marriage. I have an Anglo friend who married an Asian woman. His chief complaint was how inflexible his wife was and how, if he had the choice to marry over again, he would not marry an Asian.

One of our most difficult challenges as a couple came when our two girls were teenagers. Through their early years, we were in complete agreement on raising our children. However, we were both surprised when we got to the teenage years and found that we had strong disagreements about raising them. I wanted to "hold the girls tight." I wanted them to be home where I could see them as much as possible. Much of this desire originated within my Asian background. Jean's philosophy was to gradually give them more and more responsibility and freedom until they were entirely independent. We had a time of much heartache and tears. I would like to say that we came to a compromise, but we really never did. It was an area where neither of us could understand the philosophy of the other. By God's grace, we all made it through that time as a family!

Dealing with Discrimination

There is not only the accommodation around the cultural differences but also the stressors from outside the marriage—the looks and comments of others who disagree or who make disparaging remarks. I found it hard to keep quiet and not respond to the discrimination. However, I also felt badly for Jean and worried that she would be embarrassed to be with me. That was never the case. From talking with other Asians, I have found that they are generally more sensitive than their Anglo partners to discrimination when these situations arise.

As my parents had predicted, when our daughters went to church and school, they were teased and called "China dolls" and treated as different from the other children. This surprised me because the taunting came from children raised in Christian homes. However, when we moved into a predominantly Asian community, my daughters were accepted, and they largely identified with Asians. They even said that they were Chinese.

The Changing Cultural Climate

Asians who marry outside their ethnic identity seem to be more accepted into the mainstream of society today. The current cultural climate has made just about all aspects of Asian culture popular, including food, fashion, tattoos, and even films. For example, many non-Asians have Asian characters for a tattoo. Whether it is because Asians are seen as the "silent" minority or the "model" minority, the acceptance has been granted. My family was unusual in that just about all of my siblings and first cousins have married outside of their ethnic background. Within my family there is now an open acceptance of this diversity. It has also been my observation that when the child of an Asian marries outside his or her own ethnic group, it frees the other children who follow to do the same if they so choose.

Jean and I have been married for thirty-three years. We have lived mostly in cosmopolitan cities where we have been accepted as a couple. It took a few years before an ethnic Chinese church would call me to pastor. Of course, the church knew Jean was Anglo. Even so, some of the immigrant families had difficulty with our relationship because they felt it was wrong to send a message to their children that interracial marriage was permissible.

Some Cautions about "Intercultural" Marriages

Cultural, rather than racial, differences constitute the biggest hurdles for interracial couples. It is important to understand the norms and values of the culture of the person you are marrying. We hope that this chapter has provided some insight about Asian cultures in general as well as identified possible barriers that interracial couples with an Asian partner will have to overcome.

When we counsel couples considering interracial marriage, we emphasize that it is especially crucial to recognize the adjustment struggle they might have if one was born and spent his or her childhood in one country and the other spouse was born in another country. The cultural differences are greatest when, for example, one person was born and raised in Hong Kong and another was born and raised in the U.S. This is a problem even if both are ethnically Chinese. While the families might approve of this marriage, and while from outward appearances there would be no discrimination, since they are both Chinese, the difficulty will come in their relationship in blending two different cultures.

I believe our marriage has not only worked but has thrived because of the total commitment Jean and I have made to each other. Part of our commitment was demonstrated by trying to learn and understand our ethnic and cultural differences. I believe our lives have been enriched because of this. However, the biggest factor that helps our marriage thrive is our commitment to making Jesus Christ the Lord and center of our home. Looking back, Jean and I both know we made the right decision.

Discussion Questions

1. Why do you think that immigrant Asians are especially likely to try to maintain their own native culture?
2. Bob was raised in an environment where there were relatively few non-Asians. How does living in such an environment affect attitudes toward marrying outside one's race?
3. Why do you think Asians may be more sensitive to discrimination than whites in interracial unions? Do you think that the tendency for racial minorities to be more sensitive to discrimination than whites is true in other minority-majority pairings? Why or why not?
4. Do you think that the Chins are correct when they propose that individuals from different countries will have a more difficult adjustment to make in marriage than Americans from different races? Why or why not?
5. Are there elements of Asian cultures that the Chins did not address but that you think are important in an interracial marriage? What are they? How would you deal with such elements in an Asian/non-Asian marriage?

⚘ ELEVEN ⚘

Being Brave Enough to Love in Color

Olga Soler

SO, YOU ARE WHITE AND THINK YOU ARE IN LOVE WITH A PERSON of color. Perhaps you are intrigued, liking the otherness and difference that give you surprises on a daily basis. Maybe it is the look you like, the ethnic music, the food, or the way that person stands out in the crowd. That says some things about you, that you are adventurous, brave, and not too rigid in your own image of culture—all of which is good. You will need to keep those qualities and hone your racial awareness skills.

No one pays more attention to another person than someone who is in love. If you are in love with a multiracial person like myself, I might be able to pass on some wisdom. I can speak on this subject because I have the privilege of sharing genetic space with several bold races of people: Taino Indian, Sephardic Jew, African, French, and Moor. I know the blessing of cultural blending and the disaster of cultural clash from the perspective of a believer. You are in for many surprises, and a little homework is recommended. This essay will help you learn about racial history and cultural differences and will give you a few warnings about the repercussions of devious motivations for interracial love.

The Importance of Learning Racial History
I realize that every person carries baggage from the past, but the baggage of a persecuted minority is unique in many ways. We minorities have a history of suffering racial abuse at the hands of majority-group members. Yes, our ultimate identity as Christians is in Christ, but if you are part of the dominant culture, you may not see how important our racial identity is for us. It is more convenient for society if we forget who we racially are, but that is not good for us. Americans talk about unity in diversity, but there is still a racial hierarchy. In practice, true unity is a result of equality without racial hierarchy. If you want a pecking order, you cannot have unity or equality.

One would hope that the church would have some enlightenment on this subject, but it often mimics society. Sadly, in the area of racial prejudice, sometimes the church surpasses society. For example, Native people have had languages forbidden and names changed when we were evangelized because the languages were not "Christian." This is in direct disobedience to the Scripture that states that people of all nations are God's and that there is no language or speech in which God's testimony is not heard. Many terrible, bigoted things have been done to us in the name of Jesus that have wounded his great heart, and at times these things will cause anger to rise up within us.

Please do not take it personally when we express some of our anger. Try to understand us and guard against condescension. You must believe in the core of your being that we are not inferior to you. We are not children or substandard humanity, but we have been treated (and sometimes we still are) as if the dominant culture has all the answers and we have none. Do not make this same mistake.

You, as an individual, can do your part in the healing of your beloved of color. Whenever you can validate our suffering, confessing your ancestral or individual part in that suffering by acts of commission or omission, and whenever you comfort and support us racially, you will be doing the work of God. Sin does not just go away; it must be confessed and cleansed by the blood of Jesus. Then there can be reconciliation with God and people. Racial sin is no different. It lingers in the interactions of generation after generation, and it takes on many aberrant forms. It must be owned and confessed and purged. As a royal priesthood, all believers are called to be ministers of reconciliation (2 Corinthians 5:18; 1 Peter 2:5,9). When love compels you to cross over the racial divide, take up your priestly calling to mediate peace between your race and ours. Many of us are asking God for the power to forgive, but your repentance will facilitate our forgiveness.

My own personal racial history is made up of an unusual combination of races. I am pleased at being able to identify with many marginalized groups. I can sympathize with the wandering Jew and agonize over the centuries of persecution we Jews endured. I revel in my chosenness both as a descendant of Abraham by blood and as a descendant of Abraham by faith in Jesus. However, I have also borne the scorn of the term "Nigger" in the South and Midwest and the indignation of the term "Spick" in the North. Can you see how my multiracial emotional makeup can be such a dichotomy of shame and pride? Bigotry, reverse bigotry, and chauvinism lash out with anger and cruelty to inflict humiliation on its object of disdain. I have been that object. I hated it, and I have hated to see it happen to others. By God's grace, I have gleaned one benefit from it. It has helped me to see that people are not just equally valuable but equally sinful. You can help us silence past voices of shame. You can assist in building up what our experience has torn down.

If you love a person of color, you will also deal with adjustments to our personal history as well as our ethnic past. Sporting as rich a lineage as I do should enable me to walk proudly and richly through life. After much healing, by God's grace, I can do this, but the fact is that cultural clashes have also left many degrading scars. When I was growing up in the Bronx, New York, I only knew that I was Puerto Rican. We spoke Spanish, ate rice and beans, and danced to salsa music. When Indians were mentioned in our family, they were spoken of in condescending terms as poor, ignorant hill folk. We were Spaniards, I was told. Otherwise, there was silence. It was the racial pecking order in Puerto Rico that contributed the most to my family's hushed tones on race. The fact that Grandmother was black was never spoken of. My mother, who was fair skinned like her blue-eyed father, would comb my hair in the morning, cursing the fact that it was *pelo malo* (bad hair belonging to black people). She attributed my hair to Grandmother's side of the family, but if I ever said that Grandmother was black, my mother would deny the plain fact.

Mixed parentage has its blessings and curses. My own stability as a human being seemed to be lacking because of the cultural void I felt. To explore the truth, I would need tools that were not then available to me. Being raised in the South Bronx, I was well acquainted with the social problems of the day: racism, drug addiction, prostitution, domestic violence, superstition, crime, and alcoholism. A brake was applied to my own downward spiral by my acceptance into the High School of Performing Arts in Manhattan. I was told that I was the only freshman from the Bronx to be chosen that year out of five hundred applicants. But my Bronx experience was useless at that school. I felt the full impact of being a minority and found that silence was my best ally. My olive skin and thick brown curls were often mistaken for being of Semitic instead of Caribbean origin. The whites who "adopted" me would exhibit me like a trophy in their collection of forbidden cool. The Jewish boys I became infatuated with returned the admiration but would never take me home.

In my junior year I got tired of the silence and of feeling like I had to prove I was good enough to be in anyone's company. I decided to join a group of communist radicals who wanted Puerto Rican independence. I quit hanging out with light skins and wanted to only live the Latin way. When I first tried to join this group, they were suspicious of me. I did not act like a Rican and I had the light complexion of "the oppressor," as one sister vehemently reminded me. So again I had to prove myself, until I found myself in the middle of a bloody riot. I got out, I got high, and I went back to the theater. I thank God for the arts, which helped me to defuse some of that anger. But the real answer was in God alone.

I became a Christian and found roots for a new identity. Years into a more stable kind of life, I felt the need to look deeper into the past. In the foliage of my family tree, I discovered many things, both wonderful and terrible. In researching my roots, I discovered that only four generations separated me from Spain. The Spanish culture is ancient, fierce, and splendid. I found a Moor ancestor of nobility and three Sephardic Jews. Some of these had turned to Catholicism through persecution and others had turned for profit. No one said the past would be without its skeletons. I also discovered that three-quarters of my ancestors had intermarried with Taino Indians. Ironically, my relatives had always minimized the island Indians, but they were all over my genetic landscape. These Native islanders were rich in origins, having hailed from the highly civilized Andean Collas tribe, with whom the Incas consulted for their building projects. I had been led to believe indigenous people were ignorant savages with whom we had nothing to do. These were the Natives who met Columbus and who first received the brunt of European imperialism. I felt stunned, excited, relieved, and enraged by what I found.

It is important for white people who love us to understand that there is much about ourselves that may be hidden and that we must discover. The rainbow spectrum of human color in my own family (blond, blue-eyed cousins, dark Indian uncles, black grandmother, and everything in between) now made sense. Jesus says we must love others as we love ourselves. We must have an ego before we can humble it to love, and we must have a healthy view of our history before we can join with other histories peaceably.

Cultural Differences

Accepting cultural differences, rather than judging those differences, may lead you to a colorful and exciting friendship. For example, at the last indigenous conference I attended, I shared a room at the Marriott with a woman friend and a married couple. We all took care to behave with decorum and dress modestly, but still, there was a man in my room. What would your pastor say? The man in my room was a pastor. We may have been at the Marriott, but we were still camping out Indian-style. Suffice it to say, our social boundaries may not be the same as yours, and you might enjoy trying something beyond your own cultural comfort zone.

Cultures are different from each other. Some are more gregarious; others, more reserved. Some think collectively; others, independently. We may all be equal in the eyes of God, but that does not mean we are or should be the same. To whites, indigenous preoccupation with honor and gift giving and lack of consideration for time may not be profitable. Conversely, capitalists' time constraints are equally senseless to the indigenous way of thinking. Kosher practices may seem oppressive to the Christian, but to many Jews, they are part of their identity.

Even if there were no history of oppression to affect relations between Natives and Europeans, and between Christians and Jews, important adjustments would have to be made in order to get along. For example, I invited a white friend to my house for dinner, and my family was having a simple discussion. We were using our normal tones to emphasize our remarks. He thought we were having a heated argument. He did not know that some languages emphasize vowels and use a more rapid delivery, with more pronounced tones, than does English. This makes them sound like they are angry when in fact they are not. The expression of emotion and anger is a cultural shock for some that is difficult to surmount. Some Jewish humor involves a great deal of sarcasm. How do Gentiles receive that? Indians tend to listen more than they speak, and European Americans tend to speak more than they listen. Is there a right or wrong way to express one-self? These are big questions that must be discussed for honest interaction between potential mates with cultural differences. Communication styles are vital to good relations.

Normal urban life is enough to send some cultures into posttraumatic stress. For example, when Columbus came to the Caribbean and encountered the Taino Indians, he observed that they were happy and very generous.[1] He later said they would make good and intelligent servants.[2] After a while, the Spanish imported black slaves because the Tainos refused to work. I wonder why? They were later slaughtered. Now there are no more pure Tainos but only mixed bloods like myself. You can call us lazy if you like, but there are places in the Caribbean where people live to be older than one hundred. They do what they need to do to live and do not sweat the rest. They do not get stressed out. Do you want to tell them their way of life is wrong? Which would you choose: hard work and a midday siesta, producing a simple lifestyle with close relations, or constant nervous activity and endless deadlines, producing material wealth and superficial relationships you seldom have time to enjoy? "Welcome to America," you say. Do not say that so glibly if you love a person of this ethnicity. Remember, indigenous people were here first, and if we were making the rules, lots of things would be different.

If you are prepared to think outside your own cultural box and not be quick to judge people's behavior, you may do well in your mixed relationship. If you are inflexible, you will surely break under the strain of adapting to the new cultural differences.

Devious Motivations to "Love" Interracially

You must want to be with us for the right reasons. For instance, I heard two white, single brothers talking. They were complaining about their social life. One said to the other, "I don't even try to date white girls anymore. If you want someone who will submit, you need a black, Latin, or Oriental girl." It is truly a sad thing when a man's top priority in a mate is expected submission. It is sadder when you think that many Christians will read the above and not see the danger in it at all. When there is a hidden agenda of guilt, shame, control, or animosity, as there is when racism bonds with an attitude of masculine superiority, it goes to a whole new level of pain.

When the sin of racism combines with chauvinism, it gets particularly ugly. For example, when I married my ex-husband, he convinced me he was a believer. I soon discovered he was not. With tears I asked him why he would even think of courting a believing woman, knowing that it would hurt her to realize he had no spiritual interest. He said, "I knew a Christian would not divorce me and that she would submit." As a white male, he, too, felt his chances of dominance would be better with a woman of color. He had a lot of anger at women, people of color, and Christians (his former wife ran off with her minister). I bore the brunt of that anger.

If you want to marry out of your ethnicity, do everyone a favor. Make sure no anger, revenge, shame, or other negative emotions are driving your romance. I have seen lovely unions between people of different hues. Children born to these relationships are well adjusted, creative, and happy. But those tainted by their parents' devious baggage do not find peace as long as these issues remain. With few exceptions, these interracial relationships turn into terrible power struggles and become abusive. The children born to them are also terribly impacted. When they meet with prejudice outside the home, they need much support from within their home. If there is no peace to be found there, the tragedy of bigotry is amplified.

Conclusion

Where can your interracial relationship take you? It can take you to the glorious unknown beyond your racial confines, to the joy of knowing and loving someone different and remarkable like me. I can say I am remarkable because, despite the outside voices that have told me I am inferior, the voice of Messiah has told me the truth in my innermost being.

I am an indigenous black Jew. Your loved one may be indigenous, black, Jewish, or whatever. Enjoy the journey of discovery. I am as affectionate as a casique (Taino noble) and as philosophical or funny as a rabbi. I keep Jewish and Christian holidays. I speak the name of my Lord in Hebrew, Spanish, Taino, and French, and I can read the holy language of Hebrew. I can dance in African, salsa, and Israeli worship styles. I have learned from exploring Taino culture that God's arm is not shortened, that it can reach the most remote corners of the earth with the revelation of the Creator. (In Taino lore there were many signs of God's revelation. We even had a flood account in which the people who survived escaped in a giant coconut.) I am not ashamed of being tribal and believe community (kibbutz or Christian) is the way we should live. I do not care if they serve yautia or gefilte fish. What is yautia? It is a kind of root that is a staple of the Tainos. No, you cannot get it at the Jewish deli, but it is still kosher, and so are all the other wonderful things I cook and eat.

Interracial marriage can be a beautiful thing when two people recognize and appreciate each other as people and when their differences can be enjoyed and respected. This and other wonderful experiences await you if you are brave enough to love someone in color.

Discussion Questions

1. Are there aspects of other cultures that are attractive to you? What are they and why are they attractive?
2. Why do you think that the history of racial minorities is so important to them? Do you think that this history is also important to European Americans? Why or why not?

3. When is it healthy for a person of color to express his or her anger about racism to a white partner? Are there inappropriate ways that this anger can be expressed? If so, what are they? What are the best ways a white romantic partner might help a person of color deal with this anger?

4. How does our society shame people of color? How can a white romantic lover of a person of color help to overcome that shame?

5. All cultures have sinful aspects within them. How can we discern whether the actions or norms of a culture are sinful or merely different? How can we discern whether to accept cultural differences within another Christian or to confront them about a possible sinful practice?

Notes

1. *Kenneth F. Kiple and Kriemhild C. Ornelas, "After the Encounter: Disease and Demographics in the Lesser Antilles," in* The Age of European Expansion, *eds. Robert L. Paquette and Stanley L. Engerman (Gainesville, Fla.: University of Florida Press, 1996), 50–67.*

2. *Ibid.*

parenting issues

❦ TWELVE ❦

What If Our Children Date Interracially?

Michael O. and Joni M. Emerson

AFTER WE HAD TAUGHT A SUNDAY NIGHT DISCIPLESHIP CLASS AT our church, an Anglo woman came up to talk to us. The class was focusing on issues of race and religion, and the topic evidently got her thinking. Specifically, she told us—in a hushed tone—that she was increasingly concerned about her daughters, who were nearing dating age. Her concern (or as she expressed it, her fear) was that in our multiracial church her daughters might date boys of a different race.

"I just need to be blunt with you," she shared. "I hope you won't think less of me, but I need to talk to someone about this. I am worried, scared even, about my daughters dating interracially. To be honest, I have a ranking in my head. I am sort of okay with them dating a Hispanic man. It's harder for me if he is an Asian. And my biggest fear is if they date a black man. What will people think? What will they say? I shouldn't say this, but sometimes, in my weaker moments, I think about leaving this church, just to be safe."

It would be easy to dismiss this woman as a racist or as ignorant or as a weak Christian. She is none of these, in our opinion. We can benefit from her candor, her willingness to share honestly what many people think and feel but will not discuss.

Interracial dating concerns a great many people of all races, for many different reasons. Based on experience, we think it safe to say that it concerns even many of us who are quite sure it is a nonissue. In the powerful 1960s movie *Look Who's Coming to Dinner,* the progressive parents, who taught their daughter to love and respect all people and that color does not determine a person's worth, suddenly find that when their daughter brings home the man she is dating and wants to marry—a black man (played by Sidney Poitier)—they are not as open as they thought. It is a great good to love and respect everyone (Christians are commanded to do so), but when that principle leads to interracial dating and the possibility of interracial marriage, people are often surprised by their own negative reaction.

To fully understand how we think and feel about such issues, it is necessary to separate two important components: (1) our own position on the issue, and (2) the position of important others, such as relatives and the larger society. Because we live within a social network of others, what others think is of much importance for our own reactions.

We have four children, all Anglos like us. By conscious choice, we live in a neighborhood that is 80 percent non-Anglo (about 30 percent black, 25 percent Hispanic, and 25 percent Asian). Our children attend the local school, which is also 80 percent non-Anglo. Our church has people from thirty different nations in it, with all the racial groups represented. The racial mix in the places where we spend most of our time translates into a high probability that at least some, if not all, of our children will date interracially. What do we think of this?

We have at least two sides to this answer. Because we are committed to living interracially and having our children grow up in such environments, the thought of their dating interracially is a natural and positive extension to our commitment. From this perspective, we would be somewhat disappointed if they did not date interracially. Because the probability is so low for them all to date people of their same race by accident, if they did date whites only, it would mean that race still matters to them and that a key wall God told us to knock down through his Son still will be standing.

But there is another extremely important side to our answer. Race is so very real and so influential in so many areas of American life that we have to wonder. What consequences will there be for our children to date across racial lines? What barriers and struggles will they face? Will we be equipped and prepared to help them with those struggles? Can we really help them, given that we ourselves are not in a mixed-race marriage and never interracially dated? Can we truly understand the conflicts that will arise? If they marry, where will they live? Where will they go to church? In what culture or cultures will they raise their children? If grandparents stop talking to our interracially dating child and us, are we ready to face the rejection and family disruption?

Family reactions in such situations are always important, for both our children and their future spouses. Will our extended families eventually accept interracial dating, or will they reject us all together? After all, dating and marrying across racial lines will change the way the family looks. To be perfectly honest, it has taken us a long time to adjust to living contrary to the way we grew up (only around whites), and we can only imagine how long it will take and how tumultuous a ride it will be for our extended families to embrace this change.

In each of our extended families, there is currently only one interracial relationship. On one side of the family, a woman dated and had children with a man of another race. This woman, an aunt, is never mentioned in family gatherings, does not have any photographs in family houses, and has essentially disappeared from all family life. We can safely conclude either that she rejected the family or that the family rejected her. We think it is some of both, but it is hard to know for sure because no one will talk about her.

On the other side of our extended family, the lone interracial relationship caused the family great concern even during the courtship period, as the parents thought of the tremendous difficulties this couple would face. The couple eventually got married, with the parents' blessing. It was a difficult adjustment for the extended family, to be sure, but over time they and their marriage became accepted.

We tell you about these two cases to say that we have seen firsthand that interracial dating and marriage cause a family to examine itself, often split people into supportive and oppositional camps, and place stress on the interracial couple. No matter what we think as the parents, this will likely be the reality.

As our children move into dating ages, we are aware that race is very real and has profound influences for life in our American culture. Those influences make dating and marrying across race much more difficult than marrying within one's own race. But easiness, difficulty, simplicity, or complexity are not the issues on which to focus. God calls us as Christians to live, work, serve, and be together. That is our witness to the world.

We, as so many Christian parents, teach our children to come back to God's Word. As we counsel our dating children, we shall remind them that what God has brought together no one is to put apart. The way our children have been raised will make them fluent in a variety of cultures. But society, especially important loved ones in the extended family, will still react negatively to interracial dating and marriage. Our children then will learn, in a profound way, the difficulty of making one's own choices while living in a social world. If they make the choice to date interracially, they will face rejection by some. If they do not date interracially, they may lose out on a special someone, perhaps even the one God has chosen for them.

Such issues are complex; by their very nature they provide no easy answer. But therein lies the beauty. What a tremendous time to lean on God, to need

God, to search God's heart, to be in communion with God, seeking God's will! These are the very things for which we were created. Now that is living!

Discussion Questions

1. Can a person oppose interracial dating for his or her children without being a racist? Why or why not?
2. The Emersons contend that if none of their children interracially date, given their racially integrated lifestyle, they will have failed to teach them certain important lessons about race. Do you agree or disagree? Why or why not?
3. What is the best reason you can think of for discouraging your child from interracially dating?
4. What is the best reason you can think of for encouraging your child to interracially date?
5. Which of these reasons is the more powerful for you? Why?

§ THIRTEEN §

Do I Have Your Blessing?
Fred Prinzing

AWAKENED BY THE RINGING OF THE TELEPHONE AT 5:00 ON SUNDAY morning, I was certain a member of my congregation was experiencing a crisis. The call, however, brought a unique crisis to my own life. Our son, Mark, was calling from England, where he was stationed in the United States Marine Corps. After we exchanged greetings, he went directly to the purpose of his call. "I'm getting married," he informed us. "I want to know if I have your blessing."

Although still not fully awake, I responded without hesitation, "How can I give my blessing? I've never even met the girl!"

I am not sure which part of Mark's question surprised me more: the fact that he was planning to get married or the fact that he was asking for our blessing. He was not asking for our permission; he was asking for our blessing. My family was not in the practice of asking for blessings. As far as I can recall, I had never been asked for a blessing until that telephone conversation.

My parents had grown up in Chicago and attended the same church. My mother, the youngest of twelve children, was born to parents of Scottish descent. My father, the oldest of ten children, grew up in the home of his German parents. Not only did my parents have an interethnic marriage, but in fact three of my mother's nephews married three of my father's sisters!

I was reared in a strong Christian home. Even though my brothers and sisters and I all lived at home until we were married, we had more social mobility than our parents had. This was partially the result of four of us attending college and my brothers serving in the military. All five siblings, however, married someone from our local church or the evangelical colleges we attended. Choosing a marriage partner was not discussed in our home. We knew it was expected that we would marry within our own group.

My mother had often said that when it came to choosing friends, "Birds of a feather flock together." She meant that people who came from different religious, racial, cultural, and economic backgrounds were not marital prospects. They were not "our kind of people."

My parents' philosophy regarding choosing a mate became my philosophy. As far as I can remember, we never had a discussion with our own children about the kind of persons they should marry. Intermarriage, especially interracial marriage, was not only unacceptable; it was unthinkable.

That is why Mark's telephone call from England in 1981 was such a shock. When I commented that we had not met the young woman, his response was "It's the girl I told you I was dating when you visited me last Christmas." I remembered that conversation. In fact, Mark had told each of us (his mother, sister, brother, and me) separately, "I'm dating a girl here. Let's just say Granddad wouldn't approve." We all knew what he meant. His girlfriend was black.

Since it was inconceivable that Mark would seriously consider marrying someone of another race, we had dismissed the relationship as simply a fling. Mark had assured us that the relationship would be over by the time he returned to the States for a furlough in three months.

That early Sunday morning call helped us realize that it was not a fling but the real thing. "We're getting married in June!" he stated emphatically.

As our conversation concluded, he asked me a pointed question that still rings in my ears: "What's the problem? She's a Christian."

Was there a problem? If so, whose problem was it? Was the problem society's or ours? There was no question that the possibility of our son marrying interracially created a problem in our lives.

After we got over the initial shock, my wife, Anita, and I went on an emotional roller coaster. We desperately needed information and support. A library search on the subject of interracial marriage brought little material other than a few magazine articles about marriages of famous athletes and entertainers.

Who could we talk to? What would we say? How would we introduce the subject? Did we want approval or sympathy?

Anita decided to share her secret with a friend whose son was engaged to an Asian American girl to get some insight into our struggle. "I know your son is engaged to someone of a different race. How are you handling the situation?" she asked.

Her friend informed her she was doing okay. "At least she isn't black!" That ended their discussion.

The topic of interracial marriage was still considered one of the last taboos. *Newsweek* magazine addressed the issue ten years after Mark and Martha started dating.[1] Their outdoor wedding took place in rural Louisiana in the heat of summer in 1982. It was the longest day of my life.

Within the next year, the unthinkable happened again. Our daughter, Debra, informed us that she was getting married to a man she had met at a college friend's wedding. He also was African American.

We were confused. What had we as parents done wrong? Should we have discussed the problem of interracial marriage before our children chose marriage partners? During this period of introspection and analysis, we began to search for answers. We had prayed that God would guide our children in their choices of mates. Could this possibly be God's will? These and other questions seemed to go unanswered.

One night after I went to bed, Anita was reading her Bible, searching for some resolution to her struggle with resistance to interracial marriage. She cried out to God, "I need something to hang on to. Please help me to accept my children's decisions and have peace about them." Just then God directed her eyes to a passage in the book of Colossians.

> You are living a brand new kind of life that is continually learning more and more of what is right, and trying constantly to be more and more like Christ who created this new life within you. In this new life one's nationality or race or education or social position is unimportant; such things mean nothing. Whether a person has Christ is what matters, and he is equally available to all. (Colossians 3:10-11, TLB)

If God approved, then we needed to approve. Theoretical approval proved to be much easier than personal acceptance, however. Personal acceptance was a longer, more difficult process.

I was much less emotional about my personal struggle, but not necessarily more accepting. Could we give our blessing to this marriage? Before coming to a decision, it would be important to examine the issues of intermarriage, our personal viewpoints, and how we were going to respond to the situation.

Understanding the Issues

I decided to research the subject from several perspectives: theological, social, psychological, anthropological, and historical. I came to the conclusion that none of these areas presented insurmountable obstacles to interracial marriage. The biggest obstacles were personal prejudice and racism.

Although these terms are related, they are not synonymous. All of us tend to exhibit some forms of prejudice. It simply means "prejudging," or as someone has said, "Prejudice is being down on what we are not up on." Prejudice can be changed through education, experience, and exposure.

Racism, on the other hand, is sin. It is a condition of the soul that believes one person or group is superior to another because of skin color, physical features, or heritage.

Several people encouraged me to speak and write about the subject. A friend cautioned me, however, not to write about the topic until at least five years after we had first faced the issue.

Some time later I was asked to write on the subject in our denominational magazine. The article, "It's Still a Black-White Issue," created quite a mixed response, the vast majority favorable.[2] One man, however, expressed a negative reaction to his pastor. "I could see how it might happen to them once. But how could it happen twice?"

As a result of that article, people from across the country contacted us about their struggles with interracial dating and marriage. Most of the inquiries came from parents of children who were in interracial relationships.

Anita and I were urged to write a book on the subject. Although the book, *Mixed Messages,* was written for anyone interested in the subject, it was basically written from parents to parents.[3]

It is important that parents determine what constitutes an acceptable marriage before they grant their blessing upon their children's marriages. Since all marriages are mixed, the question is *how* different marriage partners can be and still be acceptable. Marriages with the fewest differences, at least genetically, would be between siblings or close relatives. Since this is illegal, other criteria for blessing children's marriages need to be considered.

"Interracial marriage" is the most emotive description, but it is not the most helpful categorization of mixed marriage. A dictionary definition of race is "Any of the different varieties or populations of human beings distinguished by physical traits such as hair, eyes, skin color, body shape, etc. Traditionally the three primary divisions are Caucasoid, Negroid and Mongoloid."[4]

Newsweek magazine printed a special issue in September 2000, "Redefining Race in America." Jon Meacham reports that in the 2000 Census there are thirty categories for race, including eleven subcategories under "Hispanic ethnicity."[5] Another article in that same issue suggests that Americans are redrawing the color lines—redefining the meaning of race. It is not just about black and white, since the nuances of brown and yellow and red mean "more—and less—than ever."[6] It becomes increasingly difficult, scientifically or socially, to make distinctions based on traditional definitions of race. Although there appear to be many differences among people, evidence seems to indicate that there is only one race: the human race.[7]

The term that is emerging to describe intermarriage is "intergroup marriages." Differences among groups can be distinguished in many ways. After reading material on the subject and discussing it with those interested in the topic, I believe there are four primary categories of intergroup marriages. It is helpful for parents and other interested parties to understand these distinctions.

Cross-color. Of all the differences among people, color is the easiest to identify. Both in the white community and in communities of color, a value is placed on pigmentation. When our son married an African American woman, we frequently were asked, "How dark is she?" When our grandchildren were born, again we were asked that question.

In some communities of color, skin color is understood by the following saying: "If you are yellow, you are mellow; if you are brown, stick around; if you are white, you are all right; if you are black, get back." Think of the ways we use the terms black and white in conversation. Black is often associated with something dirty, questionable, or illegal—black market, blackhead, black sheep, blackmail, black heart, black eye, blackball, etc. White, on the other hand, describes something pure, lovely, and clean—snow white, white collar, white knight, etc.

The browning of America is taking place. Projections indicate that shortly after 2050, whites will be in the minority. In many metropolitan areas, whites are already in the minority.[8]

The younger generation is not nearly as color-conscious as their parents and grandparents. My five-year-old granddaughter and I were coloring pictures. I wanted to ask about her views on color. "Honey, what color is Papa?" I asked.

"White," she replied.

"What color are you?" (Her mother is black and her father is white).

"Black and white," she answered.

"Which color is your favorite?"

Without hesitation, she answered, "Pink and purple!" She never understood my question. My granddaughter has grown up in neighborhoods of color and has gone to schools where there are many differences but few distinctions. Color continues to matter in our society, but its importance has changed.

Cross-culture. A white couple in a church I pastored adopted a Korean girl when she was six months old. One day when she was a teenager they were discussing the subject of marriage partners. The girl surprised her parents when she said, "I'd never marry a Korean!" As their daughter wasn't prejudiced against Koreans, her parents wondered why she would make such a statement. When questioned, the girl explained, "I'm not Korean; I'm American." Her statement did not refer to her country of origin but to cultural differences. Living in America almost all of her life impacted her views on such areas as time, finances, role expectations, extended family, etc. Her views were quite different than they would have been had she been raised in Korea.

Cross-class. One phenomenon of black-white marriages is the increase in the number of black women who marry white men. It is estimated that 32 percent of twenty- to twenty-nine-year old black men—the prime marrying age—are in prison, in pretrial detention, or on parole or probation. Furthermore, the number of black women attending colleges is greatly outpacing the number of black men (nearly two to one). It has also been estimated that two-thirds of black professionals are women. So more and more black women say they feel they have little choice but to marry outside of their race.[9]

Most parents (no matter what group they are part of) do not want their children to "marry down." Parents prefer that their children marry someone with the same or greater professional, financial, educational, or social standing.

Cross-convictions. One of the most debated and most volatile types of intergroup marriage is the one known as interfaith marriage. As intergroup marriages increase, the likelihood of interfaith marriages will also increase, especially among those from different countries of origin.

Although cross-conviction is a broader category than simply religious beliefs, differing religious convictions are the primary source of tension. Some religions strongly discourage, or even forbid, interfaith marriage because it means compromising or altering an individual's core values.

It should be recognized that there are different degrees of convictions: strong, indifferent, nominal, etc. Even a person who is an atheist or an agnostic may have strong beliefs about his or her views.

The major struggle for parents of most intergroup couples usually comes before marriage. The most difficult struggle in an interfaith relationship usually comes when it is time to train children in the area of beliefs.

As I reflect on the four primary classifications, I realize all of them have unique tensions. Our son's marriage is cross-color, cross-culture, and cross-class, while our daughter's marriage is primarily cross-color. I have come to the place where I can personally accept cross-color, cross-culture, and cross-class marriages, but as an evangelical Christian, I cannot accept a cross-conviction marriage if it means compromising or denying one's core beliefs.

Even as I struggle with the implications of my own convictions, I strongly believe a child does not need his or her parents' permission to get married unless he or she is legally underage. I also am committed to doing everything I can to support the marriage after the wedding ceremony takes place.

Differing Viewpoints

As you wrestle with the realities of intergroup marriage, you not only need to identify the different categories; you also must identify your personal viewpoint. As a parent or other significant person connected to those in the relationship, can you identify your personal viewpoint toward the subject of why you believe what you do? There are four basic viewpoints: two favorable and two unfavorable.

Approval as normal and healthy. Various groups and individuals promote intermarriage, especially among races, as not only a positive step but also as an essential dynamic in achieving unity among humankind.

From a biological perspective, some people believe that all living organisms—plants, animals, and humans—are strengthened by mixing different strains within the species. According to this viewpoint, both cross-color and cross-cultural marriages produce stronger and healthier offspring.

Others view intermarriage as the only way to achieve equality among the races. Religious groups, such as Baha'is and Sun Myung Moon's Unification Church, believe intermarriage is a step toward achieving human oneness. Sun Myung Moon states, "The quickest way to unite mankind into one family is by intermarriage of the different races."[10]

Approval as special and unique. Those who espouse this viewpoint believe that a marriage that has many characteristics in common has a better chance of success. It is preferable that partners have similar backgrounds, social standing, and racial identities. However, when a couple are in love and willing to work hard to make their marriage succeed, they deserve to be supported and encouraged.

The Reverend C. Eugene Askew reflects this attitude in an article, "Should My Daughter Marry a Negro?" "I hope [my children] will seek suitable dates and/or marriage partners among young people most like themselves religiously, culturally, economically, and racially. But if our children and circumstances decide otherwise, my wife and I hereby pledge love and understanding to them, their in-laws, their friends, and grandchildren."[11]

Those who hold this view recognize there will be many pressures and problems for those who choose this path. When couples make this choice, they are to be respected and admired for their willingness to go against conformity in marital relationships.

Disapproval as questionable and problematic. Individuals holding this viewpoint do not do so because they believe in the biological inferiority of any specific race. Their viewpoint is based on sociological and/or cultural dynamics. Many such forces may prevent or undermine a mixed marriage.

For instance, even though the couple may seem to be compatible and are personally willing to face opposition, what about their children? They will become innocent victims of racial slurs, stereotypes, and mistaken identity. Others will question the sincerity or motivation of intermarried couples. The bottom line for individuals holding this viewpoint is their belief that, however sincere the couple's intentions are, the cost is too great.

Disapproval as neurotic and destructive. People of differing philosophies and beliefs hold this viewpoint. They agree on one thing: mixed marriage is wrong. Some believe mixing the races weakens individuals physically. White supremacists, such as the KKK and skinheads, want to protect the notion of

TABLE 4: Viewpoints Regarding Intergroup Marriage	
APPROVAL	
Normal and Healthy Variety of characteristics is not only acceptable but highly desirable. The widest diversity possible makes for the best long-run outcome of the species.	**Special and Unique** While it is best to have as many commonalities as possible, diversity can be worked with. True love, commitment, and hard work can make the difference.
DISAPPROVAL	
Questionable and Problematic While all races are equally viable, differences may provide obstacles difficult or impossible to overcome. However noble the intentions or sincere the efforts, the cost inevitably will outweigh the benefit.	**Neurotic and Destructive** Mixed marriage is simply wrong under all circumstances. God is against it and it is harmful to the race or society in general.

racial purity. Others, including minority groups, are fearful that mixed marriages will eventually lead to loss of racial identity or cultural extinction.

Many people object to mixed marriage for biblical or theological reasons. Dallas Jackson, author of *Whom Has God Joined Together?* writes, "I want to emphatically state that there is not one scripture to support interracial marriage."[12] He concludes his discussion with "Furthermore, I want to state that miscegenation is genocide; it is annihilation through assimilation."[13]

After you understand the four primary categories of intergroup marriages (color, culture, class, convictions) and have identified your viewpoint, you need to decide how you will personally respond to those concerned about mixed marriages. Information without demonstration leads to frustration.

It is one thing to speak theoretically about a concept, an idea, or an issue; it is quite another matter when the decision is personal. Intergroup marriages are not going to decrease in the coming years; in fact, all indicators point to a dramatic acceleration in this phenomenon. Most of us, if not all, need to decide how we will respond. In the next few years, a relative or friend will most likely be contemplating intermarriage.

Different Responses

Although you cannot choose your children's or grandchildren's partners, you can decide how you will respond to their choices. Responses may differ, depending on your relationship with the couple, but your responses should be consistent with your beliefs, values, and viewpoints. There are four groups of people to whom you will need to respond: society, family and friends, your child, and the couple.

Response to society: ignore or interact? What does society think about intergroup marriages? Because there are so many variables and conditions, a simple answer is difficult. Our age, education, economic status, ethnicity, and beliefs condition us all. In addition, our experiences and exposure to intergroup couples, especially those of differing colors, shape our views.

Although a growing majority of the U.S. population may accept intergroup couples, many groups and individuals do not personally approve of such relationships. Expressions such as "Not with my daughter you don't" and "But just don't marry one" still reflect the feelings of a large segment of society. In some areas of our country where there is greater diversity in the population, acceptance of mixed marriages tends to be greater. These areas are often located in metropolitan centers where universities or military bases provide greater exposure to intergroup relationships.

None of us can predict or control the reaction people will have to the presence of intergroup couples. However, those who are involved in an intergroup relationship can decide how they will respond to people's attitudes or comments. Unsolicited comments may come from complete strangers. For example, while taking care of our grandchildren, we have had people stop us while we were shopping and comment about the color of our grandchildren.

Basically, there are two ways to respond to societal attitudes to intergroup relationships. The first approach is simply to ignore the comments. Most people who make negative comments, racial slurs, or jokes have already made up their minds. Society generally questions the motives of anyone who marries a person from a totally different background. The assumption is that people who marry outside of their own group do so because of rebellion, because they want to prove a point, or because they have a poor self-image. Those who choose to ignore negative comments believe that people who hold these views do so because they are ignorant. (By the way, the term ignore follows the word ignorance in the dictionary.) The problem with ignoring negative and derogatory remarks is that silence perpetuates the negative stereotype and also gives people the impression that you agree.

A different response to comments is one of interaction. Although some people might need to be challenged when they make unwelcome remarks, it is usually possible to interact with people in a nonthreatening manner. Much of an individual's prejudice is based on negative experiences or a lack of exposure or education. Asking questions and listening helps people express their fears about intergroup dating and marrying. Usually negative viewpoints on this subject are not based on logic or facts but come from tradition and emotions. Any comment, whether positive or negative, provides an opportunity to share your story of how you have grown and benefited from having a family member from a different background. Societal views will not change overnight but likely will be altered one person at a time.

Response to family and friends: proud or ashamed? One of the first questions from a family member about our children's mixed marriages was "Why are your children trying to hurt you?" Although we never attributed our children's motives to negative or bitter attitudes, this was obviously a concern of other members of our family.

Who do we tell and how do we tell others about our children's mates? These and many other questions Anita and I often discussed. Would we tell people our child's fiancé was black, or should we wait until someone made a comment?

If we informed people that our children were marrying persons of color, did we want their sympathy or their support? During the dating stage of our son's relationship, I remember watching the 1967 movie *Guess Who's Coming to Dinner?* Prior to their dating, I had watched that same movie and thought it was hilarious. Watching the film a second time did not seem nearly as funny. Now I identified with the parents of the middle-class white child and the difficult decisions they faced.

A friend of Anita's shared a comment her daughter had made upon hearing of the mixed marriages in our family: "How did they raise their children so that they felt open to an interracial relationship?" That comment, along with other positive ones, helped us become proud of our children. We began to display pictures of the married couples in our home and carry photos in our wallets. Instead of feeling we had done something wrong, we started believing we must have done something right.

Response to our children: communication or condemnation? The Bible speaks clearly about children being obedient to their parents. When a child comes of age and chooses to become independent, the relationship with the parents changes. Parents are no longer responsible for the child but to the child. While children live at home, parents are primarily responsible for giving direction. When children leave home, the parents' role changes to one of counseling.

During the dating years, parents should actively screen all of their children's relationships, both male and female. Parents should identify their children's friends who are dishonest, immoral, or lack integrity. Then parents should share their observations with their children and take appropriate actions.

No matter how opinions and feelings are conveyed, the approach should be one of communication, not condemnation. This is achieved by parents listening as well as talking and by children listening as well as talking. If a child senses that a parent is censuring or forbidding a mixed relationship, the result often is that the child goes underground. The forbidden relationship may continue and sometimes intensify under a cloak of secrecy.

Response to the married couple: support or avoidance? We first met our daughter-in-law the night before the wedding. She and our son, both serving in the U.S. military, were stationed in England. The wedding took place at her home in Louisiana, twenty-five hundred miles from where we lived.

On the other hand, we got to know our son-in-law during the two years he and our daughter dated. During that period of time, we exchanged letters and spent holidays together. Needless to say, the time spent together before the wedding provided all of us with an opportunity to process the issues and implications of their intended intergroup marriage.

Regardless of our level of comfort, once the weddings took place, we took the initiative to celebrate the differences. It takes hard work to create positive relationships with couples whose backgrounds are different. Anita invested many hours in sending letters, gifts, and cards. Whenever our daughter-in-law or son-in-law visited our home, she prepared her or his favorite foods. You can choose to avoid nurturing the relationship because of misunderstandings and past hurts or you can work toward becoming encouraging and supportive.

In our retirement years we chose to relocate from our home in the Midwest to the Pacific Northwest to live close to our four grandchildren. Although we still struggle with differing cultural values and traditions, we also have been enriched by the infusion of new ways of doing things.

We decided to work hard at maintaining, not burning, the bridges that connect our relationships. By God's grace, we are determined to give our children and their mates our continual blessing, even as they have blessed us.

Discussion Questions

1. How important is it to get a parent's blessing before marrying? How is gaining a parent's blessing different from gaining a parent's acceptance?
2. Four types of intergroup marriages (cross-color, cross-cultural, cross-class, cross-convictions) were discussed in this chapter. Which type is the easiest for prospective marital partners to deal with? Which is the hardest? Why?
3. Four different viewpoints (normal and healthy, special and unique, questionable and problematic, neurotic and destructive) were outlined in the chapter. Honestly, which viewpoint is the closest to your own outlook?
4. The chapter discussed the need to respond to society, family and friends, children, and the married couple. If your children were interracially married, which of these groups do you think it would be easiest to respond to? Which would be hardest? Why?
5. What can you do to nurture your relationship with your child's spouse in an intergroup marriage?

Notes

1. *Jack Kroll, "Tackling a Taboo,"* Newsweek, *June 10, 1991, 44.*

2. *Fred Prinzing, "It's Still a Black-White Issue,"* The Standard, *June 1987, 4–9.*

3. *Anita and Fred Prinzing,* Mixed Messages *(Chicago: Moody Press, 1991).*

4. Webster's New World Dictionary, *3d college ed., s.v. "race."*

5. *Jon Meacham, "The New Face of Race,"* Newsweek, *September 18, 2000, 60.*

6. *Ibid., 59.*

7. *Boyce Rensberger, "Roaming the World, Thriving on Diversity,"* St. Paul (Minnesota) Pioneer Press, *January 8, 1995, 16A.*

8. *Meacham, "New Face of Race," 60.*

9. *Steven A. Holmes, "Marriages between Blacks and Whites Increase Rapidly,"* San Diego (California) Union Tribune, *August 3, 1996, A26.*

10. *Sun Myung Moon, "The Heart of Reunion" (speech delivered September 11, 1977), quoted in Dallas Jackson,* Whom Has God Joined Together? *(Royal Oak, Mich.: Jackson, 1990), 233.*

11. *C. Eugene Askew, "Should My Daughter Marry a Negro?" in* Marrying across the Color Line, *ed. Cloyte M. Larsson (Chicago: Johnson, 1965), 33.*

12. *Jackson,* Whom Has God Joined Together? *199.*

13. *Ibid., 219.*

§ FOURTEEN §

When Our Children
Do Not Look Like Us:
Transracial Adoption in the Church

An Interview with Deborah H. Johnson

COULD YOU PLEASE EXPLAIN WHY KIDS THAT ARE OF MINORITY OR BIRACIAL *descent are considered special needs children even though they may not have serious medical problems?*

Generally, they are not classified as special needs anymore. Part of President Clinton's Adoption and Safe Families Act was the Multiethnic Placement Act (MEPA) and the Interstate Ethnic Placement Act. It came in the late 1990s and removed race and culture as a special needs placement factor.

Does MEPA work for or against the need to find adoptive parents for children of color?

Well, that is being debated. There are a few lawsuits around the country trying to challenge MEPA. It does not apply to Native American children, because of a federal law, the Indian Child Welfare Act. But all other children of color are covered under MEPA. Interestingly, religion can be considered as a placement factor, but not race or ethnicity.

How did this come about?

I believe MEPA is the result of some legal battles where Caucasian families wanted to adopt their foster children, who were children of color. In Minnesota, we had what was called the Minority Heritage Preservation

---

Editor's note: Deborah H. Johnson is currently the executive director of the Minnesota Adoption Resource Network. The editors wish to thank Deborah for her insightful, sometimes startling comments, which come from her expertise in working with adoption and diversity issues. The following interview with Ms. Johnson was conducted by Sherelyn Whittum Yancey on March 6, 2001. Sherelyn's questions are italicized.

Act that had race as one of the primary placement matching factors. So first, every effort had to be made to find relatives; next, people from the same race or culture; then, people who had a prior relationship with the child; and finally, what we call a stranger adoption—anyone who is interested in adoption. What MEPA did was take out the racial/cultural piece. Now priority is given to relatives or people who have had a prior relationship with the child. There are approximately ten matching factors, and race cannot be the primary factor anymore. In the past, children of color were automatically considered special needs. For our program purposes, special needs is whoever has been placed under the guardianship of the commissioner of the State of Minnesota. The old terminology labeled these children as "state wards." That's the population we serve. These children range from having very few problems, or special needs, to children with real severe medical or emotional issues.

So for people who want to adopt children of color, "special needs" would have been a good route to go because there are no fees as compared to private adoption. In Minnesota you're saying that kids of color are no longer considered special needs. Have you seen a backlash to MEPA?
I think it boils down to the interpretation and implementation of the Multiethnic Placement Act (MEPA), what its spirit and intent are, and then how it filters down into actual practice. Some people are going do their work the same way they've always done it, and that's why there are all these lawsuits going on, because people are challenging that. States could lose their federal funding if they are continuing to use race and culture as the primary matching factor. One of the good things that has happened is kids sometimes will move through the system quicker because they are not waiting to find an African American family or a Hispanic family, etc. They're looking at a variety of other matching factors, so the kids are not waiting for a racial match, which did happen in the past. Often children would wait in hopes that they would find the perfect racial match. The downside is, you may have kids who have grown up in a very urban, inner-city environment being moved out to small farm towns, where they are the only child of color and they face all the issues with families who may not necessarily have the wisdom, education, or insight to really grapple with those issues. We may have a whole generation of transracially adopted children who have significant identity issues as they get older.

How does your agency help prepare both the kids and the prospective parents for transracial adoption?
We have an annual, half-day training that is a mandatory component of our adoption preparation process. But with such a huge issue, really, that's a drop in the bucket. Ideally, we should have a half-day training once a month to deal with these issues. We do provide resources for ongoing issues, but we have difficulty getting people to comply with the minimal mandated half-day training.

Why is it that adoption fees are less for adopting children of color than for adopting white children?
I think that may be true in some states. It is not true in Minnesota, and it's not true in our agency. I think that's a practice that is disappearing, but I know that it exists in some places. When you talk about adoption and the politics that dictate it, it is regionally influenced. In places where it is heavily urbanized, agencies may have a large population of children of color that they are desperately trying to place, so they may charge a lesser fee to attract a wider population of adoptive parents.

Are you saying private agencies lower their fees to reach minority parents that may not have the same family resources or income level white families tend to have for adoption expenses?
Yes, that may be one of the recruitment strategies an agency could use. I think, in part, that is an outdated belief, but I think that it's rooted in some ongoing economic realities. In our special needs program we don't charge any fees, so that's a moot issue. The state is subsidizing all the costs for the adoptions.

Your agency doesn't charge any fees?
No, I work with special needs adoption, so all of our children are state wards and the state pays for an agency to do all the work. It's a pilot program, about three years old and very innovative. I think there is some hot discussion in the adoption community about fees in general for placing children.

Previously, you said race is no longer considered a matching factor but religion can be. How does that affect Christians who want to adopt children?
Well, it can be as simple as a child that has been involved in a Baptist church and a possible requirement the agency can put on is matching that child with

a Baptist or a Protestant family. Or if the child is Muslim, they have to narrow it to a Muslim family.

Why are parents in transracial adoption more likely to be white than nonwhite?
People have the perception you need to be a certain kind of family to adopt. We work hard to demythologize that assumption. You don't have to be a two-parent family living in the suburbs with the house with a white picket fence, a dog and a station wagon—that has been the traditional picture. I think the majority group has more access to resources, and let's just say it, money. It costs money to raise kids, and taking in additional children is in some ways a luxury. The fact that you can choose to add members to your family takes economic resources and a sense of empowerment. You can have five kids and financially be able to support them. A lot of the recruitment materials have been targeted toward that population as the best kind of family.

Who are the good parents? I used to do a lot of recruiting for a foster care agency, and I had a Latino child I was trying to place. I called another county and they said, "We don't have any Hispanic foster homes. I don't even know any Hispanic people who would make good foster parents." I thought, In the whole county? You can't think of any? Then she said, "Besides, they all live in trailers." I thought, Oh, a good family couldn't live in a trailer?

We're really looking at materialistic resources as opposed to who nurtures the children, who loves them unconditionally. Who will give them the opportunities to build their potential as opposed to who has the minivan to drive them back and forth? We have single parents who adopt. We have people in apartments—you don't have to own your own home. We also have students who adopt. We look at every kind of combination, because it's really about which needs of a child an adult can meet best.

When you talk about mythology, are you talking about the idealism of white middle-class values that's held up as the role model?
If you look back, it's the 1950s mentality. We don't even have a majority of white families in our country anymore that reflect this mythology. That's the ironic thing. The American dream hasn't changed even though it's not even close to the demographics of the actual American population.

Why do minority parents adopt so few white children?
It does happen, but it's a rare occurrence. I think it's the mentality that a white child needs to be with white parents, but a white family can also raise a black

child. The system may see black parents raising a white child as second best. The reality is that there are many families that would adopt a white child and there are so many children of color that, ironically, when we get a family of color in our agency, we have ten referrals for them. Everybody wants to place with them, whether the child is biracial or a child of color. Families of color are eagerly received!

On the other hand, I worked with a single white woman. She is a biological parent of a young boy who is African American and Native American. I placed a two-year-old that is African American and Native American in her home. The county was thrilled even though she was a white single parent; the siblings would share a biracial mix. Now, we could never say that's why we placed him there, because that would be placing based on racial or cultural reasons, but of course, that was one of the most appealing factors. Her biological son was African American, Native American, and Caucasian. He is really triracial, in a sense, so the combination was a good match for them. It's interesting because this child and her son's baby pictures look like they could be twins.

Why don't minority parents adopt more minority kids, if that's the best fit?
They get screened out in an institutionally discriminatory practice/system. Also, I think that, unlike in our program, other programs charge fees. They are also not actively recruited. There tends to be a lot of informal adoptions, a lot of kinship caregiving that happens that's not formalized. I know lots of children who have been raised by Grandma and Auntie and cousins. There's a lot of "adoption" that happens, but it's not in the white framework where they went before a judge and had a legal procedure. It's more informal, community, extended family in both the African American and Native American families. It's very typical and accepted. A lot of people have been raised by extended family.

How legitimate are the Association of Black Social Workers and American Indian tribes' objections against transracial adoption by white parents?
I think it comes from a historical perspective of cultural genocide. They may see this as another way for whites to rid themselves of ethnic cultures by taking the children and raising them in white culture and brainwashing them to think they are white, taking away any sense of cultural history. These groups feel that they are losing their history and fear there won't be anybody left to be the culture bearers for the next generation.

I think that was a legitimate concern historically the way transracial adoption was done. For instance, the Indian boarding school system intentionally destroyed cultural identity. We took kids away, we took away their culture, and we tried to make them think they were white. If you talk to an adult who was transracially adopted a generation ago, that's what they thought. Some of them are really are messed up! They get to a certain age in their life where they realize, "Wow, I'm not white. What am I?" Then you get anger, grief, loss, and all those pieces of the identity puzzle.

Are children better off staying in a foster care home of their same race or being transracially adopted, and for what reason?
I think the key part of that is the difference between foster care, which is temporary, and adoption, which is permanent. The need for permanency for children is so crucial. I think that permanency is a priority. When it's possible, we do some racial/cultural matching [with adoptive families]. But when that's not possible, to leave kids in limbo literally leads to adults who were foster children telling us that once they are an adult, they have nowhere to come home to. They have no family. What is it like to operate in our society with no family? That's not about race; that's not about culture; that is about a sense of belonging somewhere. Our human condition and need transcends racial matching. The best of all possible worlds is to match children's needs with a family's skills, talents, experience, and background. I really think that children need to feel with certainty "This is my family. Come hell or high water, we're in it together."

Even though the adoptive parents don't look like the child racially?
Yes. They love me and they care for me. It's that commitment piece. People are committed to them. For example, I just did an adoption of an eighteen-year old girl who had been in this foster home for years. They had asked if she wanted to be adopted at age twelve, and she said no. When she turned eighteen, she got scared and she said, "I don't have anybody." She asked her foster parents if they would adopt her, and they said, "Of course we will. You are a part of our family." So as she matured, she realized, "Wait a minute! This is something I need before I launch off into adulthood."

What was the racial composition in that situation?
She was Native American and her foster parents were Caucasian. She said, "You have always been my family for the past six years. I want to have

balance. I want my kids to have grandparents." She wanted that whole inter-generational piece as well. She needed that place of belonging. Before arriving at this conclusion, however, she had lived previously on the reservation for a couple of months when she had some problems with her foster family. They had encouraged her to explore her roots. She thought that was where she wanted to live. She went there and didn't find any real connections. She didn't have "family" there.

She didn't have any extended family?
No. There wasn't anyone. The tribe embraced her on a cultural/community level, but there was no one that she felt bonded to or attached to in an intimate way. She came back to her foster family, because she felt they were the people who would take care of her.

With all those risks, do you believe being adopted by white parents is still better than remaining in limbo and not getting adopted?
Yes, but only if it's done right—if there's education, if there's a commitment to diversity, and if there's an understanding of the complexity and challenge that you're taking on. I know families who have adopted transracially, and they do a beautiful job. Just like in an interracial family, they really have to pay attention. It's not just like any other family—it's not better, it's not worse, but the challenges are different and unique.

When we work with our adoptive families who are thinking about tran-sracial adoption, we tell them they really are becoming an interracial family. That is your new social status, like it or not. The things interracial families are interested in, those are going to be your issues because those are going to be the issues for your children. This really needs to be grasped. We're not a white family that took in children of color. It's our new status and it changes all of us. We may need to make some very different choices than we would have before. We may need to move, change churches, seek out new friends, and confront the racism in our own families.

When you are frank about counting the social costs, have you had white parents back off and say that they did not want to go ahead with the transracial adoption?
We haven't had a lot of people back off, but we've had people slow the process down and really take some more time to be thoughtful. We talk a lot about the intergenerational pieces.

189

For example, one of the adoptive fathers I was working with is a minister in a very small, rural town. They transracially adopted the most beautiful biracial African American girl. They have one other adopted child who is Caucasian. I asked the father, "What do you think about this? You've got this beautiful little brown baby in your family."

He said, "I need some time to process that."

About a month later we had another meeting and he said, "I really thought about what you said. I didn't think of her that way. I just saw her as our little baby girl. I went back to my church and I asked to meet with the elders and we sat and talked about it and their reactions. I fantasize about the future. I'll be up in my cabin up north, sitting near the lake in my rocking chair on the porch with all of my family around me—my grandkids, my great-grandkids— having a good picnic." Then he said after talking with me that picture changed. Some of those kids in that picture were brown; some of them were black. He said, "It occurred to me that I could have a black son-in-law." He said at first that was a little disconcerting because that was not the picture he had envisioned of his life. Not better or worse, but just really different.

He struggled and grappled with it and then realized, Wow, how cool! How fun would that be to have that kind of diversity within his family. How interesting. How challenging. And then he realized it was going to be okay. He said, "It took me a while to think through what that would mean intergenerationally. I could have a black son-in-law; I could have black grandchildren. What is that about? It's looking a generation ahead and changing my vision. My dreams changed and they literally look different." Then he said, "I had never thought about that. I'm glad we had this conversation and I'm okay with it. I've talked with my elders about this; we've discussed it, and they are all really supportive."

Being a minister, was he able to say anything about how his faith helped him be willing to alter his dreams?

That was his point. He thought about it as exciting and challenging, but it was very different from his original vision. That's what happens when we work with families: a transformation begins to happen.

I teach parents that as you go through this process and become sensitized to these issues, the world is going to look like a very different place to you. Some parts of it are going to be really ugly, and you're going see things that you have never even noticed before. You're going to hear things in a very different way.

Once you have your children, people usually go through a phase where they are super sensitive. It's like walking around without your skin on. Every little comment, even little compliments, such as "Oh, she has such beautiful skin," pushes buttons. What do you mean? That she's dark? New adoptive parents seem to be waiting to be socially hit, and so they are just trying to be prepared.

You will go through things that you never would have imagined, like a spiritual awakening via the transracial adoption experience. How do we feel connected to people? How do we feel attached? Is it because we look alike? Is it because we share the same general history, or is it about a commitment to one another, to go through the challenges? That is adoption. It's accepting that commitment to love and to parent, to bond, to attach. It's something that you do. We're not a family because we have the same genes; we're family because we committed ourselves to become a family.

I think that's why people who understand commitment on a spiritual level realize that relationship and intimacy on a spiritual level have nothing to do with biology. For example, look at marriage. We create family, and we're okay with two unrelated people calling themselves family in marriage. But in adoption we ask, "Is this a real family?" People who do have some sense of spirituality already get that part. We feel attached. We have relationships based on spiritual things that can transcend racial stereotypes and embrace these kids.

There seems to be a trend for some white Christian couples to adopt internationally, especially from nations where the children are fair skinned. Could you comment on the pros and cons?
We have resources regarding international programs here as well. However, I think that when you have families that are selecting international adoption, you really have to examine motivation. Are they escaping the boogeyman of open adoption where birth parents are met? Are they trying to escape the racial issues? Even if you go to Russia or Bulgaria, there's that cultural piece where race and culture are still valid. If you adopt a same-race child, are you going to pretend that they are not adopted? Is it going to be like back in the 1940s where we just pretended everybody was biologically connected because they shared the same complexion? Is there going to be some shame attached to the fact that they are adopted?

The reality is that even with an international adoption, there may be issues of search and reunion. We've seen this in Korean adoptions particularly. In the most unlikely of circumstances, a lot of international adoptees are still searching for and finding biological parents.

So, both domestic and international adoptees are driven by a need to search out their biological parents?
Exactly. It is not about which kind of adoption you do. It's part of our human composition to want to know our roots. "Where did I come from? Who was responsible? Why was I placed for adoption?" It's part of the whole psyche formation that adoptees go through. The whole journey includes understanding their individual story of why they were placed for adoption. It doesn't matter whether you were adopted from Milwaukee or Moldova.

It's this internal drive in the child that adoptive parents may have the most struggle with. It's probably one of the most feared but also most crucial elements for adult adoptees' mental health. If parents are not open to that search and not supportive, they become the "enemy." Parents can actually push their child away because of the very issue that they were trying to not lose them over. So, many parents will do an international adoption, yet because they can't be supportive of a later search for biological parents, they lose their child.

When transracially adopted children with white parents reach adulthood and want to seek out their biological parents, do they tend to identify more with the people of their same race, or will they still feel bonded and want to identify with their family who raised them?
I think how young adults understand and move through that process is really intrinsic to how adoptive parents have worked with this issue all along. If you have not talked about it, if you have not worked with your child in understanding why they were placed for adoption or why you chose to adopt, then for adult adoptees, it becomes a loyalty issue. "Am I going to love my white family, or am I going to look for another avenue here? Does this feel like an either/or situation when really it's not?" Because of their lack of insight and understanding, I've seen white adoptive parents frame it as an either/or loyalty choice.

Can you think of some examples?
Yes. I know adult adoptees who will do their entire search and reunion process but never tell their adoptive parents. They sever the relationship with their adoptive family. They will have nothing to do with them, which is most adoptive parents' worst fear. On the other hand, I have seen adoptive parents literally hold their kids' hands, pay for everything, and go through this entire process with them. They cried with their kids when they found their birth mother; they've gone to the reunion, embraced the whole family together,

and considered them extended families. I have seen everything in between these two extremes.

Wouldn't you rather be standing next to your child, hugging her and her birth mother in the same embrace, rather than being left in the cold? When parents avoid the search process with their child, I think it's sad that they have been there for their child through everything possible and then, at the most critical time in their identity formation, they are absent because of their own fear of losing their child.

Do they have to choose between loyalty to their adoptive parents and loyalty to their birth race?
I think in families where it's been done right, children don't have to choose. I know families that have been very successful. If you already see yourself as an interracial family, kids don't have to choose. It's your family, and if your community is multiracial anyway, there isn't this sudden initiative to find these things. If that has been a part of your life all along, there's no drastic, dramatic break. If you go to a racially diverse church, if your house is filled with multiracial artwork, symbols, acknowledgment, when will a child ever have to choose? It's already there.

Many white Christian couples might not grasp the importance of taking on an interracial family identity through adoption. Can you give me another example of this?
It's just as if you were to marry interracially. If you married someone from Somalia, you wouldn't say, "Okay, now you have to stop being Somali today because we're getting married. So forget your traditional clothing, foods, all of that. You married me. I'm white, so now you're white." That's the message children of color have gotten for years from white adoptive parents. "You're in a white family now, so you need to adapt to our ways, our things, our culture, our beliefs, our values and forget all that other stuff you were connected to." But then they grow up and go out into a society who lets them know that they are not white!

But if children are in a family that embraces who we are collectively, that your culture is just as much valid as mine is, then we're going to find a way to integrate your traditions. I know transracial adoptive families that celebrate Kwanza because they have African American children in their home. They also go to a play called the *Black Nativity*. This is a regular part of their family traditions now.

Are you saying white middle-class Christians cannot expect to simply form their transracially adopted child into that white middle-class mold—that the parents are the ones who must be willing to change?

You can try to make the child conform, and it may work until you go through an experience like I had with my son. When white parents have to go up to the school because your son was called a "nigger" or a "Chink" or a "gook" or a "spick," how do you deal with that from your white, Anglo-Saxon, Protestant perspective? I think that's where the rubber hits the road. Your child is experiencing a completely different life reality than you know, than you live in, than you've ever experienced, than you understand. Suddenly you are going to be out there protecting, advocating, educating, going to the principal and explaining what these words mean and why they are harmful. That becomes part of your job as the parent.

That's one of the things in this parental role that some people are really uncomfortable with. For example, when a shy, quiet woman says, "I'm not an outspoken person. I'm not assertive and I don't stand up for things," I say, "You'd be surprised when you become a parent!" When parents see some-one attacking their child, I've seen the meekest, mildest women (and it's usually women) who suddenly become ferocious—fearless even. They are a little shocked themselves, but they have to be well prepared to do it.

What else have you noticed about the mothers of transracially adopted children?

I find it really interesting that often when mothers are out with their children, the broader public assumes that the mother is in an interracial marriage. They may hear disparaging comments or questions. My challenge is, if you find it so offensive (the assumption that you are interracially married), then why would you adopt transracially? I recommend that if you wouldn't marry interracially, you shouldn't adopt interracially. You can just forget it. When I presented that at one of my workshops, I was really blunt! I believe that if you have some negative attitudes about interracial marriage, then you shouldn't be considering transracial adoption.

Tell me more about the connection between interracial marriage and trans-racial adoption.

It is very basic because it's about respect, dignity, understanding, and struggle (because interracial marriages are a struggle). That same level of intensity needs to be present in a transracially adoptive family. In adoption circles we haven't wanted to say that, we haven't wanted to frame it that way, but it is true.

It probably takes more flexibility on the part of the adults than it does on the part of the children, and up until recently, it's been the children who have had to be flexible. They have had to learn, they have had to become accustomed, they've had to compromise, and they've had to accommodate. Now we are flip-flopping that and saying, "No, it's you as the adult, as the parent, who has to accommodate. You are making this choice; you are changing this child's environment. You are the ones that need to look at your lifestyle and who you are in a very hard way."

For example, one of the things I say to people who live in very homogenous communities is "You live in a small town and don't have any people of color; do you ever think of moving? If your husband or wife were offered a job that would triple your family income, would you consider moving for that job?" "Oh yeah, we would consider that," they reply. "Well, you're going to adopt a child whose mental health hinges on the environment that they live in, and you know that they would be healthier in a more racially diverse community; would you consider moving? Can you ask yourself if your financial health is more important than your child's mental health?" They look at me like they have never thought of it like that. We have to ask ourselves: Why are we willing to move to make more money but not willing to move to create a healthier environment for our child?

You have provided me with guides you use in your work to assess adoptive parents' ability for cross-racial parenting (see Appendix B). One of the questions asks, "Are you willing to change your church to a congregation that is culturally diverse?" What has been your response?
We have a lot of families who will not change churches. So we really scrutinize them when it comes to transracial adoption, because they convey, "We're really connected. That's our community; that's who we feel comfortable with." "Okay," I say, "but you're an adult, you know how to form attachments, and you know how to create relationships. We're not saying that you have to do that, but it speaks to your willingness to adapt to your child's needs."

What benefit would a white couple gain from being willing to go to a multiracial church?

When you look at what churches do, in addition to the spiritual aspect, they are really a social institution. If a child's environment isn't comprised of social institutions that reflect, validate, and empower them, then what are those institutions doing? They are negating, they are devaluing, they are disempowering, and they are minimizing the child. His or her reality isn't being validated.

I believe children of color need to have healthy environments where they have similar values and good ethics and beliefs that are faith based. That should be in the church life. That's the natural place for those mores and those insights from a spiritual base to come from—other people of faith whose racial diversity validates the child and parents.

A place to spiritually grow?
Exactly. Your racial identity, your self-esteem, and your spiritual development are so intertwined; they are inseparable. You cannot say that we'll work on this now and we'll work on that later; it's all so integrated. For efficiency's sake, why not be a part of a social institution that has a spiritual base that can help you?

By Christians remaining in same-race churches, have we been doing a disservice to multiracial families?
Yes. Of all the natural places for a family to get support to deal with whatever life challenges they come across, your church family is the place where you would want to go. But if your church family says, "Well, I don't get it. What's the big deal? Why are you upset about that?" If it's a racial incident, suddenly you feel like, Oh, okay, so this is not a place to go to when I am hurting and I'm a Christian. Our kids learn that.

How do faith communities developmentally influence racial identity formation; for example, when kids are part of Sunday school or a youth group?
Most people are shocked how early this stuff starts. It's close to two and three years old when they start to understand racial differences. Families say to me, "Oh, my kids never say anything; they never talk about it." I ask them if they are giving the kids the language to talk about it. Are you giving them the opportunity to talk about it? Three-year-olds will look at their family, asking, "Why does Mommy have black hair? yellow hair? brown eyes? blue eyes? Why does Daddy have blue eyes? Why does Daddy have yellow hair?" These questions are not attached to any value system, just descriptions of what his

or her world looks like. But as adults, we are so freaked out about race that if somebody points out any kind of difference, we say, "Oh, shhhh, we don't talk about that," or we minimize it, or we just don't make it something important. However, immediately we should start explaining to kids that Mommy has black hair because she is Korean and Korean people have black hair. It's very benign. It's informational; it's not a value statement. It's not a prejudicial thing.

We're so uncomfortable with grappling with race that we don't want our kids to notice that some people are brown. "Oh, shhh, don't call attention to that!"

Or we don't want to offend by pointing out the difference instead of allowing diversity of hair, eye, or skin color to be a normal thing.
Right. Kids will point out that that person is really black. OK, let's talk about why people are that black. It can be a very enlightening conversation, but because we're so concerned about what kind of values are projected, what kind of prejudices we might attach to it, we either don't deal with it or we deal with it inappropriately. Of course, there's the other extreme where you don't like them because they are different.

It starts at these very early stages when kids are first learning how to talk. Language is a mental processing function. Their thought processes are forming, and we need to teach kids literally how to think about things. Then they can observe things without attaching values to them. That's our job as parents or in children's ministries, to help our kids interpret what they see.

Could you speak to a major challenge white parents transracially adopting may face because they do not have that language since our society stresses being color-blind?
That's common. We need to ask ourselves: "Am I uncomfortable talking about how or why people's skin color differs? Why is that uncomfortable for me? How do I explain this, and where do my perceptions come from?"

For some families who live in a very diverse area, there is a lot of explaining that needs to happen. A funny example occurred when my daughter was really little, about four years old. We were at one of those playland places and I heard her very loudly say to this girl, "Well, what are you?" I thought, Hmmm, what is she asking? Was she asking, "Are you Korean?" The girl looked like she might be of Asian descent. I heard the other little girl run out of the play area and run to her parents. I didn't hear their answer, and then she ran back and said, "I'm Filipino!" She was so happy that she had a good answer at that point. Why didn't her parents tell her she was Filipino? She didn't know it, perhaps, because we, as a society, do not want to talk about it. If I thought she was just too little, well, you're never too little to start forming your identity. What kids learn is that if we don't talk about it, it's a bad thing.

Should white adoptive parents teach their minority children to be color-blind, to act as though their race doesn't matter?
No, stop, no, no, stop doing that! When I see these T-shirts that say, "Love sees no color" or "Love is color-blind," I just want to rip the T-shirt off of them! Why would you want to be color-blind?

Let's look at the word *color-blind*. It seems to *want* to not see things as they really are, which then implies there is something wrong with being different. I think we need to totally reframe that approach. That is really pretty naive—isn't it?—because you have to completely divorce that person from who they are. For example, that's like saying, "Let's pretend that there's no difference between men and women; I didn't even realize you were a woman." Well, gee, is that a compliment or an insult? I think we can acknowledge and really enjoy and appreciate those things as opposed to pretending that they don't exist.

I see so much denial and ignorance. If I say I see you in lots of different ways, then I can appreciate all the different components and complexities as part of who you are as a human being. I don't think any of us want to be pigeonholed in one very narrow category, but to say I don't see any of those things, I am blind to your color—how boring is that? I understand the well-meaning intent of that, but it also strips away people's individuality.

Transracially adopted kids often have their racial differences minimized because the adoptive parent just loves them and says, "I don't think about their race; they are just my son or my daughter. We're all one in Christ, so race doesn't matter." What do you think?
We have to incorporate our racial identity. The fact that we don't even recognize that there might be a problem with color-blindness, or pretending that racial differences don't matter, speaks to the very core of the issue. What's wrong with saying, "I'm African American; I'm proud of my identity." Not that it's more or less than the fact that I'm a Christian, but it's the visible nature of who I am. I am much more than that, but when I walk into a room, the first thing someone notices is that I am an Asian female. I have to be com-

fortable with my racial and gender identity so that it doesn't become an issue. If I'm in denial about that, it's going to be an ongoing issue.

How would you help white parents prepare their children of color for inevitable experiences of racism in our churches or society?
What is really tough is that many white foster/adoptive parents have a belief that it just won't happen in their community or in their family. Once we break through that denial, there is now a sense of responsibility that if they really see the world full of institutional racism and prejudice, what is their role in that as a majority white person? What do they have to do about that now that they know about it? Is there some shared responsibility? Is there some guilt and shame? My point is not to shame white people about what they may or may not have done but to say you have to see the world the way your child is going to see the world. See the world as it truly is, not how we wish it was. These are very different perspectives. Your child of color is going to notice things; they are going to be a target of so many attitudes, beliefs, and experiences that you, as a white person, have never been exposed to.

How can white parents gain that wisdom to prepare their adopted children of color for these racialized attitudes, beliefs, and experiences they them-selves have never encountered because they are white?
I think part of it is really breaking through one's own denial that racism exists. We invite parents who have already transracially adopted to come in and speak about what their child is experiencing—what they deal with on a daily basis.

I do a major portion on preadoptive cross-cultural training. I talk a lot about my own experience, raising my biracial children and what that's like. We use a lot of person-to-person connecting. My kids go to a nice suburban, middle-class school, and this is what we're dealing with. I pump up my kids every morning that they are the most fabulous children on the planet and no one should say anything to devalue them. Then they go out in the world and they get squashed flat every day. Then when they come home, we pump them back up again.

As a parent, that is what you do every day, minute by minute. Your kids are dealing with this racial stuff on a conscious and subconscious level, and the media in particular is so negative. There is a constant barrage of negative perspectives and stereotypes and images that our kids constantly have to guard against, and they need our support.

How can prospective adoptive white parents help with the attachment issues of adopting older children of color who have already bonded with their birth mother, even though she may have been an inadequate mother, and they've been in the foster care system for years?

There are a lot of different variables, and some of it is the mental health history. Some of the kids are going to be predisposed to having more difficulties. It has to do with what kind of care they received, whether they were nurtured. I don't mean whether they had a really nice nursery or the fancy things, but were their needs met? Were their emotional needs responded to? Were they loved and nurtured?

The kids who I feel have the most difficult time are those who have multiple transitions—in and out, in and out, back and forth—and it's that intermittent sort of nurturing that probably creates the most difficulty with attachment. Kids can experience attachment and then it's broken, but they can reattach. It's amazing. Children are much more resilient than you would ever imagine, given that they have a fairly solid mental health history. Kids who were already fragile because of heredity on the mental health issue may have more difficulty with resiliency. I have seen seven-year-olds who have had multiple placements yet have attached beautifully when everyone said it would never happen.

Can you think of a specific situation?

Yes. I placed a nine-year-old whose history was horrendous. He was a sexual abuse victim and perpetrator. He had several attachment disorder diagnoses—disturbed attachment behavior, fire setter, impulsive, destructive, all of these things. He was in a residential treatment center at the time and had a deliberately slow transition. The family started going to family therapy together before he even left the institution. The adoptive parents went to his school meetings and doctor's appointments. They had him every weekend, and so by the time he moved into their home, he was just like their son.

The healing that has happened in that circumstance is nothing short of a miracle. Everyone involved said we would be lucky if this worked for six months. The mom continued to reinforce, "He's our son; he's part of our family," and they just have not seen the extreme behavior problems.

I think that really speaks to the healing that happens when a kid believes "This is permanent, this is my family, and these people are committed to me no matter what I do." I remember that at one of their preplacement meetings he asked them, "Do you know about me?"

They said, "Yes, we know about you."

"Do you know all the bad things that I have done?" he asked.

They replied, "Well, we've read your history."

He asked, "You still want me?"

They reassured, "Yes, we want you to be our son."

He said, "OK, I'll be your son."

The child wants to know if you will accept all the good, bad, and the ugly and still want him or her. You are still committed, and if the commitment is there, then it's safe. This boy finally found someone who was willing to accept him on that level.

That brings us back to that sense of belonging and permanency that transcends race.

Yes. Think of the spiritual sense of your relationship with Christ. The Lord is someone who loves you, knows you—and still wants you after all that! That's the amazing thing. What's sweet about this little boy is that he had so much potential in light of all the negative things. When he was five years old, he led a church choir. At his adoption ceremony, he did the opening and closing prayer. I sat there and said to myself, He is a preacher in the making because he is up there preaching about his life and about his adoption and his great family.

Was this an interracial couple?

Yes. The mom is African American and the dad is Caucasian. They've been able to do this role modeling with Christ; they've been able to share God's love, their love, and their commitment. They are very committed to their church and their minister. They did a baptism-dedication-adoption combination ceremony. They sent out engraved invitations celebrating their new family. They had a reception, and it was really about them becoming a family. They wanted all their friends who supported them to celebrate with them. Their church really embraced their unique family.

Were they in a multiracial congregation?

Yes. Their church was on the corner of the block where they lived, and so they would just go down the street for church.

Do you believe he feels secure and there has been a real healing in his spirit?

Yes. Not a lot of people want to take a nine-year-old boy out of residential treatment with a tremendously difficult history of five disrupted foster/adoption placements. Some kids just have that spark, and he was always very tied to the church. In all of these circumstances, he was always going to and involved in a church. Through all of these transitions and trials, his faith and spirit survived.

Discussion Questions

1. How important should income be in determining whether a family can adopt a child? How does our value on materialism discriminate against people of color who want to adopt?

2. What can white parents do to help children of color develop a healthy racial identity?

3. How may white parents of children of color experience racism? How can these parents prepare for these racial encounters?

4. Do you think that Johnson is right when she argues that people who would not interracially marry should not transracially adopt? Why or why not?

5. If you transracially adopt, what changes are you willing to make to ensure that your child will be exposed to people of his or her race? Will you move to an integrated neighborhood or join a multiracial church? What else might you do to help your child?

appendixes

Resources

WE HAVE READ AND SEEN MANY OF THE FOLLOWING RESOURCES. However, we cannot endorse the content of each selection. At the time of publication, websites were verified as active, but they may not be current by the time you read this section. Since Christians have been late in creating any resources for interracial families or multiracial individuals, most listings are secular, yet even so, they are helpful in addressing common issues.

Websites

Center for the Study of Biracial Children
> http://www.csbc.cncfamily.com/
> An organization that seeks to provide material for and about interracial families and biracial children.

Frontline
> http://www.pbs.org/wgbh/pages/frontline/shows/secret/
> A Frontline story of a racially mixed daughter, plus other stories of multiracial people and several links.

International Christian Adoptions
> http://www.4achild.com
> A nonprofit California Christian adoption agency.

Interracial Adoption
> http://www.adopting.org/inter.html
> The section of an adoption assistance organization that deals with transracial adoption.

Interracial Adoption
> http://ww2.netnitco.net/users/tank/adopt3.htm
> An extremely colorful website that provides advice and support for those who want to transracially adopt.

Interracial Haven
> http://users2.ev1.net/~crusader/irhaven/
> A website by Allen Steadham that is designed to support those in multiracial families. (At the time of this writing the site also contained the Christian testimony of Steadham.)

Interracial Singles
http://www.csbc.cncfamily.com/
An online dating service for those who seek interracial romantic relationships.

Interracial Voice
http://www.webcom.com/~intvoice/
A bimonthly newsletter with numerous links to other websites that would interest multiracial families and singles.

Multiracial Churches
http://www.congregations.info
A valuable resource for helping multiracial families locate multiracial churches nationally. It also features results from research on multiracial congregations.

MAVIN
http://www.mavin.net
A Seattle-based multiracial site that features the magazine *MAVIN* (the magazine is very Gen X in its focus and may not interest older interracial couples, but it is still a helpful resource, especially for college students).

Mixed Folks
http://www.mixedfolks.com/community.htm
A website designed to supply multiracial individuals with role models and the opportunity to interact with other multiracial people. The list is inclusive of all different types of racial combinations.

My Shoes
http://www.myshoes.com/myshoes.html
This site is set up to provide multiracial adults and youth chat rooms and support groups.

Mulatto People
http://www.mulatto.cjb.net/
A group that seeks to define black/white multiracials as their own cultural group. There is even a mulatto flag at this website that is meant to represent black/white multiracial people.

New People Magazine
http://www.newpeoplemagazine.com/
An interracial e-magazine designed to supply resources such as interracial greeting cards, movie reviews, articles concerning interracial people, etc.

Our Blended Family
http://go.to/interracialblend

A place for interracial couples, racially blended families, and any others with open minds to share stories and support.

PACT

http://www.pactadopt.org/

A comprehensive site addressing the adoption of children of color and providing many resources for those involved in transracial adoption.

Race and Adoption

http://racerelations.about.com/cs/raceandadoption/

An online clearinghouse of a variety of articles on transracial adoption.

Transracial Adoption

http://www.transracialadoption.com/

The name of the website says it all. This is probably the best place to begin your search for support materials on transracial adoption.

Urban Mozaik Magazine

http://www.urbanmozaik.com/

A multicultural e-magazine that promotes cross-cultural understanding and celebrates cultural diversity.

You Don't Look Japanese

http://www.angelfire.com/or/biracial/

A rather unique website that includes information on interracial relationships that other websites do not always contain, since it also includes links to some of the criticisms of interracial relationships.

Interracial Family Support Groups

Ameurofian Heritage Foundation
Valerie Wilkins-Godbee, P.O. Box 859, Peekskill, NY 10566
v_wilkins1@hotmail.com

Association of MultiEthnic Americans
P.O. Box 66061, Tucson, AZ 85728-6061
1-877-954-AMEA
http://www.ameasite.org/

Biracial Family Network of Chicago
Box 2387, Chicago, IL 60690-2387
773-288-3644, xmen3@netzero.net

Brown Organization of Multiracial and Biracial Students—Shirley Johnson
68 Brown Street, Providence, Rhode Island 02912
BOMBS@brown.edu
http://www.brown.edu/Students/CONMAG/gsa/43.html

Carri Uram
    103 Green Lake Dr., Greenville, NC 29607
    864-233-4872, speclink@greenville.infi.net
Center for the Study of Biracial Children
    Dr. Francis Wardle, 2300 South Kramaria St., Denver, CO 80222
    303-692-9008, francis@csbc.cncfamily.com
    http://www.csbc.cncfamily.com/
Families of Color
    Dr. C. Lessman, Box 478, Fort Collins, CO 80522
Getting Interracial/cultural Families Together (GIFT)
    Irene Rottenberg, P.O. Box 1281, Montclair, NJ 07042
    973-783-0083, NJGIFT@aol.com
    members.aol.com/NJGIFT/index.html
Hapa Issues Forum, Berkeley Chapter
    ASUC Box 401, Bancroft Way/Telegraph Ave., Berkeley, CA 94720
    510-466-5859, ucb@hapaissuesforum.org
    http://www.ocf.berkeley.edu/~hapa/
Hapa Issues Forum, Los Angeles Chapter
    231 East Third St., Suite G-104, Los Angeles, CA 90013-1493
    213-694-0286, socal@hapaissuesforum.org
Hapa Issues Forum, San Francisco Chapter
    1840 Sutter St., San Francisco, CA 94115-3220
    sf@hapaissuesforum.org
Hapa Issues Forum, Southern California Chapter
    231 East Third St., Suite G-104, Los Angeles, CA 90013-1493
Hapa Issues Forum Stanford University Chapter
    Jaci Lew, P.O. Box 11562, Stanford, CA 94309
    crane314@stanford.edu, http://hapa.stanford.edu
Hapa Issues Forum, University of California, Irvine Chapter
    c/o Office of the Dean of Students, Irvine, CA 92697-5125
Honor Our New Ethnic Youth
    P.O. Box 23241, Eugene, OR 97402
    541-343-4023, ayanna@angel.mailcity.com
Interracial Club of Buffalo
    Mary Murchison-Edwards
    Box 400 (Amherst Branch), Buffalo, NY 14226
    716-875-6958, MEdwo32688@aol.com
    http://folksites.com/Interracial-Club/

Interracial Family Alliance
    Nathaniel Brown, Box 9117, Augusta, GA 30906-9117
    706-793-8547, Brown0524406@cs.com
Interracial Family Circle
    Valerie Center, Box 53291, Washington, DC 20009
    1-800-500-9040, 202-393-7866
    info@interrfamilycircle.org
    www.interracialfamilycircle.org
Interracial Family Connection
    Pat Barner, P.O. Box 7055, Norfolk, VA 23509
    757-622-9260, cffssunshin@aol.com
    http://groups.hamptonroads.com/IFC
Interracial Intercultural Pride
    Stacy Bell, Box 11811, Berkeley, CA 94712-2811
    510-663-0975, IPrideCA@aol.com, www.I-pride.org
InterRacial Life
    Dave Seibel, 2 George St., East Brunswick, NJ 08816
    732-390-7316, david_seibel@ml.com
Interracial Lifestyle Connection
    Gary Bowden, 4406 North 54th Street, Fort Smith, AR 72904
    501-785-4304 (call between 11:30 A.M. and 1:00 P.M.)
Lifeline for Children
    P.O. Box 17184, Plantation, FL 33318
    a032725t@bc.seflin.org
Multiracial Americans of Southern California
    Nancy Brown, 12228 Venice Blvd., #452, Los Angeles, CA 90066
    310-836-1535, NGBrown173@aol.com
Multiracial Family Circle of Kansas City
    Kevin Barber, P.O. 32414, Kansas City, MO 64171
    816-353-7602, MFCircle@aol.com
    www.cdiversity.com/mfc
Multiracial Group at U. of Michigan
    Karen Downing, 122 Undergraduate Library, Ann Arbor, MI 48109-1185
    313-763-5084, 313-764-4479, kdown@umich.edu
National Advocacy for the Multi-Ethnic
    N.A.M.E., P.O. Box 11756, Murfreesboro, TN 37129
    Info@namecentral.org
    http://www.namecentral.org/

National MultiEthnic Families Association
2073 N. Oxnard Blvd, Ste. 172, Oxnard, CA 93030
yaz@earthlink.net
New England Alliance of Multiracial Families
Ellen Rollins, P.O. Box 833, Natick, MA 01760
781-488-5468, info@neamf.org
http://www.neamf.org/
One Love
104 Brookwood Drive, Seneca, SC 29678
People of Every Stripe
Ed Cooper, P.O. Box 12505, Portland, OR 97212
850-894-8540 (fax)
Project Race
Susan Graham, 2910 Kerry Forest Parkway, D4-129, Tallahassee, FL 32309
503-282-0612, projrace@aol.com
http://www.projectrace.com/
Rainbow Families of Toledo
Nancy Shanks, 1920 S. Shore Blvd., Oregon, OH 43618
419-693-9259, Minan04@aol.com
Students of Mixed Heritage
SU 3187, Williams College, Williamstown, MA 01267
Students of Mixed Heritage at Amherst College
Amherst College, Amherst, MA 01002
413-597-3354, smhac@amherst.edu
http://www.amherst.edu/~smhac/
Swirl, Inc.
Jen Chau, 16 W. 32nd Street, Ste. 10A, New York, NY 10001
212-561-1773, jenchau@swirlinc.org
www.swirl.org
The Interracial Family Alliance of Houston
Chris Townsend, 281-579-9005
info@ifahouston.org
www.ifahouston.org
Triangle Interracial and Multicultural Experience
Marsha Alston, 15A Woodbridge Drive, Chapel Hill, NC 27516
Unity Multiracial Social Group
B. J. Winchester, P.O. Box 2902, Orange Park, FL 32073-2902
BJW007@bellsouth.net

Videos

Videos tend to be expensive. Some, however, can be purchased and/or checked out at schools or public libraries. George has used the following videos in his sociology class on multiracial families.

Domino: Interracial People and the Search for Identity. 45 minutes. Films for the Humanities and Sciences, 1995. This video is situated in Canada and contains the interviews of six multiracial people, exploring their experiences in racial ambiguity.

Interracial Marriage: Blending the Races in America. 52 minutes. Films for the Humanities and Sciences, 1992. This is a documentary that interviews several people on the subject of interracial marriage. The interviews include academicians as well as those in interracial families.

The Politics of Love—In Black and White. 33 minutes. California Newsreel, 1993. This film explores interracial dating and marriages on college campuses. The film not only examines the attitudes of supporters of interracial unions but also explores the views of blacks and whites who oppose these relationships.

A Question of Color: Color Consciousness in Black America. 58 minutes. California Newsreel, 1992. This one explores how African Americans discriminate against other blacks based upon how light or dark they are. It is useful for showing the absurdity of the concept of race and how blacks have accepted the philosophy of racism, even though they may be the group that suffers the most from this philosophy.

Books on Interracial Unions and Multiracial Identity

Blassingame, John W. *Slave Testimony: Two Centuries of Letters, Speeches, Interviews, and Autobiographies.* Baton Rouge: Louisiana State University Press, 1977. This book offers a vast collection of slaves speaking for themselves about their lives, including interracial sexuality and mixed-race lineage.

Blumberg, Rhoda G., and Wendell J. Roye, eds. *Interracial Bonds.* Bayside, N.Y.: General Hall, 1979. Somewhat outdated, but still insightful. This book describes positive interracial bonds on both institutional and intimate levels.

Brasseaux, Carl A., Keith P. Fontenot, and Clause F. Oubre. *Creoles of Color in the Bayou Country.* Jackson: University Press of Mississippi, 1994. Here is the first in-depth historical examination of antebellum

Louisiana's three-tiered society: whites, free people of color, and black slaves. It demonstrates how interracial families operated inside and outside the confines of white social and legal systems.

Clinton, Catherine, and Michele Gillespie, eds. *The Devil's Lane: Sex and Race in the Early South.* New York: Oxford University Press, 1997. Seventeen contributors present new research in the overlapped areas of sexuality, race, and gender from the seventeenth to nineteenth centuries.

Dalmage, Heather. *Tripping on the Color Line: Black-White Multiracial Families in a Racially Divided World.* New Brunswick, N.J.: Rutgers University Press, 2000. Dalmage's book explores the racial ambiguity interracial marriages and multiracial people introduce to Americans.

Davis, James F. *Who Is Black? One Nation's Definition.* University Park: Pennsylvania State University Press, 1996. This work makes a persuasive argument that the one-drop rule has only been applied to blacks in the United States. This is an excellent source for those who want to investigate the implications of the one-drop rule.

Driskill, J. Lawrence. *Cross-Cultural Marriages and the Church: Living in the Global Neighborhood.* Pasadena, Calif.: Hope, 1995. This book contains a compilation of several stories of Christian interracial couples. Many of the couples are missionaries. This work is useful for helping Christians see role models of interracial families.

Frazier, Sundee. *Check All That Apply: Finding Wholeness as a Multiracial Person.* Downers Grove, Ill.: InterVarsity Press, 2002. The first of its kind, this is an excellent Christian book that can help multiracial people fully explore their racial identity. A multiracial person herself, Frazier utilizes the personal experiences of other multiracial individuals and current scientific data to help assure multiracial people that their racial identity is a gift from God.

Ferber, Abby. *White Man Falling: Race, Gender, and White Supremacy.* Lanham, Md.: Rowman & Littlefield, 1996. Here is a disturbing but well-written book documenting the fact that much of the hatred in white supremacy is based on the fear of interracial sexuality.

Forbes, Jack D. *Africans and Native Americans: The Language of Race and the Evolution of Red-Black Peoples.* Chicago: University of Illinois Press, 1993. Forbes documents scholarly research on the constantly changing use of language to describe and define race by color classifications. His work is especially enlightening regarding mixed-race people's identities and where they fit in North, Central, and South American cultures.

Funderburg, L. *Black, White, Other: Biracial Americans Talk about Race and Identity.* New York: William Morrow and Co., 1995. The book contains interviews of several black/white multiracial individuals divided up into topical sections.

Haizlip, S. T. *The Sweeter the Juice: A Family Memoir in Black and White.* New York: Simon & Schuster, 1994. This is the true story of the author's multiracial heritage and her search through six generations of African, European, and Indian parentage for meaning to America's obsession with race, color, and family ties.

Hodes, Martha. *White Women, Black Men: Illicit Sex in the Nineteenth-Century South.* New Haven: Yale University Press, 1997. Hodes provides groundbreaking historical documentation of southern white women and black men's sexual liaisons from colonization through the end of Reconstruction. Her stories illustrate the evolution from toleration to violence for these relationships as a cover-up for white patriarchal control of southern society.

Katz, William Loren. *Black Indians: A Hidden Heritage.* New York: Alladin Paperbacks, 1997. The book offers a historical look at an exceptional multiracial population—the blending of Africans and Native Americans—that has been largely neglected in American history.

Katz, William Loren, and Paula A. Franklin. *Proudly Red and Black: Stories of African and Native Americans.* New York: Ethrac, 1993. This is a children's book appropriate for ages eight to twelve, profiling black Indian real-life heroes.

Korgen, Kathleen Odell. *From Black to Biracial: Transforming Racial Identity among Americans.* Westport, Conn.: Praeger, 1998. Tracing the development of biracial identity among African Americans, this book illustrates how multiracial identities are unable to develop until social conditions materialize that allow for their emergence.

Leslie, Kent A. *Woman of Color, Daughter of Privilege: Amanda America Dickson, 1849–1893.* Athens, Ga.: University of Georgia Press, 1995. This is a sensational biography of the biracial daughter of a wealthy white planter and his mulatto slave. Although a slave, Amanda was socially acknowledged as a white daughter of privilege before and after the Civil War. She fought for her half-million-dollar inheritance as a woman of color despite the lawsuits of her white patriarchal family.

Mathabane, Mark, and Gail Mathabane. *Love in Black and White: The Triumph of Love over Prejudice and Taboo.* New York: HarperCollins,

1992. The authors have penned a dual autobiography of a black African man's courtship and marriage to a white American woman. Mark Mathabane is famous for his previous book, *Kaffir Boy.*

McBride, James. *The Color of Water: A Black Man's Tribute to His White Mother.* New York: Riverhead, 1996. Here is a brutally honest autobiography chronicling a black man's search for his poor, white mother's Jewish past, the rejection she suffered for interracially marrying, the shame and pride he felt about her, and the success she instilled in her many children.

McNamara, Robert P., Maria Tempenis, and Beth Walton. *Crossing the Line: Interracial Couples in the South.* Westport, Conn.: Greenwood, 1999. The authors interviewed several black/white interracial couples in the South who face unique challenges from living in that region of the United States.

McRoy, R., and L. Zurcher. *Transracial and Inracial Adoptees: The Adolescent Years.* Springfield, Ill.: Charles C. Thomas, 1983. This work examines the psychological development of black and black/white multiracial kids who have been adopted by white and black families. It documents the fact that there is little psychological difference between those adopted by each racial group but that those adopted by whites are less likely to develop a black racial identity.

Moran, Rachel F. *Interracial Intimacy: The Regulation of Race and Romance.* Chicago: University of Chicago Press, 2001. Written by a biracial law professor, this insightful, factual overview of customs and laws supporting racial discrimination explains many of the "whys" behind American society's link between racism and laws against interracial intimacy.

Nash, Gary B. *Red, White, and Black: The Peoples of Early America.* Englewood Cliffs, N.J.: Prentice-Hall, 1999. In these pages are historical accounts of cultural, social, religious, and sexual interaction of Europeans, Africans, and Native Americans.

Prinzing, Fred, and Anita Prinzing. *Mixed Messages.* Chicago: Moody Press, 1990. This was the first Christian book to take an honest look at the issue of interracial marriage. It is a valuable resource for Christians who want to understand issues surrounding multiracial marriage. Now out of print, the book can be obtained by contacting Fred Prinzing at fzing@aol.com.

Rockquemore, Kerry, and David Brunsma. *Beyond Black: Biracial Identity in America.* Thousand Oaks, Calif.: Sage, 2001. This is an excellent study of the various ways that black/white biracial people may develop different types of racial identities. It illustrates the truth that it is a mistake to reduce all multiracial people to a certain stereotype.

Root, Maria P. P. *Love's Revolution: Interracial Marriage.* Philadelphia: Temple University Press, 2001. Root uses this book to report her research on interracial couples. She argues that external social rejection, rather than internal relationship dysfunction, is the only major distinguishing quality between interracial and intraracial marriages.

————. *The Multiracial Experience: Racial Borders as the New Frontier.* Thousand Oaks, Calif.: Sage, 1996.

————. *Racially Mixed People in America: Within, Between, and Beyond Race.* Thousand Oaks, Calif.: Sage, 1992. Both of these last two books by Root consist of a series of edited articles about multiracial individuals by researchers, activists, and academics. The strength of these books is the diversity of topics covered.

Rosenblatt, Paul C., Terri Karis, and Richard D. Powell. *Multiracial Couples: Black and White Voices.* Thousand Oaks, Calif.: Sage, 1995. This book is built upon research done with twenty-one black/white couples who live in the Minneapolis/St. Paul area. This research allows us to understand some of the internal dynamics of multiracial families.

Russell, Kathy, Midge Wilson, and Ronald Hall. *The Color Complex: The Politics of Skin Color among African Americans.* New York: Harcourt Brace Jovanovich, 1992. This work examines the phenomenon of color discrimination among African Americans, showing that blacks are not immune to the societal norm of racial prejudice.

Simon, R. J. *The Case for Transracial Adoption.* Washington, D.C.: American University Press, 1994. Simon argues that transracial adoption does not harm people of color despite the concerns of certain minority groups. Simon reviews current research literature on the topic and assesses her own longitudinal study.

Spickard, P. R. *Mixed Blood: Intermarriage and Ethnic Identity in Twentieth-Century America.* Madison: University of Wisconsin Press, 1989. Providing the best historical treatment of interracial relationships available, Spickard uses white/Japanese, white/Jewish, and white/black unions to test certain theories about interracial unions.

Tizard, Barbara, and Ann Phoenix. *Black, White, or Mixed Race: Race and Racism in the Lives of Young People of Mixed Parentage.* London:

Routledge, 1993. Here is a treatment of the subject of black/white multiracials in England.

Washington, Joseph R., Jr. *Marriage in Black and White*. Lanham, Md.: University Press of America, 1970. Washington's is a classic study of interracial marriage. It is somewhat outdated but still delivers a good historical analysis. It is useful for understanding some of the early theories of interracial marriage.

Books on Racial Reconciliation by Christians

If Christians want to serve those who are in multiracial families, then they need to educate themselves about racism. Below is a list of books that deal with issues of racial reconciliation from a Christian perspective.

Cassidy, Michael. *The Passing Summer: A South African's Response to White Fear, Black Anger, and the Politics of Love*. Ventura, Calif.: Regal, 1989.

DeYoung, Curtiss. *Coming Together: The Bible's Message in an Age of Diversity*. Valley Forge, Pa.: Judson, 1995.

Emerson, Michael O. and Christian Smith. *Divided by Faith: Evangelical Religion and the Problem of Race in America*. New York: Oxford University Press, 2001.

Ham, Ken, Carl Wieland, and Don Batten. *One Blood: The Biblical Answer to Racism*. Green Forest, Ark.: Master, 1999.

Park, Andrew Sung. *Racial Conflict and Healing: An Asian-American Theological Perspective*. Maryknoll, N.Y.: Orbis, 1996.

Perkins, Spencer, and Chris Rice. *More Than Equals: Racial Healing for the Sake of the Gospel*. Rev. Ed. Downers Grove, Ill.: InterVarsity Press, 2000.

Usry, Glenn, and Craig Keener. *Black Man's Religion*. Downers Grove, Ill.: InterVarsity Press, 1996.

Ware, A. Charles. *Prejudice and the People of God: How Revelation and Redemption Lead to Reconciliation*. Grand Rapids: Kregel Publications, 2001.

Washington, Raleigh, and Glen Kehrein. *Breaking Down the Walls*. Chicago: Moody Press, 1993.

Woodley, Randy. *Living in Color: Embracing God's Passion for Diversity*. Grand Rapids: Chosen Books, 2001. See also www.eagles-wingsmin.com.

Yancey, George. *Beyond Black and White: Reflections on Racial Reconciliation*. Grand Rapids: Baker, 1996.

Go to www.racialreconciliation.com for purchase.

Research Articles on Interracial Adoption

As a sociologist, George believes academic articles are the best way to disseminate the knowledge that dispels rumors and myths. But not everyone enjoys such articles. Those who wish to find less academic writings can find them at the websites cited in the first section of this appendix.

Alexander, R., and Carla Curtis. "A Review of Empirical Research Involving the Transracial Adoption of African American Children." *Journal of Black Psychology* 22, no. 2 (1996): 223–5.

Brooks, Devon, Richard P. Barth, and Alice Bussiere. "Adoption and Race: Implementing the Multiethnic Placement Act and Interethnic Adoption Provisions." *Social Work* 44, no. 2 (1999): 167–78.

Curtis, Carla. "The Adoption of African-American Children by Whites: A Renewed Conflict." *Families in Society* 77, no. 3 (1996): 156–64.

Deberry, K., Sandra Scarr, and Richard Weinburg. "Family Racial Socialization and Ecological Competence: Longitudinal Assessments of African-American Transracial Adoptees." *Child Development* 67, no. 5 (1996): 2375–99.

Hollingsworth, Leslie Doty. "Effect of Transracial/Transethnic Adoption on Children's Racial and Ethnic Identity and Self-Esteem: A Meta-Analytic Review." *Marriage and Family Review* 25, nos. 1–2 (1997): 99–130.

Macey, M. "'Same Race' Adoption Policy: Anti-Racism or Racism?" *Journal of Social Policy* 24, no. 4 (1995): 473–92.

Research Articles on Interracial Children

Brandell, J. "Treatment of the Biracial Child: Theoretical and Clinical Issues." *Journal of Multicultural Counseling and Development* 16, no. 4 (1988): 176–86.

Neto, Felix, and Lizalia Paiva. "Color and Racial Attitudes in White, Black, and Biracial Children." *Social Behavior and Personality* 26, no. 3 (1998): 233–44.

Saenz, R., Sean-Shong Hwang, Benigno Aguirre, and Robert Anderson. "Persistence and Change in Asian Identity among Children of Intermarried Couples." *Sociological Perspectives* 38, no. 2 (1995): 175–95.

Wardle, Francis. "Meeting the Needs of Multiracial and Multiethnic Children in Early Childhood Settings." *Early Childhood Education Journal* 26, no. 1 (1998): 7–11.

Winn, N., and R. Priest. "Counseling Biracial Children: A Forgotten Component of Multicultural Counseling." *Family Therapy* 20, no. 1 (1993): 29–36.

Research Articles on Interracial Dating

Fujino, Diane C. "The Rates, Patterns, and Reasons for Forming Hetero-sexual Interracial Dating Relationships among Asian Americans." *Journal of Social and Personal Relationships* 14, no. 6 (1997): 809–28.

Lavilla, Stacy. "The Minority Interracial Couples: Dating Someone of a Different Race Who Isn't White Can Be Difficult." *Asian Week* 19, no. 33 (1998): 12.

Nguyen, Ly Thi. "To Date or Not to Date a Vietnamese: Perceptions and Expectations of Vietnamese American College Students." *Amerasia Journal* 24, no. 1 (1998): 143–69.

Yancey, George, and Sherelyn Yancey. "Interracial Dating: Evidence from Personal Advertisements." *Journal of Family Issues* 19, no. 3 (1998): 334–48.

Research Articles on Interracial Marriage and Family

Aldridge, Delores P. "Interracial Marriage: Empirical and Theoretical Considerations." *Journal of Black Studies* 8, no. 3 (1978): 355–68.

Baptiste, D. "Marital and Family Therapy with Racially/Culturally Intermarried Stepfamilies: Issues and Guidelines." *Family Relations* 33, no. 3 (1984): 373–80.

Brown, John A. "Casework Contacts with Black-White Couples." *Journal of Contemporary Social Work* 68, no. 1 (1987): 24–29.

Davidson, J. "Black-White Interracial Marriage: A Critical Look at Theories about Motivations of the Partners." *Journal of Intergroup Relations* 18, no. 4 (1991–92): 14–20.

Hendriksen, Richard C., Jr., and Richard E. Watts. "Perceptions of a White Female in an Interracial Marriage." *Family Journal* 7, no. 1 (1999): 68–70.

Lewis, Richard, Jr., George Yancey, and Siri S. Bletzer. "Racial and Nonracial Factors That Influence Spouse Choice in Black/White Marriages." *Journal of Black Studies* 28 (1997): 60–78.

Luke, Carmen, and Allan Luke. "Interracial Families: Difference within Difference." *Ethnic and Racial Studies* 21, no. 4 (1998): 728–54.

Rankin, Robert P., and Jerry S. Maneker. "Correlates of Marital Duration and Black-White Intermarriage in California." *Journal of Divorce* 11, no. 2 (1987): 51–67.

St. Jean, Yanick, and Robert Parker. "Disapproval of Interracial Unions: The Case of Black Females." In *American Families: Issues in Race and Ethnicity,* ed. C. Jacobson. New York: Garland, 1995, 341–51.

Stephan, Walter G., and Cookie White Stephan. "Intermarriage: Effects on Personality, Adjustment, and Intergroup Relations in Two Samples of Students." *Journal of Marriage and the Family* 53, no. 1 (1991): 241–50.

Sung, Betty L. "Chinese American Intermarriage." *Journal of Comparative Family Studies* 21, no. 3 (1990): 337–52.

Tucker, M. B., and Claudia Mitchell-Kernan. "New Trends in Black American Interracial Marriage: The Social Structural Context." *Journal of Marriage and the Family* 52, no. 1 (1990): 209–19.

Research Articles on Multiracial Identity

Deters, Kathleen A. "Belonging Nowhere and Everywhere: Multiracial Identity Development." *Bulletin of the Menninger Clinic* 61, no. 3 (1997): 368–84.

Funderburg, Lise. "Crossing the Demographic Divide: The Otherness of Multiracial Identity." *American Demographics* 20, no. 10 (1998): 24–25.

Hall, Christine C. Iijima. "Best of Both Worlds: Body Image and Satisfaction of a Sample of Black-Japanese Biracial Individuals." *Amerasia Journal* 23, no. 1 (1997): 87–97.

Herring, R. "Developing Biracial Ethnic Identity: A Review of the Increasing Dilemma." *Journal of Multicultural Counseling and Development* 23, no. 1 (1995): 29–39.

Kahn, Jacks, and Jacqueline Denmon. "An Examination of Social Science Literature Pertaining to Multiracial Identity: A Historical Perspective." *Journal of Multicultural Social Work* 6, nos. 1–2 (1997): 117–39.

Kerwin, C., and J. Ponterotto. "Biracial Identity Development: Theory and Research." In *Handbook of Multicultural Counseling,* eds. Joseph G. Ponterotto, J. Manuel Casas, Lisa Suzuki, and Charlene M. Alexander. Thousand Oaks, Calif.: Sage, 1995, 199–217.

Williams, Carmen Braun. "Claiming a Biracial Identity: Resisting Social Constructions of Race and Culture." *Journal of Counseling and Development* 77, no. 1 (1999): 32–35.

Assessment Guide: Capabilities of Persons Who Parent Cross-Racially or Cross-Culturally

Introduction

When an applicant for adoption indicates an interest in parenting inter-racially or interculturally, an assessment is to be made to determine his or her capacity and disposition to value, respect, appreciate, and educate the child regarding the child's racial, ethnic, and cultural heritage and background.

Parenting Ability

1. How will you respond to the child in your home if the child is called racially derogatory names?
2. How will you teach coping skills to a child of a different race or mixed-race background?
3. What problems do you think might come up in school or in the neighborhood? How will you handle social mixing and dating?
4. How might the issues for the child change as the child becomes older?
5. Have you considered that your child may resent you for making the decision to adopt cross-racially? How will you deal with it?
6. Discuss what you know about the music, entertainment, and eating preferences of the child's race or ethnic group.
7. Discuss what you know about the skin and hair care and dietary and health needs of the child.
8. How will a child in your home learn about his or her own race, culture, history, and customs?
9. How will you, on a regular basis, provide this child with exposure to positive role models from his or her race?
10. How do you feel that your decision to parent cross-culturally will benefit you? How do you feel that it will benefit the child?
11. How do you feel your decision to parent cross-racially might negatively

affect you? How do you feel that it might negatively affect the child? How will you handle the negative effects and hurt?

12. Do you have toys, books, and games available that reflect the child's racial and cultural heritage? Why would this be important for the child's development?

13. Do you have substitute caregivers who are of the same race of the child you wish to adopt?

Motivation and Support

1. Why are you considering cross-racially parenting a special needs child?

2. Are there individuals of other races within your family? If yes, . . .
   a) What have been your experiences with them?
   b) How have they been treated within your family?
   c) Are there any family members who have not accepted the individual?

3. Have you discussed your interest in parenting cross-culturally with your family, friends, and neighbors? What were their reactions? Give examples of statements they have made.

4. Do you have friends of different races? If yes, . . .
   a) How often do you socialize with them?
   b) How long have you been friends?
   c) If you have friends or relatives of different races, have you overheard racist comments made about them or witnessed ways that they were treated differently than you in a public or private setting? Give examples of incidents of racism. How did you handle the situation? What could you have done differently?

5. What cross-cultural activities do you participate in? How often?

6. Do you have neighbors who are of the same race as the child you wish to parent? Do you socialize with them? How often, and what activities do you participate in?

7. What is the cultural makeup of your church? How do the church members embrace and celebrate diversity?

8. Are you willing to switch to a congregation that is more culturally diverse?

9. Are any of the references you listed individuals of the same race as the child you wish to be considered for? If so, list the individual's name and length of relationship.

10. Children of color are often labeled within the educational system as behavior problems or as having limited academic skills. Given this, how will you be an advocate for the child you wish to adopt?

Experience and Understanding of
the Role of Race and Ethnic Heritage

1. Discuss when you first became individually aware of cultural differences and similarities.
2. What is your earliest memory of a person of a race other than your own? What race or culture was that person a member of?
3. What have you done to learn about other races and cultures? What are you willing to do to learn about other races and cultures?
4. What do you know about other races, especially the race of the child you are interested in parenting?
5. Who could you access as positive role models for the race(s) or culture(s) of the child you are interested in?
6. Are there role models whom ethnic groups may consider positive but whom members of your family, community, friends, or you, consider negative? How do you feel about teaching the child about these role models? How would you go about teaching the child about these role models?
7. What do you know about how racial identities develop?
8. Are there similarities and differences between your lifestyle and that of the child's racial and ethnic group? How might a child in your home feel about these differences?
9. Have you had any experience of being oppressed due to your own racial and ethnic heritage? Describe the situation and feelings. What did you learn from these experiences?
10. What are some thoughts or biases regarding the culture of the child you wish to parent that you are aware you have?
11. Please list national historical leaders who were of the same race as the child you wish to adopt. In addition, please list the contributions they made to society.
12. What privileges do you have that a person of color does not have?

❦ APPENDIX C ❦

Controversial Issues
George A. Yancey

INTERRACIAL FAMILIES AND MULTIRACIAL IDENTITIES BRING ABOUT controversial racial issues in America. This section will outline the pros and cons of four of these controversial issues: the 2000 Census; the social construction of race; assimilation versus pluralism; and race and the multiracial family.

The 2000 Census
Several organizations that serve multiracial individuals have worked to place a multiracial category in the U.S. Census. As a result of their efforts, the race category was changed to allow the respondents to the 2000 Census to mark more than one race to describe themselves. This "Check All That Apply" response is seen as a compromise between these multiracial individuals and the civil rights organizations that have opposed using a multiracial category. The debate that led to this compromise is discussed below.

Some multiracial individuals do not believe that their racial identity would be represented in the American Census if they were limited to only one race. In that case, if a person has a white father and a black mother, for example, then that multiracial person would have to either choose "white" (denying his or her connection to the mother) or "black" (denying his or her connection to the father). The person would have the option of choosing the "other" category, but many multiracial individuals perceive this choice as dehumanizing. This complaint is, in fact, common among multiracial people, since they often are forced to use monoracial categories (when applying for a job, enrolling in school, filling out government forms) to describe their multiracial reality. For these individuals, a multiracial category is an important way for them to meet some of their needs for self-definition. They want the same freedom of racial self-determination that monoracial people have and perceive attempts to deny them the multiracial category as an unfair imposition of an identity by those who do not understand their multiracial lives.

On the other hand, many minority civil rights organizations have opposed the multiracial category. They argue that Census data is vital for constructing educational and governmental programs as well as being important for assessing the effectiveness of antiracism efforts such as affirmative action. For example, if we do not have an accurate count of the percentage of blacks in a given city, then we do not know if companies hiring workers from that city are hiring enough blacks. If 20 percent of the manual laborers in that company are black, then it matters if 25 or 50 percent of the city is black, if we want to know how good of a job that company is doing in hiring black workers.

Given this dynamic, it is easy to see why civil rights organizations fear the multiracial option. They fear that many multiracial minorities will choose the multiracial category, which will lower the count of racial minorities from measures such as the Census. Some activists contend that certain racial minorities will see multiracial identity as a way to escape minority status, thus decreasing the number of specific monoracial minorities included in a census count. They further argue that this process will harm multiracial individuals, since they are not counted as a racial minority but as a multiracial person, even though such individuals still face discrimination as a racial minority instead of as a multiracial person. Thus, they perceive the multiracial category as a disservice to the cause of civil rights.

The current system of "Check All That Apply" is seen as a compromise because it allows multiracial individuals to represent their entire genetic lineage while also enabling bureaucratic organizations to count the number of individuals who are represented by a given minority group. Like many compromises, individuals on both sides of the issue are less than totally happy. Some individuals in multiracial organizations are concerned that when it comes to actually counting individuals, European Americans in their genetic lineage will be ignored and that the number of racial minorities might be maximized. On the other hand, some civil rights organizations fear that more people will be encouraged to look for whites in their genetic background (since most blacks have whites in their ancestry) in order to mark down more than one race in the census. If this practice becomes commonplace, these organizations fear, we may start underestimating the number of racial minorities in America. Either way, this debate is not going away soon.

The Social Construction of Race

Interracial families and multiracial individuals are controversial because our presence reminds others about the fallacy of a biological notion of race. So much of America is racialized and built upon an idea of biological racial purity and superiority. But as was noted in chapter four, "One Race," this notion is false.

Sex is a biological reality. By definition, men are physically different than women. Women can potentially bear children, whereas men cannot. Men have different sex organs than women. Thus, we can set up objective standards by which we define men differently than women. However, there are no such objective physical standards by which we can determine the racial group an individual belongs to. Race is a dimension created in society; how we define the race of certain individuals is arbitrary. For example, we typically think of Hispanics as being a separate race from whites. Yet a Latino is a person with European and Native American lineage. Biologically, Hispanics are the offspring of Europeans, not a separate race apart from Europeans. Our American society has decided that Hispanic Americans are a separate race, and that decision, not any biological differences, is what makes them a separate race.

Here is another exercise to illustrate the social constructive nature of race. Determine in your mind the answer to the following questions: Are African Americans and European Americans members of different races? What about European Americans and Mexican Americans? Asian Americans and Native Americans? Mexican Americans and Puerto Ricans? Japanese Americans and Korean Americans? Irish Americans and Italian Americans? English Americans and German Americans? There have been times in American history when the entire list of groupings above was thought to represent members of different races. In fact, even today there is no agreement about which of these groups is racially distinct. So, to reiterate, we can agree upon biological differences between men and women, but we cannot agree upon how we define racial groups as being different from each other. This is because how we define race is due to a social process, and unlike sex, it is not a biological reality.

Race as a social construction has some very important implications. First, it means that a biological basis for racial differences cannot exist. And since we cannot define race in biological terms, it is impossible for us to argue that differences between individuals are based upon race. We know that on average men are taller than women. We can calculate this because we can biologically assert who is a man and who is a woman. But this is impossible for racial differences because we do not have a neat way of sorting out who belongs to what race. For instance, to test a hypothesis that blacks are taller than whites, I would have to decide if people like Halle Berry, Rick Fox, or Tiger Woods is biologically black, white, or Asian. I can only do this through an arbitrary social definition of who is black, not by any objective standard.

Therefore, when it comes to measuring height, I am unable to determine if biological racial difference exists.[1]

We must live with the reality that race is socially constructed. Yet some people use the fact that race is a social construction to argue for a color-blind society. While race is a biological falsehood, race and racism are still social truisms. For instance, I have white and Indian genetic ancestry but live in an American society that will treat me as an African American. Discrimination based upon perceived biological differences still exists. The fact that these differences are not significant does not eliminate this discrimination. An important challenge that Americans will have to deal with is the reality of racism and the social lie of race. Those of us in the forefront of the multiracial community must think about how we can deal with the reality of racism even though that reality is based upon the social lie of biological differences. Furthermore, it is the responsibility of all Christians to combat American racism even as we recognize the fallacy of racial purity.

It is not right to unfairly judge Americans who are wedded to the idea of racial purity. We have an entire racial history based upon this notion. It is only relatively recently that Americans have begun to question the notion of racial purity. Educating the general public about the arbitrary manner by which race is defined is going to be a difficult task. Those of us in multiracial families are part of this educational process. We did not enter into these families to make a political or social statement; we did so because we made a commitment to love someone of another race. Now that we are in these families, though, we can help illustrate the fallacy of racial purity. When we recognize this possibility, it may make it easier for us to handle those uncomfortable questions that inevitably come our way and that challenge our racial loyalty and identity. These questions are the result of an American society that is in the middle of a paradigm shift—a movement from reliance upon racial purity to an acceptance of the subjective nature of race. We must help our fellow Americans handle this transition with patience—and with firmness, in asserting the legitimacy of our decision to marry or adopt across racial lines. Likewise, as Christians, we must help our fellow brothers and sisters in the Lord prepare the church for the racial changes that are coming as we in multiracial families continue to grow in numbers.

Assimilation vs. Pluralism

Some people believe that the best solution to racism in America is assimilation, which can best be conceptualized as the merging of different cultures.

When you have multiple immigrant groups coming together at a specific time and place, a certain degree of assimilation must always take place. For example, to thrive in America, it is important to learn English. Language attainment then becomes a way that people from different cultures can become partially assimilated into American society. But while many first-generation immigrants maintain knowledge of their native tongue, often their children and grandchildren are less fluent in that language. After several generations, the descendants of immigrants lose that language and speak only English. At that point, as it concerns language, they have been completely assimilated into mainstream American culture.

Of course, individuals do not have to assimilate with every aspect of the mainstream culture. In America people often eat the food, celebrate the holidays, and practice the religion of their native cultures. But some assimilation is likely if a group remains in the United States for an extended period of time. For some groups this assimilation may be so complete that they lose their entire ethnic heritage. The German, Welsh, English, and French Americans of the 1700s lost their cultural traditions as they assimilated into what today we call "whites." The fear of losing their racial heritage has led some members of racial minorities to reject this total assimilation and embrace a different goal for race relations—cultural pluralism.

Theoretically, cultural pluralism means that racial groups will be able to maintain their own cultures but do so in a society that treats all races equally. The main emphasis of cultural pluralism is to have a society in which all racial cultures coexist and are maintained. This means that even as members of different races may interact in organizations where secondary, or superficial, relationships are formed, more intimate types of relations will tend to occur only among members of a single racial group. For example, in some American high schools there are two proms. One is for whites; the other prom is for racial minorities. This separation is not enforced by law but by the custom of pluralism. At the prom for European Americans, "white" music, such as a country/western or rock, is performed, while at the minority prom, a more ethnic flavor of music is exhibited. In this way, the purity of each racial culture can be maintained. This is a great example of cultural pluralism as students of different races go to the same school and thus develop superficial relations with each other, but when it comes to deeper levels of interactions—dating and dancing—then racial purity and separatism become the norm.

It is a mistake to think about the differences between assimilation and pluralism as an either/or concept. It is not the case that we must have either total assimilation or total cultural pluralism. As I asserted earlier, a certain amount of assimilation has to take place for our society to work smoothly. The real question, then, is how much assimilation we should have and how much cultural pluralism should take place. By our very nature, interracial families and multiracial individuals demonstrate assimilation in America. However, this does not mean that we cannot also embrace some of the concepts of pluralism. An Asian/white couple may decide to raise their children culturally as Asian, rather than as members of the majority group, to help maintain the notion of cultural purity within the Asian framework. However, despite this possibility, the presence of those of us in the multiracial community will continue to challenge the dogmatic attitudes of some pluralists toward intimate relationships between people of different races. Therefore, to some degree, those of us in interracial relationships are probably going to be more likely to favor assimilation than pluralism in this important societal debate.[2]

Race and the Multiracial Family

The previous discussion on assimilation and pluralism brings up another controversial topic about multiracial families: how we are to be classified. Since I am in a black/white interracial marriage, is my family a "black" family or a "white" family? Are we supposed to live among blacks or among whites? These questions emerge from a society that likes to place people and families in racial boxes that do not easily apply to us. They also emerge from a society that tends to create racially segregated schools, churches, and neighborhoods. Those of us in multiracial families are a reminder of how artificial this segregation is.

Historically, majority/minority multiracial families have tended to live within the minority community, rather than among whites. Part of the rationale for this may have come from the majority community, which sought to punish the white partner. It was not uncommon for whites who dared to intermarry to be ostracized by their families, to be abandoned by the European American community at large, and if the marriage failed, to face rejection from potential white romantic partners. However, as the old structures of white supremacy have undergone challenge from civil rights groups, this type of banishment has become less "politically correct." Now multiracial families have more freedom to choose where they may live. But issues of acceptance are still not always clear-cut. In a society that regularly demands racial loyalty, the desire to place multiracial families within a given racial community will continue to put those families under pressure.

To date, there is little research that suggests how multiracial families tend to identify themselves and which racial communities they are most comfortable in. Ideally, many members of interracial families desire to live a multiracial lifestyle that incorporates neighbors, schoolmates, coworkers, friends, and fellow church attendees of different races. Such a lifestyle matches the experience we have with our immediate nuclear and extended families. However, since there are few stable racially integrated neighborhoods in America, living a completely multiracial lifestyle is difficult. Yet many multiracial families have been able to compensate for this difficulty by incorporating other dimensions of a multiracial lifestyle through joining multiracial support groups, joining multiracial churches and clubs, and sending children to integrated schools. Hopefully, as racial segregation becomes less commonplace in America, multiracial families will find it easier to maintain a multiracial lifestyle and attempts to racially classify us will become less controversial.

Notes

1. *It can be argued that we can make such a comparison if we eliminate all multiracial individuals. There are two problems with this argument. First, very few people know their genetic lineage well enough to determine whether they are of a "pure" race, making it impossible to determine who to include in the comparison. Second, the number of "pure" races is so small among certain groups (most notably African Americans and Hispanic Americans) that it would be difficult to find enough individuals to make a meaningful comparison.*

2. *In fact, one of my graduate students has just completed a paper in which he finds that people who have interracially dated are systematically more supportive of assimilation than pluralism. Even when he controls for other variables (age, income, education, etc.), this tendency does not go away. While I want to make sure that the reader understands that I am not asserting that all individuals in interracial relationships support assimilation, this research does suggest that being in a multiracial relationship is connected to a desire for societal assimilation.*